TRIBALISM AND THE TRAGEDY OF THE COMMONS

Land, Identity and Development: The Manipur Experience

TRIBALISM AND THE TRAGEDY OF THE COMMONS

Land, Identity and Development: The Manipur Experience

Edited By

CH. PRIYORANJAN SINGH

AKANSHA PUBLISHING HOUSE
NEW DELHI-110002 (INDIA)

AKANSHA PUBLISHING HOUSE
4649-B/21, Ansari Road
Darya Ganj, New Delhi - 110 002
Ph.: 23263193 / 9811582579 / 09435116718
Telefax: 011-23263193
Email: ektabooks@yahoo.com
www.akanshapublishinghouse.com

Tribalism and the Tragedy of the Commons:
Land, Identity and Development: The Manipur Experience

First Published 2009
ISBN 978-81-8370-181-5

PRINTED IN INDIA

Published by Akansha Publishing House, New Delhi and Printed at Aryan Enterprises, Delhi.

CONTENTS

SECTION II
HISTORY, POLITICS AND DEVELOPMENT

SECTION III
TRIBAL LAND SYSTEMS, IDENTITY AND CHANGE

FOREWORD

It gives me immense pleasure to write the Foreword to this volume entitled *Tribalism and the Tragedy of the Commons: Land, Identity and Development – The Manipur Experience* published by the Indian Council of Social Science Research, North Eastern Regional Centre, Shillong.

India's Northeast remains much misunderstood in the rest of India although a great deal of national attention has been received in the past few years. A separate ministry has now been formed – Ministry of Development of North Eastern Region (DoNER) – to address the special needs of this region. The Ministry has prepared a Vision-2020 document. However, the question of land, identity and development which is of utmost importance in the entire Northeastern region and more particularly in the State of Manipur, has often been a bone of contention.

Manipur is, indeed, a land scarce State. Ninety percent of the total geographical area of the State belongs to the tribals. All the Scheduled Tribes reside in the hill areas. The Hindus, Muslims and Scheduled Castes belong to the valley area which accounts for only 10% of the total geographical area. The density of population in the valley was 631 per sq km in 2001 as against the density of population of only 44 per sq km in the hill areas. It is also true that less than 10% of the area is found suitable for productive agricultural activities.

The Manipur Land Reform and Land Revenue Act, 1960 is extended to the whole valley but applies only to a negligible portion of the hill area. The land system in the tribal areas is different in terms of ownership, transfer and use. Land is used in the hill areas as a mere piece of community property - not as a source of enterprise and income. Of course, the valley is not an exception to the concept of treating land as a piece of idle property. But increasing commercialization of agricultural activities is taking place to a large extent. The crucial issue before the State is how to make best use of available land in order to produce enough to meet both consumption and investment requirements. Land development demands institutional credit. The legal title of ownership duly authenticated by the competent authority according to the law (i.e., Manipur Land Reform and Land Revenue Act, 1960) of the State is a necessary condition for financial support from organized financial institutions. There is thus a contradiction between the terms of land ownership on the one hand and the terms and conditions of banking institutions on the other. The need for a new policy of optimum Land Resource Management is being acutely felt.

The people in the hill areas of Manipur by and large, do not encourage the extension of Manipur Land Reform and Land Revenue Act, 1960 to the hill areas. They feel that their livelihood opportunities and identity may be threatened with the influx of rich private owners. Hence they prefer community ownership to individual ownership. Besides, political leaders of the hill constituencies also prefer the *status quo* of the traditional system. Although the present form of land ownership may be socially acceptable, yet it goes largely against the spirit of competitive development and diversified activities. There is a contradiction between development interest of hill areas and system of land ownership at the moment. The emotional attachment of the tribal people to the land perhaps needs to be reassessed in terms of its various implications on the development process of the State of Manipur. I am happy to note that this book has dwelt on this very important issue. Certainly there is a need for land reform in the hill areas of Manipur through appropriate laws by taking into account the need and aspirations of the people.

The papers put together in this volume with great care by Priyoranjan and published by the ICSSR North Eastern Regional Centre, are a major step towards such an awareness.

Bhaskar Chatterjee
Planning Commission
Government of India
Yojana Bhavan
Sansad Marg
New Delhi - 110 001

PREFACE

This book is the outcome of a seminar, organised by the Indian Council of Social Science Research, North Eastern Regional Centre (ICSSR-NERC), Shillong, in collaboration with the R K Sanathombi Devi Social Science Research Institute at Imphal. The seminar brought on a common platform, perhaps for the first time, the key opinion leaders, social activists and academicians of the various ethnic communities of the region, to deliberate upon the tricky issues of land, identity and development.

The new thinking among policy planners of the Northeast Region of India is, veering around a consensus that in the multi ethnic region, culture and identities have to be adequately factored in, in the design of development policies. However, policy planners and academics are not yet clear of the structures of the cultures and identities of the region and how they interact with development at the ground levels. Policy planners need theoretical frameworks as well as ground level understanding of identity and cultural politics in the region, to evolve effective cultural and identity management norms that have a bearing on development. This book is a modest step towards a conceptual understanding of the complex relationships between land, identity and the development process, with Manipur as the context. It gives insights into the land systems of the tribes of Manipur and seeks to unravel the roots of identity politics in the state, in the larger context of a development process that is leading to unimagined poverty and deprivation of a growing mass of the denizens of the blue mountains, that we have allegorically termed as the 'Tragedy of the commons'.

I record here my thanks to Dr. C. Joshua Thomas of the ICSSR-NERC for having reposited his faith in me in editing this book. The venture would be rewarded adequately, if it generates further debate amongst all concerned.

Ch. Priyoranjan Singh

ACKNOWLEDGEMENT

We appreciate much the valuable support which we received from Mr. Bhasker Chatterjee, IAS, Additional Secretary, Planning Commission, Government of India, New Delhi and the Department of Land Resources, Ministry of Rural Development, Government of India for their support and the financial assistance extended towards the *National Seminar on Land, Identity and Development: Manipur Experience*. We are grateful to Mr. Falguni Rajkumar, IAS., Secretary, North Eastern Council, Government of India, Shillong for inaugurating the Seminar and also extending the intellectual input in the programme. Professor Gangumei Kamei, noted historian and former Cabinet Minister, Government of Manipur deserves special appreciation being the moving spirit behind the different tribal groups and the movement and his active intervention in the seminar and the publication of this volume. We are grateful to Padmashree Th. Haridas Singh, Chairman, R.K. Sanatombi Devi Research Institute of Social Sciences, Imphal, Manipur and Justice Manisena, former Chief Justice of Gauhati High Court, Professor Mohindro Singh and the staff of their Institute for their excellent support that they had extended towards this programme. We do acknowledge with thanks the support which we received from Professor Amuba Singh, Vice-Chancellor, Manipur University in various ways towards this Seminar. Lastly we are grateful to Professor Pramod Tandon,

Vice-Chancellor, North Eastern Hill Unversity (NEHU) & Chairman, ICSSR North Eastern Regional Centre, Shillong and the staff of the regional centre for making this exercise a grand success.

Editor

LIST OF CONTRIBUTORS

1. **Samir Kumar Das**, Professor, Department of Political Science, University of Calcutta, Kolkata, West Bengal.
2. **Prasanjit Biswas**, Reader, Department of Philosophy, North-East Hill University, Shillong, Meghalaya.
3. **Pradip Phanjoubam**, Editor, The Imphal Free Press, Imaphal, Manipur.
4. **Gangmumei Kamei**, Formerly Professor, Department of History, Manipur University, Canchipur and Cabinet Minister, Government of Manipur.
5. **Ch. Priyoranjan Singh** Associate Professor, Department of Economics, Manipur University, Canchipur, Imphal, Manipur.
6. **Bhabananda Takhellambam**, Lecturer, Department of History, C.I College, Bishnupur, Manipur.
7. **Mangi Singh**, Associate Professor, Department of Political Science, Manipur University, Canchipur, Imphal, Manipur.
8. **E. Bijoykumar Singh**, Professor, Department of Economics, Manipur University, Canchipur, Imphal, Manipur
9. **N. Vijayalakshmi,** GNC, NERCORMP/IFAD, Shillong, Meghalaya.

10. **N. Bhupendro Singh**, Lecturer, Department of Humanities and Social Science, National Institute of Technology, Silchar, Assam.
11. **K. Gyanendra Singh**, Research Scholar, Department of Humanities and Social Science, National Institute of Technology, Silchar, Assam.
12. **U.A. Shimray**, Assistant Professor, Institute for Social and Economic Change, Bangalore, Karnataka.
13. **H. Phomrong**, Lecturer, Mount Everest College, Senapati, Manipur.
14. **D.Hangsha**, Research Scholar, Department of History, Manipur University, Canchipur, Imphal, Manipur.
15. **Samson Chiru,** Social Worker, New Delhi.
16. **S.R. Tohring,** Research Scholar, Jawaharlal Nehru University, New Delhi.
17. **T.T. Hoakip,** Lecturer, Department of Political Science, North-East Hill University, Shillong, Meghalaya.
18. **S. Kipgen**, Lecturer, Manipur College, Imphal, Meghalaya.
19. **T. Misào**, IPS(Retd), Senapati, Manipur.
20. **D.L. Hoakip**, Research Scholar, Department of History, Manipur University, Canchipur, Imphal, Manipur.

SECTION I

IDENTITY POLITICS AND RALLYING OF THE TROOPS

1

INTRODUCTION

The Northeastern region of India is considered by many as an enigma that responds to development initiatives rather slowly and most of the times, does not respond at all. The setting up of the North Eastern Council (NEC) at Shillong for accelerated development of the region and many other Northeast specific development programmes of the Government of India, backed by liberal funds, have not translated into strengthening the productive base of the region nor rising the income and employment levels to that of national benchmarks. The per capita income gaps between the region and rest of India has progressively widened from around twenty percent in the early nineteen nineties to around thirty percent in 2007. The ***Vision 2020 document*** for the development of the region prepared by the Ministry of Development of North Eastern Region (DoNER) and released by the Prime Minister in July 2008 estimates the Northeast needs to grow at a scorching pace of 11.8 percent growth for thirteen years, to merely catch up with the rest of the country.

Many reasons have been given for the developmental failures in the region, some of them apparently impromptu. Inappropriate policy frameworks, governmental failures, insurgency and roving banditry, dependency and rent seeking cultures, market failures and negative incentive structures et al, all representing facets of the proverbial elephant's anatomy, as perceived by blind men but non describing the anatomy itself. Some have been bold enough to assert that the failure of "imposing new institutions" for the functioning of market forces is the main stumbling block and that a 'cultural approach" with "special solutions" is only sinking the region further. Other more politically astute observers have tried to jump the gun and deflect harder questions of political irresponsibility and economy management by raising the bogey of partition that is assumed to have taken the Northeast some twenty five years backwards. More serious writers have however pointed out to the fact that policy planners, academicians as well as thinkers on the Northeast, have singularly failed to adequately locate the problems of the Northeast in its factual political economy context and resorted to textbook economics or conventionality, which are in the nature of 'impositions'. Thus Prabat Patnaik writes, "They nowhere take into account what the people of the region want or feel. They internalize the perspective of the outsider, and are hardly different from what a visiting economist from New Delhi or Washington DC would have said". Respecting the wants and feelings of the stakeholders/peoples, is the morality of all democratic regimes and impositions are but colonial thinking that can only be termed as reactionary and is likely to 'play havoc with the lives of the local people, without achieving the desired objectives'. The crux of the matter here is simply that for too long the structural dimensions of the region has been sidestepped, either by design or as a matter of brazen dishonesty or both. After all, where development funds are put into, how sectoral allocations are prioritized and how issues of equity and inclusiveness are addressed, are political decisions that are fundamentally decided by the structure of power and division of wealth. The sooner this blind-spot is unravelled and then factored in, the more productive will be the outcome of development in the Northeast.

The larger issue however is what the common people of the region really 'want and feel' and whether the people of the region live in an environment of cultural liberty, where each individual can make his own choices under his own free will. The people of the region live under excruciating circumstances of repression by both state and non-state actors where the expression of the free will in terms of what one wants and how one feels, are bludgeoned by cultural and identity politics which have turned violent and flowered into insurgencies, some ideologically moored and most, blatantly opportunistic and contrived. Cultural identities are narrowed down to exclusive territoriality and ethnicity, artificially codified into rigid norms and impulses of progressive changes are coercively being blocked. In a domino effect of one cultural and identity fundamentalism giving rise to another, the identity conflict in the region is giving ride to cultural killing fields where the minuscule uniqueness of cultures are magnified manifold and aggressively erected in confrontational postures, whereas the universal, the humane and the moral elements of all cultures are deliberately being put on a tight leash. The fall out is that the 'commons' make cultural or identity choices that are against the imposed ones, at great risks of social alienation, treachery or outright physical violence. Public expressions of what one wants and how one feels have therefore a tendency of being tainted by elements of compulsion. The vehement pronouncements and claims of opinion makers and civil society organizations of the Northeast as representing the feelings or choices of the 'commons', needs to be taken with a pinch of salt.

Culture, Identity and Development

The role of culture in economic development has had a long history of intense debate among social scientists. Starting from Max Weber's The Protestant Ethic and the Spirit of Capitalism, the causal relationship between culture and development has had its adherents as well as opponents. Cultural determinism in economic development however is little evident from statistical analysis or historical studies. If Protestantism was at all the reason for the emergence of modern economic development in Europe, a counterpoint is always there in the spectacular economic performances of Confucian societies like China, Japan and others in South East Asia. However it is also true that empirical evidence suggests that economic development is associated with shifts away from absolute norms and values towards values that are increasingly associated with shifts away from absolute norms and values towards values that are increasingly rational, tolerant and trusting, and participatory. The impact of economic development on culture is quite apparent whereas the impact of culture on development is still debated. Institutional economists like Douglas North (1990), emphasise that "institution (i.e. formal and informal rules) were critical in 'reducing transaction costs and thereby promoting economic efficiency. Institutional economists have brought to the forefront the role of history, culture and other 'path dependent' factors in shaping economic behaviour and development. The Asian economic miracle and experiences in Eastern Europe have made cultural and institutional factors as key explanatory variables in successful economic transition. The social resources of a community or 'Social Capital', embodies many aspects of the cultural traits of a society and affects development. What is relevant for developing societies is the realization that unlike the Weberians, there is a necessity to focus more on the positive aspects of culture, and all cultures, to enrich our understanding of development."

The explicit recognition that cultures have a positive role to play in development has become a widely accepted ideology in recent times. Political theorists and leaders had for long shied away from accommodating diverse ethnicities, religions, languages and values as they feared and theorised threats to the concept of the Nation State. The result was the widespread suppression of cultural identities and in extreme cases, the brutal resort to ethnic cleansing or religious persecution. On the flip side, however, the explicit accommodation of diverse ethnicities, have on the other hand, given rise to identity politics along ethnic, religions, racial and cultural lines. The Human Development Report, 2004, had brought to the forefront the place of cultural liberty in today's diverse world and how cultural liberty has become an essential ingredient of human development. The report also emphasises how identity politics are turning into sources of instability, polarization, hatred and conflict, and are retarding peace, development and human freedoms. Identity politics have in the extreme, turned into retreats to conservatism and rejection of change, social, economic and political. Identity politics is no doubt a historical process of social change that are founded on human freedom and democracy but they have the potential to turn into threats to human freedom itself if the interpretations and meanings one gives to identity and cultural liberty are not founded on universal and moral moorings. Indeed, cultural liberty—the freedom to choose how one lives, 'is a simple idea but profoundly unsettling'. The need for astute management of cultural and identity politics can hardly be ever underemphasised.

Writing in the same report, Amartya Sen had problematised the concept of cultural liberty in the larger context of human development. Sen writes that 'the central issue in cultural liberty is the capability of people to live as they would choose, with adequate opportunity to consider other options'. The success of socio-economic and political spheres hinges upon cultural freedom. However the glorification of cultural conservatism and unreasoned endorsement of inherited traditions leads to curtailment of cultural choices and freedom. Participation exclusions in education, employment, decision making etc., based upon gender, religion, ethnicity etc., and Living Mode Exclusion—denying life styles that one chooses or being forced to other's lifestyles, are fall outs of cultural fundamentalism or cultural conservatism. In multicultural societies, group rights are often championed as a corollary to the wider acceptance of cultural diversities as a social and political regime. Sen rightly points out however, that group rights in multicultural societies should be tested against their role in enhancing freedoms of human beings. If group rights block individual choices that amounts to imprisoning not only the individuals within the group but also amounts to imprisoning the group itself. Thus "nothing can be justified in the name of freedom without actually giving an opportunity for the exercise of that freedom". Sen therefore writes that the defending of social arrangements and institutions should depend upon what they do to human freedom.

Communitarian theories claim that identity is a matter of discovery and not a matter of choice; one is borrn into a cultural milieu, its affiliation and its attachments. But this primal identity is only one of the many identities that an individual can choose to have. The pitfall of communitarian conception of identity is that newly asserted identities can tyrannize by eliminating the claims of other identities. Identity politics and the politics of recognition often lead to "Rapid fire cultural generalizations" and serve as "tools of sectarian prejudice, social discrimination and even political tyranny". Cultural bigotry leads to inefficient and iniquitous tyrannies and even government failures. Sen concludes that individuals belong to many groups and have many ways of identifying themselves and "To deny choice when choice exists is not only a factual mistake, it can have grave moral consequences in a world where identity- based conflicts and brutalities are common. 'Reason before identity' and role of choice are vital ingredients of inclusive development.

Identity Politics in the North-East

The movement for separate States, homelands or outright cessation from the nation is the singular characteristics of the northeast that defines it to the rest of the country and to some extent to the rest of the world. Except for Sikkim and Arunachal Pradesh, all the States in the region have had or are having multiple insurgencies or armed movements that has thrown the region into political turmoil and violent conflicts. All the conflicts somehow or the other, have been linked to the question of land or questions of identity, the distinction between land and identity being blurred or no distinction being recognized. In the absence of any normative discourse on the issue of land and the identity question, land based or identity based conflicts are breeding like rabbits in most of the states of the region, especially in the State of Manipur. Development has been the immediate casualty amidst all this chaos.

Territoriality of homeland demands that cross each other, necessarily have conflict built into them. Samir Kumar Das compares this to the peeling of the onion that ends only with the end of the onion itself. The principles upon which these demands are anchored, first settlement, length of time, ancestry or historical isolation from the mainland, each distinct in itself, are deployed in a manner that privileges a particular community as much as it dis-privileges and censors the claims of the others. As such there can be no end to the present-day territorialisation. Das points that land or homeland has been an integral part of nationalist imagination throughout history and that 'the modern state has emerged with the claim of embodying a nation within itself or having homogenized the people living within its ambit as a single nation'. Land then becomes territory as the state or the nation 'monopolized' or 'captured' it. Territory is an object of ownership, while land is not; land is sharable while territory is not. Transforming land into territory facilitates ownership of resources, supervision and colonization at will. Ethnic or nationalist aspirations in the northeast have a common bond of territoriality that is exclusive of the other and has resulted in fallouts like tragic ethnic cleansing and mass displacements of the non-ethnic, claims over land in other administrative divisions and amputing away land to others, in order to preserve ethnic majority in one's homeland. Ethnic demands for homeland challenges and contests the territoriality of the adversarial nation state. Das describes this as 'the mimicry by the ethnic community of the territoriality of the adversarial nation state'; territoriality has therefore, anarchy built into it.

Group and community based identities are political constructs and therefore have prejudices and biases ingrained in them to empower the elite to 'rally the troops'. Therefore, which community or group claims a homeland is less important than the rationale behind the claim. Elaborating a self chosen norm to further one's claims is one thing and finding the universal norm for conflict resolution is quite another. Hypothetical norms are caused by desire whereas categorical or universal norms are not caused by subjective desire. This singular failure to distinguish between the two is at the core of the failure to resolve inter community or group conflicts. There is as yet no answer as to how to make the transition from the hypothetical to the categorical norms in the northeast.

Partition of the Indian sub-continent led not only to the emergence of two and more states but also created permanent divides between the Hindus and the Muslims. The moral indifference involved here equally applies in the case of the partition of the northeast into administratively separate homelands. Multi-ethnic and multicultural nations have always found their own ways to live together in a democratic process that laid emphasis on the role of understanding and appreciation. Village or local level solidarities and sociality, concrete universality a la Gould, are the product of the people's democratic struggle to live in harmony and peaceful co-existence. Das feels that civil societies in the region, albeit in reformed *avatars*, have a crucial role to play in addressing the issues of land, identity and the development problems in the Northeast.

Pradip Phanjoubam questions the notion of civil society in Manipur and how these civil societies have subverted the very moral roots upon which they should be drawing their credibility from and how these organizations tend to become tools or proxies of conflicting parties rather than be neutral mediators. There is a crying need to restructure our notion of the civil apace so as to distinguish between 'the tools of war' from those of peace, unambiguously. Civil societies in the Northeast, have acquired 'ethnic tints' and become organizations that have narrow sectarian agendas as against the universal and the moral, like that of the International Red Cross Society for example. This lack of humanitarian and universal moorings in either, youth, women, student or other civil societies has only compounded the problems that they are purportedly set to address. The political structure is liberal and has allowed the mushrooming of civil societies. But the civil societies claiming to represent public interests have become authoritarian and intolerant to dissent. Experts and the intelligentsia who are better equipped to show the way and policy measures, have been marginalized and not listened to. Civil societies in the State live in a time warp of bygone days, cultures, society, values et. al. There is a missing sense of the contemporary world. Phanjoubam notes that ethnic politics in Manipur is showing the glaring chinks in democracy. Democracy has made India accommodative to various identities and cannot this be a ground to work on for solutions in the State, Phanjoubam adds.

Going deeper into the issues of land, identity and development, Prasanjit Biswas believes that the defining characteristics of the relation between land and labour is that communities are embedded in a marked social boundary. In this pre-political state, boundaries of communities remain unalterable. As a result the State and the market jointly act as an adversary to presumed social boundaries of communities. The State supports movement of peoples across social boundaries from the position of weakening social boundaries. The State 'sees' these boundaries as alterable for purposes of resource management and inter- community relations. The undermining of community oriented values by extraneous forces is sometimes given the legal force to limit indigenous rights over land behind a veneer of land reforms and agrarian reforms.

Land use in the hills is patterned after kinship relations within the community. Land belongs to the community. Land thus becomes not only a material resource but also a symbolic domain that regulates social exchange, livelihood and political power. The social symbolic value determines material value. Converting land into property subverts the social symbolic value of land and segregates land from communal labour. Land becomes a commodity and gives rise to differentiation and landlessness, also to sale outside the community. In spite of the Sixth Schedule, landed gentries have emerged in these areas. Intrusions of market forces have changed the perception of 'social boundaries'.

Inter-ethnic de-legitimization within a democratic liberal set-up is sought to be a demand for right to life and livelihood. Majoritarian homeland claims exclude others. Is there a notion of homeland that includes others in a liberal democratic sense? Micro distinction of communities based on linguistic and cultural identities has led to alienation of land and a counter rise of other identities. Biswas emphasises the need to evolve a non-ethnocentric positioning of identity politics.

This would require a greater sensitivity towards the others. What is more required is sensibility which can restore an ethical paradigm in the resolution of land related conflicts in the shaping of a territorial identity.

Land related conflicts amongst the Nagas and the Kukis, the two major umbrella tribes of Manipur, has a long history in the State. While stressing upon the role of the colonial policies of divide and rule in Manipur that inevitably initiated macro level tribal conflicts, Bhabananda Takhellambam writes that the foundations of Kuki and Naga nationalism was laid in the Kuki and Zeliangrong rebellion in the early part of the twentieth century. The anti British rebellion also spawned large scale inter tribal conflicts between the Nagas and the Kukis. After Independence in 1947, and before the formal merger of Manipur with the Indian union, the Manipur Constitution Act 1947 was in force. The constitution making body included the representatives of the Kukis and the Nagas. After the subsequent general election in 1948, the Maharaja of Manipur became the symbol of unity of the kingdom. The plural and ethnic dimensions of Manipur and the likely conflicts that was likely to set in, was foreseen by the great patriot Hijam Irabot and he attempted to forge the United Front of Manipur in the 1948 elections. The paper asserts that it was a combination of State inaptitude, Central blunder and the forceful National Socialist Council of Nagalim(NSCN) politics that has brought the ethnic conflicts in the State to a head. Jawaharlal Nehru refusing to entertain the Naga Nationalist Council memorandum at Kohima in 1952 when he was in Kohima with Nu Win , is cited as an example of state political failure that led to the explosion of the Naga insurgency in the region. The inaptitude of the State and Central government at each opportunate and timely moments are cited by the paper as the main reason for the State to be sinking deeper and deeper into the quicksand of ethnic conflicts that is engulfing the state in the post independence era. Ethnic homelands, armies and civil societies are mushrooming in the State in a mad rush for counterweight measures to protect ethnic and communal interests. Amidst all this, the efficient use of the State's human resources, are in shambles and development is the casualty.

The Kuki-Naga conflict in Manipur is the standing example of how homeland demands in one State can affect ethnic relations in neighbouring States. The rise of Naga insurgency in the 1950s and the evolution of the concept of Greater Nagaland and Nagalim, infringing upon the Naga inhabited territories of neighbouring States, hardened and galvanized Naga ethnic and sub-national aspirations. The peace agreement of 1964, between the Government of India and the Federal Government of Nagaland was extended to the Naga inhabited districts of Manipur. When the NSCN (IM) was formed in1980, the implications of the Naga insurgency on inter tribal relations in Manipur became quite concrete. Ethnic cleansing, impositions, monetary and otherwise, uprooting of villages and restrictions in movements became the rule of the day in the Naga and Kuki inhabited areas of Manipur. The Kuki-Naga clash of the early 1990s, led to the death of twenty thousand tribals, uprooting of fifteen thousand families, burning of seventy thousand houses and violence in five hundred villages. The Kukis assert that the Kuki-Naga conflict is a direct fall out of the political machinations inherent in the concept of Greater Nagaland and more importantly that it would be misleading to call it an ethic conflict. S. Mangi examines the various dimensions of the Kuki-Naga conflict and tries to locate the reality in the ground level mirror of electoral politics. In the last assembly elections, the twenty assembly seats in the hill districts were shared equally among the Kukis and the Nagas. What was significant about these elections was that the United Naga Council (UNC) had sponsored twelve candidates but won only six seats. This was against the back drop of the UNC *dikat*, physical and otherwise, asking others not to contest. The authoritarian and undemocratic move of the UNC, exposed the deep divisions among Naga tribes and put in stark relief, the aspirations of the people and the imagined political roots of the purportedly civil society. Mangi concludes that 'Loosing sight of this fact while negotiating any issue which concerns ownership rights of land in one way or the other, and also the territorial integrity of the state, will be the height of lack of political far-sightedness'.

Land Identity and Develoment in the Tribal Regions of Manipur

Manipur has two distinct physiographic divisions of the hills and the plains. The plain area mainly consists of the valley region right in the heart and centre of the State and this valley is surrounded by the hills where the tribes of the State resided since pre-history. Legends and folklore of the tribes as well as Meiteis of the plains trace their common origins to the hill settlements in the mountains, until the three brothers separated and branched out as the Kukis, the Nagas and the plains living Meiteis. There is no doubt that the present day major ethnic communities of the state had throughout history, evolved social solidarities that was strong enough to deem it fit to weave in stories of their oneness in their narratives of creation itself, which after all largely defines a people's identity. And how these social solidarities are broken, how age old trusts and the practiced universal values of peaceful co-existence are laid asunder, are the stories of a development process in the State, that was iniquitous, non-inclusive and largely catering to the political elites, both in the plains and the hill regions.

Gangmumei Kamei, with a broad brush, paints the political economy of development in the State and illustrates how acts and regulations of the State concerning tribal land, ill judged, misinterpreted, or politicised, has sown the seeds of conflicts on land in the State. To the tribals, the issues of ethnicity, identity and land ownership are built into their psyche in such a way that their identity binds them to their land and territory which are the vanguards of their sustenance and livelihood as a community. Ethnicity and the tribal mode of production and the nature of the ownership of the resources of the community are the basis of the tribal identity. Tribal polity in the State, historically, did not grow beyond the village level and did not grow into a tribal polity formation. The polity is based on the village and the land holding system. Intensive studies on the tribal land holding systems are lacking. This is reflected in the varying versions of the tribal land system at any point of time.

The tribal land system and the village polity remained undisturbed through time, during the native period and also during the colonial period. The Manipur Hill People's Regulation 1947 and the Manipur (Hill Areas) Village Authorities Act, 1956, diluted the village polity by instituting the Village Authority. But this institutional change did not affect the land holding system of the tribes in the state. However the introduction of the Manipur Land Revenue and Land Reforms Act, 1960, raised fears and apprehensions among the tribals that the extension of the Act in the tribal areas would alienate tribal communities from their land. According to this Act, land was to be cadastral surveyed, ownership rights conferred and revenue assessed and collected. The Act was partially introduced in the plain areas of some four hill districts, effectively introducing privatization of land in the hill areas, albeit in the plain areas of the hills. The Act therefore had the salutary effect of disruption of the tribal land system in the plain areas of the tribal region of the state. Another Act, The Acquisition of Chiefs Rights Act 1967, sought to abolish the Chiefship among the Kuki-Chins but could not be implemented on account of strong resistance. There was another attempt by the State to introduce the MLR and LR Act during 1989 through an amendment in the Act but was also rebuffed. This last attempt of the State was responsible for the great mistrust that has been imbibed by the tribals against the MLR and LR Act.

The much maligned 'Act' however, categorically states that the transfer of land from the tribal to the non-tribal is subject to the permission of the Deputy Commissioner of the district and the concerned district council. This provision contains the leeway for settlement of the non-tribals in the tribal areas and at the same time protects the interest of the tribes from being inundated by outsiders. The ramifications of the act was clearly politicised and unduly ethnicised thereby snuffing out sane debates. The heat of the debate has gone down as opinion leaders and scholars stepped into the debate. Kamei feels that there is now a consensus that there is a need for legislation for tribal land tenure in the hill areas. A change in the tribal mindset among the intellectuals are visible and the progressive community leaders are raising the issue of a suitable land law for the tribal hill areas to pave the way for institutional finance and investments for development in the hill regions. The tribes should not fear of loosing their identity and they should 'respond to the call of the changing times', asserts Kamei.

The existing land system in the hill region of Manipur becoming hurdles to the general development is further examined by E. Bijoykumar. The hill regions of Manipur have abundant forest and land resources and therefore large scale poverty in the hills cannot be explained by the lack of resources. For the gainful and sustainable exploitation of the rich natural resources of the hills, incentive structures and good governance are required. Where the land system and ownership have large elements of uncertainty, in that the common peasants are virtual tenants of village chiefs, the incentive to invest in commercial crops and highly lucrative horticultural crops are necessarily low. Combined with market, government and other failures, there are high efficiency failures in the hill regions of Manipur, leading to high levels of poverty. Historically, individual ownership of land has encouraged farmers to move on to progressive farming and crop mixes, as the owner cultivators are ready to take higher risks and commitments. Bijoykumar feels that the evolution of property/land rights in the hills seems to have been arrested due to the interventions of the village chiefs and the elites, with grave consequences of heightened development disparity between the hills and the valley areas, leading to political claims of territorial division.

Efficient utilization of the vast land resources of the hills, require a transformation in the rigid social norms and conservatism in the tribal social and economic structures. A greater consciousness has to be aroused that land, in the broadest term, including all natural resources, is a source of heightened income, employment and general welfare. A commendable effort is being made by the NERCORMP/IFAD project in the hill regions of Manipur, to evolve a development model that seeks to improve livelihood options in a sustainable manner. Through the instrument of village resource management and self help groups, the project seeks to conserve the environment and the fragile ecology of the hills and at the same time encourage maximum utilization of resources in a sustainable manner, for heightened income and employment generation. For example, crop focused, cluster specific activities have been launched with necessary training, extension and marketing linkages. Success stories in ginger, banana and passion fruit productions are coming up.

The project is anchored on an adaptive institutional change model, that owns and structures itself into time honoured village institutions and yet manage to bring about radical changes in the way resources are managed, utilized and shared fruitfully. The more fundamental impact of the project, in the long run, will perhaps be in its ability to unobtrusively unlock institutional rigidities in tribal societies and herald the re-generation of their institutions in the post-modern context of change with continuity. Vijaylakshmi Brara highlights these issues in her paper on the NERCORM/IFAD project and points out some of the dynamics of the changing land relations and growing differentiation in tribal society and economy of Manipur and cautions that 'An essential requirement of this region is an healthy and adaptive system of land rights that can tackle the incipient problems of differentiation, jhum, inequality and the emergence of a local elite'.

Breaking down of the traditional land systems and the corruption of traditional institutions to suit the village elites in the hills are brought to the fore by T.T. Haokip and D. L. Haokip. The Kuki land system is based upon the absolute ownership of village land by the village chief and his descendents. The emergence of a strong and authoritarian chief among the Kukis, was a historical requirement for survival. The Kukis, being historically a migratory tribe, were prone to intra or inter tribal clashes, necessitating a single authoritative figure. However the pristine land system in the past was based upon moral obligations and rights of both the chiefs and the villagers, whereby the system ensured the homogeneity, solidarity and security of the village and the concept of the rulers and the ruled was not at all ingrained in their imagination of the land system. The Kuki chiefship was conceived as distributors of village land rather than as Zamindars and his functional powers were based upon consensus and customs. Drastic changes have taken place in this traditional land system in the recent times. In many villages, private property in land is a fact of life and in others the chiefs have become tyrannical, authoritarian and exploitative. Development works are being blocked by chiefs on non-payment of land compensation which he appropriates for his self. Chiefs are selling off land and new villages are being set up by the new- rich and powerful to reap governmental development funds in the name of the village and absentee chiefs are dime a dozen, spending their time and living in urban areas, while maintaining the political and economic stranglehold over the villages. T. T. Haokip narrates interesting opinions of Kuki leaders expressing their disenchantment in their own land systems and chiefs who have become exploiters and landlords.

Haokip laments that the system of 'one state, two systems' policy of the colonial times are still followed in the post-colonial and is sustaining many fresh divides between the hills and the valley peoples. High levels of dependence on land for livelihood in the face of non –availability of alternative livelihood options have created the present explosive situation whereby territorial claims are ethnicised among the various tribes of the state on the one hand and tribal-non-tribal clash of interests on the other. Thus, the modern notions of private property and territorial claims have replaced the traditional notions of land ownerships and habitations. To 'unlock the value of land, while preserving its associated traditional values', require a shift towards democratic values and processes and a land system that is suited for a modern economy.

Kuki chiefship and the land system bound around this traditional institution are a source and mechanism through which Kuki customary law as well as traditions are generated, retained and interpreted, according to S. K. Kipgen. This institution is the living force that enables the Kukis to maintain their identity. What is needed is a change from within that separates the cultural aspects of the institution from the economic aspect of absolute control over land, with a new land law for the hills. Kipgen further adds that the suppressing of shared history and the stressing upon on segregation and individual identities is only a recent phenomenon. The tribals in the hills lived under the suzerainty of the Manipuri Kings, without interference in the internal affairs of their village republics. The subjugated tribes 'shared the common joys and sufferings of the state with the Meitei Kings through the ages'. The Manipuri Kings however failed to institutionalize their political domination of the hills and the non-participation of the tribes in the political mainstream, led to the incomprehensive process of state and nation building. Historical forces have thus led to the development of isolationist tendencies and ethnic insularity among the tribals.

The resistance of the tribes to changes in their land system and common property rights has been partly fuelled by the fear of loss of their land to outsiders. T. Misao brings into perspective, ground level realities of in- migration into Kuki territory. The migration of Nepalis into the Sadar hills have displaced a large number of tribals in the Senapati district. From being lessees to village land, the Nepalis have managed to permanently settle in tribal land and now possess legal ownership rights. Villagers displaced by the Kuki- Naga conflict of the early nineties have been compelled to settle around the Nepali settlement rather than in their tribal land. The Nepali migration in the hill regions of Manipur is thus adding a third dimension into the already complex Kuki-Naga conflicts in tribal Manipur. The Nepalis are able to return a Nepali M.L.A. from the Sadar hills much to the chagrins of the tribals. If land is privatised and bought by non tribals, how the outsiders are to be accommodated in the tribal social and political structures, within the village, needs to be addressed properly. Will the village authority have the same functional controls over the migrants and whether if the numbers increase, would not the tribal way of life and polity be seriously undermined. On the issue of development in the hill areas, Misao feels that the mindset of the tribals are yet to change from the mono-cropping cycles to a more progressive multiple cropping cycle. A massive extension and marketing service is called for. As of present, the huge potentials of cash crops like ginger and cardamom are being suppressed by middlemen who pay a pittance to the farmer (Rs. 12 to 15 per kg. as against Rs. 90 in Sikkim) and in case of individual efforts of marketing, cartels make sure that the products are not bought. The rich potentials of the hills have not been properly tapped due to tribal empathy and governmental failures.

The breaking down of the traditional land system is also widely observed in the villages of the Naga tribes. U. A. Shimray writes that Naga social and cultural practices are closely rooted in their village ecology and land is intrinsically interfaced with the political cultural and economic parameters. Social and economic changes have altered the egalitarian as well as communitarian concept of land ownership such that 'elite households' and powerful sections of society have succeeded in turning community land into private land. The situation has been worsened by the fact that the land system and tenure is not codified but based upon oral traditions, which is liable to corruption by individuals.

There are a number of marginal tribes in Manipur who have become the bone of contention for affiliation to the two major tribes of the Nagas and the Kukis. Caught in the game of numbers as well as economic and political survival, these small tribes face land and identity crisises that are qualitatively different from the other tribes. The Anals of Chandel district are a distinct example. Historically the Anals are an off soot of three original villages and they paid tributes to the Manipuri kings. Villages multiplied either by consensual bifurcation of a village or by being 'purchased' by an individual or a party. The tribe now number sixty eight villages. They fought territorial wars with the Kukis in distant memories but are now settled in adjacent villages with the Kukis. In the height of the Kuki-Naga clash of the 1990s, the major tribes claimed the Anals as their own, tribal affiliation thus becoming a political decision rather than a matter of identity, ethnicity or historicity. S.R.Tohring highlights some of the existential dilemmas of the marginal tribes when drawn into the vortex of ethnic politics in Manipur. In Anal villages, the traditional land system of communal ownership has virtually given way to the individual ownership holdings and a land market has developed. Not surprisingly, land disputed are on the rise within the village community and when customary law is not able to decide things, the villagers resort to government courts. Interestingly, modern values and norms are creeping in and the inheritance right of the girl child is gradually being honoured.

The Chiru tribe is another example of how trysts with modernity can lead to the collapse of traditional institutions and land based identity. This tribe reside in the foot hills adjacent to the valley plains. Being more exposed to the market and state forces of modernization, they are a tribe that has suffered large doses of land alienations with the advent of private ownership in land. The Chirus have resorted to selling land even to non villagers, and landlessness has become a fact of life in their villages. Samson Chiru pleads for a land reforms measure that would keep the Chirus as distinct ethnic entities. H. Phomrang and D.H. Hangsha have also given an interesting account of the Khoibu tribe, another marginal tribe of the state.

The larger context within which the problems of land, ethnicity and identity has to be addressed, is the evolving nature of, Manipur's economy and the direction that it has been taking in the recent past. K. Gyanendra addresses the macro structural dimensions of the state's economy while N. Bhupendro specifically analyses the nature of agricultural development and structural changes in the agrarian sector of the economy within which is buried many of the seeds of conflicts related to land, livelihoods and social relations of production that, to many, is the womb of social conflicts in backward agrarian societies.

Village Level Realities Beyond Identity Politics

Pre-colonial and colonial Manipur was a political entity that was firmly anchored in the bed rock of a historically evolved plural and multi-ethnic society. Tribal nationalism in the Northeast, and latter on in the state, is infringing upon this shared history, polity and identity. In the valley region, the linkage between land and identity did not arise in the pre- independence period. It is only a post independence phenomenon that the issue of land and identity are assuming alarming proportions among the majority population in the valley, in the face of tribal sub- nationalism movements that apparently and avowedly draw their ideological sustenance from the vital linkages between land and identity, in the peculiar ecological as well as historical context of tribal history in Manipur. In the hill regions however, the issues of land, identity and development has indeed become a heady mix that has intoxicated a many and blurred considered and measured debates for tribal development and social change. Land as a means of production and livelihood is much more vital in the hill economy then in the valley regions. Absolute lack of general development, especially in the interiors, and negligible growth of non-farm economic activities, has made land, so much more precious. Land and land systems are therefore, sought to be sacrosanct and inalienable, in fact traditional land rights and tenure systems are sought to be the vary basis of tribal village polities and identities.

Land in the pristine traditional consciousness, was the village commons, to be enjoyed by all, inclusively as well as equitably. It was the property of non but the property of all, to be defended for, to be looked after and to be sustainably exploited for the welfare of the villagers. The authority of the Chief and village council and the intra-clan distributive power of the clan heads, were but institutional details for the smooth functioning of the land system, which was fundamentally based on community ownership, rather than private ownerships. In an ecological and moral environment of low population, vast lands, subsistence and non-monetized village economy, far removed from the forces of markets and profits, private property consciousness and accumulation, the system worked not only equitably but also morally. In fact the 'strong chief' and the common property foundation of the land system was a necessity to maximise or maintain common welfare.

With the intrusion of modern state institutional norms and market forces, private property and accumulative consciousness inevitably cut at the moral foundations of the tribal land systems. Imagine the powerful clan heads are also the members of the village council, as is in most village councils. Imagine also that populations are growing and the jhum cycles are shortening so that land has become scarce to the extent of the emergence of landless households in the villages. These were the right conditions for the emergence of a village elite, the emergence of a land market, the birth of private property in land and albeit, new colonization of land, preferably in the non-traditional, non-jhum, river valleys, beyond the control of the chief or the clan heads. In the contemporary tribal villages, a new political economy is slowly enveloping, remnants of a cherished and remembered tribal land system, towards privatization of land, land alienation, land hunger and differentiation among the villagers. This is leading to unimagined poverty and deprivation of a growing mass of the denizens of the Blue Mountains that we have allegorically termed as the 'Tragedy of the Commons.'

The groundswell of dissent against the prevailing tribal land systems that are turning into exploitative and inequitable tenurial structures, especially among the Kukis, is finding currency not only among the educated new generation of tribal opinion makers but also among a minority section of the tribal elite. However, the dissent is yet to catalyse into a popular demand at the state level as vested interests are deeply entrenched in favour of the status quo. Given the inter tribal conflicts as well as the intra village power equations, concrete proposals for land reforms are unlikely to emerge from the tribals themselves, at least in the short run. Meanwhile the ordinary tribal villagers are likely to be trapped in the time warp of a land system that has gone out of step with the demands of a modern economy, a system that is increasingly becoming parasitic of the natural resources and ecosystems of the hill regions. In the valley region, development has taken place in a distorted fashion, and the economy is hurtling down the path of tertiarization. In the absence of a healthy manufacturing sector, employment and income are getting increasingly marginalized and casualized. The impact on land and the agrarian sector development has been retrograde and the sign of a commercialized agriculture led growth is being retarded by the nature of the emerging political economy and agrarian structure. What then are the social issues that are being thrown up in the villages of the state, both in the hills as well as in the valley? Ch. Priyoranjan examines these issues with micro level data from two villages in the State.

This book is only a preliminary exploration into the politics of land, identity and development and their interrelationships that are harboured by conflicting groups and their exponents. If some of the issues thrown up in this book lead to further research and considered debate, the venture shall be adequately rewarded.

Ch. Priyoranjan Singh

2

LAND, IDENTITY AND CONFLICTS: A Plea for Rebuilding Civil Society in Manipur

—*Samir Kumar Das*

This paper seeks to point out how contentious rights claims to land made by different communities become a source of conflict between them and makes a plea for rebuilding civil societies as a means of resolving them. It further argues that the civil societies as they exist today - whether in the northeast or elsewhere in India, are only too inadequate to handle the land-related conflicts. It is important that our plea for civil society should not be construed as simply reactivating the already existing civil societies in the region, but as one for rebuilding it in a way that they are capable of handling them. Accordingly, the paper is divided into two parts: While the first part traces the roots of these conflicts, the second part explores into the possibilities of rebuilding the civil societies in the northeast in general and Manipur in particular. We seek to frame our arguments in a normative mode and the introductory part of this paper primarily aims at clarifying what it means in philosophical terms and the bearing it has for our arguments.

On Being Normative

While the distinction between the normative and the descriptive is too well known to be driven home here, it was Immanuel Kant – the famous philosopher of Enlightenment who made perhaps for the first time in the history of ideas, a very fine distinction between two kinds of normative statements or in his words 'imperatives': hypothetical and categorical. As he argues:

> Imperatives, themselves ... when they are conditional, i.e., when they determine the will not as such but only in respect to a desired effect, are hypothetical imperatives, which are practical precepts but not laws. Laws must completely determine the will as will, even before I ask whether I am capable of achieving a desired effect or what should be done to realize it. They must thus be categorical; otherwise they would not be laws, for they would lack the necessity which, in order to be practical, must be completely independent of pathological conditions, i.e., conditions only contingently related to the will (Kant 1966:131).

Hypothetical norms according to Kantian line of argument are only a means to an end – meant to be followed only to realize some desired effects. These norms therefore are specific to the subject who chooses to observe and follow them only on condition that by following them, he would be able to realize his desire. That is to say, the observance of these norms does not depend on their self-evident or any intrinsic worth, but on their instrumentality in realizing his desire. These norms, in Kant's famous language, are 'caused' by the desire. Categorical norms on the other hand are 'uncaused' by any such subjective desire. Anyone who claims to be a moral subject is called upon to observe and follow them irrespective of the desire that he might otherwise hold and harbour in his mind. In situations where the norms conflict with his desire, the former are supposed to give way to the latter. For Kant however, the distinction between the hypothetical and the categorical norms – more than the commonplace one between the normative and the descriptive, is too transparently clear to be blurred and messed up.

Kant's warning against using the norms in order to fulfill one's desire is well taken. Indeed, this will have to be read together with one of his central arguments that the categorical imperatives that apply to one must also apply to others in the same manner. As one unhinges them from one's desires, they are also meant to be followed and observed by others. This double-way formulation of norms makes them universal. Thus it becomes possible for all – irrespective of their many other differences (like class, gender, ethnicity etc), to follow and observe the same norms and be part of a 'World republic'. The presence of these norms in simple terms makes it possible for them to live together, to share exchange and communicate amongst themselves.

Before we pass on to the next section, a couple of comments will perhaps be in order. First, although Kant was referring mainly – if not exclusively to individual subject, the same can be said about groups and communities functioning as collective subjects. In the context of India's Northeast, we need to remind ourselves that the collective subjects play an important role in any form of political communication and discourse. The supremacy of community is reflected not only in its often exclusive claim to land or homeland but more often than not in basing such claims on norms that are only specific to that particular community. This entails the violation of the Kantian principle of categorical imperatives at least at two levels: At one level, it is illustrative of a community's inability to separate the norms from its desires and intentions. But at the second and at a more serious level, it implies that the community elaborates the norms in support of its claim in a manner that also censors and disprivileges the claims of others. Since the norms are driven by desire and therefore specific to a community, these rule out the possibilities of dialogue and communication between the contending communities and as a result do not lay down any universal law. In the first part of this paper we propose to show how a community's claim to homeland invokes norms that are only specific to it.

Secondly, it is not our intention to make a case for categorical imperatives a la Kant in order to facilitate any dialogue and communication between the communities. While categorical imperatives could have provided a solution, we do not know how a transition from hypothetical to categorical imperatives can be made in the present context of the North East. Following Gould, we propose to make a further distinction between 'abstract universality' and 'concrete universality' and argue that it is possible to address the vexed question of conflicting claims over homelands by way of basing the civil societies of the region on the principle of 'concrete universality'. The distinction between abstract universality and concrete universality is too serious to be wished away. For one thing, while abstract universality asks one to keep the categorical imperatives separate from a community's particular desires and intentions, concrete universality is based on the axiom that our social existence on daily basis implies considerable overlaps and blurring of interethnic divides without however making them completely obsolete and the history of conflicts in the region is albeit shorter than that of peace and cooperation. As we live in the society, we cannot afford to remain isolated and remain completely aloof from others – notwithstanding that we have outstanding conflicts with them over mutually conflicting claims to homeland. Yet our living in the same village, locality or neighbourhood makes it imperative on everyone's part to mend fences with others and to live with them. The fact of our collective existence and social living helps in generating a sociality that cuts across the ethnic divisions and boundaries—without however wiping them completely. This sociality does not rule out our differences and separate identities – but does not allow us to stretch them to a point where we are necessarily pushed into conflicts with others. Difference after all is not conflict, but is only strategic to our common existence and collective social living.

Social scientists working on the region have a tendency of blowing conflicts out of proportions in a way that interethnic conflicts are conventionally taken as the mark of the society and politics of the northeast. Conflicts are sanitized of their complexities and are defined in simple black and white terms. The absence of conflicts is read as cooperation and vice versa. We on the other hand plot conflict and cooperation along a continuum and there are vast gray areas that span between them. If there is one hallmark that is said to characterize these societies, it is conflicts between communities in the region. The history of conflicts in the region written by the scholars becomes so overbearing that it hides the history of cooperation and turns our attention away from the intricacies of conflicts that might have told a different story - had they been studied in depth. Seldom are their works informed by any serious micro-studies in conflicts and violence in the region. In course of our work on forced displacement of population induced by them, we could gather some insights into the nature of conflicts occurring in the region including Assam, Manipur, Arunachal Pradesh and Tripura (Das ed. 2007 forthcoming). The value of our work lay in an arduously conducted series of case studies on conflicts – at times more than one study on the same case made by the contributors. Although the focus of that work was more on the tales of the internally displaced persons rather than the nature of conflicts that catalyze and induce them, some of the lessons are instructive. It will not be out of place to remind us that the conflicts in the region even in very recent years are marked by the twin elements of externality and surprise: For one thing, available records on inter-community conflicts tend to suggest that the violence that takes place within a mixed locality or neighbourhood is always attributed to outside forces—that is to say, forces external to it. Even if the locals are seen to be involved in it, their involvement is necessarily explained with reference to the provocations and incitements coming from outside forces. The author's long conversations and interviews with various cross-sections of people drawn from otherwise conflicting communities seem to suggest that people have been and continue to remain in best of terms with each other, but somehow fail to explain why in times of crisis their cross-ethnic solidarities at the village or local level fail in controlling - if not stopping violence. A good deal of these explanatory endeavours is of course paranoiac: but even this collective paranoia shared apparently by two or more conflicting communities, points to a certain assertion of selfhood by a given locality or neighbourhood as a whole - of which they are only parts. Such assertion of collective self – more often than not, only a post-violence phenomenon cuts across the boundaries of conflicting ethnic communities. When we say that life limps back into the normal after fiercest of interethnic conflicts and violence, we imply that the villages and localities that contain mixed populations continue to find their ways of making people live together and carve out a niche for themselves. Secondly, while the source of these conflicts is always attributed to external forces, the communities also seem to believe that the conflicts had had no internal or local basis. In simple terms, they lack any prehistory that might explain their emergence in the first place. In the absence of any prehistory, the occurrence of conflicts and violence takes everyone by surprise: People who have been living together for generations should not have been involved in them and should not have given themselves to outside machinations and incitements. All this proves that notwithstanding these conflicts, daily life in conflict zones implies a good deal of sharing and exchange, communications and transactions. As the author has argued elsewhere, it is only with the emergence of conflicts that such local solidarities prove ruefully inadequate to withstand it (Das in Sinha & Chakrabarti eds. 2007: 245-267).

Concrete universality refers to this indistinct zone in which the very logic of daily living pushes people to enter into exchanges and transactions with the neighbouring communities almost on a daily basis and thereby cut across the ethnic boundaries. It is important that we make 'concrete universality' - a category separate from both hypothetical and categorical imperatives. While categorical imperatives are supposed to be completely 'uncaused' by desires and intentions and therefore find it difficult to fire the imagination of the entire collective subject at any one point of time, the concept of desire according to Kant is devoid of any moral connotation. Our collective existence as a group – a community or a clan also contains many desires within it; but the desires are seldom pitched at a level where we are necessarily forced into a conflict with the neighbours or engage in violence with them. Our everyday living is predicated on the principle of avoiding violence even if it involves compromising our desires and intentions - rather than being engulfed by them. Violence is after all not the lingo of our everyday social existence. In the second part of this paper, we propose to pursue the question of concrete universality further and will try to see how it can provide the basis of an emerging civil society in the northeast.

What is in a Name?

Before we begin, let us clarify another methodologically significant point: Although a new genre of normative writings has emerged in recent years in the context of India's Northeast, we continue with the old habit of referring to cases with names of different groups and communities involved in the conflicts. The act of naming comes both as illustration of the concrete case under review and as a policy response to the conflict that such a case involves. Policy Studies has been the most potent of all newly opened fields of research and investigation into the society and politics of the region. Thus we come across a new breed of social scientists, statesmen, administrators and bureaucrats, who are never at their wit's end and never short of solutions to the problems that afflict the region. The interest in the Northeast has coincided with a new glut of publications in policy vein and also a new breed of troubleshooters, technocrats, managers and policy-makers etc. The region has already become one of their favourite visiting spots in recent years. Everyone is so concerned about the future of the region and wants to be seen as caring for it. The tragedy is that the Northeast continues to reel in spite of being showered with so many policy suggestions and few policies. The act of naming comes necessarily with an entire package of policy suggestions.

It is true that the act of naming airs a sense of immediacy. One who refers to a group and community by name offers policy suggestions seemingly without any ambiguity and hardly minces words. The author sees immediacy more as a bane than a blessing. Let me explain why. For one thing, it brings with it an association of a group, community or a body of people with any given essence and helps in profiling and stereotyping it. We know that historically the identities of most of the groups and communities in the region developed as *exoethnonyms* – that is to say, names appended to them by the outsiders including the colonial rulers and their stooges. Bakhtin has made the point rather starkly when he argued that one does not name oneself. It is always the other that names one. Such essences and stereotypes have now become part of the regional lore so much so that even if you call them by different names, these essences and stereotypes remain the same. The meaning of the phrase 'What is in a name?' lies precisely in the ease and comfort that one experiences while identifying one. Naming therefore implies namelessness – the message that the being has reached certain finality preempting the possibilities of further metamorphosis and so we can be absolutely sure of what it is. Persistent naming of the being makes its identification not only possible but simple and easy and eventually renders the act redundant. Namelessness springs precisely form this recurrent act of naming it. While the act fixes and freezes the groups and communities – thanks to the modern technologies of enumeration through census and other statistical operations, it never takes note of the politically determined nature of groups and community-based identities. The assumed namelessness of beings in simple terms defines them as fully formed entities and rules out the possibilities of any future transformation of identities.

But, there is more to the problem than this otherwise well-taken point. We redefine the phrase 'What is in a Name?' as the namelessness that emerges not from the habit of persistent naming by the outsiders but from the politically contingent nature of our names and identities. Names therefore are only in constant transition: The name, one is given, is always in a state of flux - rendering one perpetually nameless. It is uneasily perched between name and the nameless. Viewed thus, names are not to be associated with essences and stereotypes. Since names are only politically contingent positions, the phrase takes us straight to the question of 'what could have happened, had we been in the position of others?' It does not matter whether X group or Y group makes a case for homeland; the point is that the case should be read independently of the subject who makes it. The value of the claim will have to be judged not in terms of who makes it but in terms of what the case is being made of. Namelessness implies substitutability of positions.

Substitutability of positions enables us to open dialogue and build bridges across the communities and groups. When mothers ask us to 'shed no more blood', they are not referring to the blood of their own biological children, but that of the children of any mother on earth. When every single woman claims that she is the mother of the victim who has been raped and murdered, the issue goes beyond the ambit of biological mother. The motherhood celebrated here is of universal nature. This is what makes social living and common existence possible for a diversity of people. In this paper therefore I have preferred to follow a writing style in which we do not name names.

Village or such local-level solidarities are not based on the pursuit of conflicting interests - but on an understanding and appreciation of each others' positions and a will to live – which effectively means a determined will to live together. Such solidarities in other words make our common existence and social living possible. Little has so far been said about the role of understanding and appreciation in mending fences between groups and communities in times of conflict. While its distinction from desires and intentions is pretty clear, it should not be confused as moral indifference. Many of the policy alternatives suggested in the context of the northeast smack of such moral indifference. Partition of the region into neat and administratively separate homelands – apart from its evident impracticalities (for the demographic composition of the region is so complex that there will remain minorities within such apparently well-defined homelands and the majorities are constantly haunted by the nagging fear of being outnumbered by others – thanks to immigration from outside the region), is also to be read as an instance of moral indifference. Partitions are likely to reduce the possibilities of communication between the communities and are unlikely to beget sociality between them. The partition of the subcontinent has not only cut it into two or eventually more states, but also created a permanent divide between the Hindus and the Muslims.

What we call everyday existence and its correlation to namelessness will have to be analyzed in proper perspective. We may make a distinction between two very different kinds of everyday existence knowing fully well that such a distinction should not be stretched beyond a certain point: One, in which we as distinct identities of people live together without any significant give and take, exchanges and transaction between us. Thus, it does not matter whether any of our neighbours dies or falls sick – we remain so obsessed with ourselves. A good deal of urban living involves such a form of common existence. The people are as it were pigeonholed into separate spaces and the urban space viewed in that sense is never continuous. It is interesting to note that Dr. Ambedkar—the principal architect of the Constitution of India, warned the Constituent Assembly against this form of social existence in which the backward sections including the *dalits*, SCs and the STs are put together by the diktats of the Constitution and law of the land, but are seldom allowed to socially mix with others. Much of our civility as Renata Markus tells us is of this nature. On the other hand, we may refer to another form of sociality in which one's commitment to others often leads one to make compromises and live with them. In Markus' words, this lays down the foundations for 'decent society' rather than the conventionally understood civil society.

The policy alternatives doing their rounds in the entire Northeast have never taken note of the role - such understanding and appreciation continue to play in consolidating the society. As a result, policies are prescribed from above and become an object of administration and government and remain oblivious to the democratic politics continued in the region in spite of its many other shortcomings. As the author has argued elsewhere, the official and unofficial processes of making peace have failed to develop synergy between them (Das 2007). Thus peace-making endeavours made by the state remain cut off from the people's democratic struggles for making social living and everyday existence possible against all travails and odds.

Land, Territoriality and the Question of Identity

Land or more aptly homeland has always been an integral part of nationalist imagination. The yearning for land that a community can claim as its own – unencumbered by and autonomous from others has catalyzed many a conflict in history and the modern state has emerged with the claim of embodying a nation within itself or having homogenized the people living within its ambit as a single nation. Whether the nation has forced the state to emerge or the reverse cannot be answered in any thumb-rule manner: it remains a historical question to be answered historically. But one point is clear: Both nation and state correspond or are supposed to correspond with each other within a determinate territory. Land turns into a territory only insofar as it is 'monopolized' and 'captured' by any state and/or nation.

Territory – unlike land, has a few characteristics: First, territory is an object of ownership and 'colonization', while land is not. In any 'communal mode of power' as Partha Chatterjee argues, one's entitlement to land follows from one's membership to a particular community. Collective ownership of land gives one only the authority of using but not owning it. In our studies in population displacement in the Northeast, we found out how difficult it becomes when a person is displaced from one's ancestral land precisely because one does not hold and possess any legal title to it. On being asked to show any legally conveyed title deed against his claim to home from which he was to be evicted, a tribal chief of Arunachal Pradesh reportedly rebuffed: "The laws came first or our ancestors?" On the other hand, the argument that private ownership of land has already become the rule in the Northeast and we need to change swiftly to a legal landownership regime (Baruah 2005) to the author's mind is not only exaggerated but paves the way to state's ultimate supervision over resources in general and land in particular. This will only facilitate the transformation of land into territory – that is to say, into a resource that can be owned, supervised and hence 'colonized' at private will. The necessity of delineating and demarcating land for the preservation of one's identity and way of life was felt in the region for the first time in the plains only in the early part of the twentieth century and in the hills much later – perhaps on the eve of Independence.

Secondly, while the notion of land is highly uneven and discontinuous, state territoriality is not. Take the example of the Khasis of Meghalaya. Their clan names bear the trace of the particular part of the hills and mountains they (are supposed to) inhabit and the clan differences coincide with the distinctions between various levels and slopes of these hills and mountains. Colonization – particularly in its early phase, too created such a differentiated space in cities: the core area of a city like Calcutta would always remain out of bounds of the natives while the immediate concentric circles were occupied by their stooges and henchmen – the Bengali clerks and managers. The natives would be pushed to the far corners of the city according to their status and class differences. State territoriality levels off such distinctions. Within the territory of the state, we are all Indian citizens and as citizens we are all equal in the eyes of law and are entitled to 'equal protection of laws' (vide, Art. 14 of the Constitution of India). Not that these and other related provisions do away with our putative differences; but that such differences are 'disregarded' and 'bracketed out' insofar as the Constitution and laws of the land are concerned. The presence of a common territory constitutes us into nationals and citizens and places us as it were on a continuous space.

Thirdly, while land is sharable with others, territory is not. The examples of land being shared by communities without dominating or being dominated by each other are not rare. Many tracts and dispatches, memoirs and autobiographies written particularly by the eminent intellectuals and entrepreneurs of the region in the early twentieth century continued to reflect on the benefits that immigration from outside has done to the region – whether in terms of spread of western education and development of languages or in terms of investment and entrepreneurship training in the region. A section of them definitely thought positively about the presence of the outsiders in the region. On the other hand, territoriality or more aptly perceived territoriality conceptualizes it in exclusive and zero-sum terms: As I win the territory, you stand to lose and vice versa. Such exclusivity is achieved in three mutually related ways: one, by getting rid of areas with a heavy concentration of the non-ethnics; two, by reunifying the areas where the members of a community remain scattered for historical reasons under one administrative unit, and three, by cleansing the areas of the others on the ground that they are outsiders to the homeland. In order to preserve its numerical superiority, a group often gives away a part of its territory where the non-ethnic other are concentrated in numbers in order to tilt the balance in its favour. We know that administrative frontiers were drawn in the region in order to suit the administrative interests of the colonial rulers. The otherwise normal rule meant for administering the plains was not applied to the hills where according to administrative authorities particularly during the initial years the establishment of colonial rule, 'primitives' and 'savages' reside. It so happens that the members of the same community as a result remain scattered between several administrative units. The demand for unification is made under such circumstances. Finally, as a community feels that it has been depleted in strength in a manner that it becomes impossible for it to regain its numerical supremacy, it resorts to ethnic cleansing almost as a last resort. This is increasingly being resorted to particularly by the insurgents since the late 1970s. To my mind, 1980 marks the watershed in this respect. To round up, the efforts at making the administrative borders coincide with ethnic or national borders has turned out to be chicken-and-egg game that the nations and ethnic groups are seen to be involved since the emergence of the nation in the seventeenth century.

Territoriality is the lowest common denominator between the mutually rivaling nationalist and ethnic aspirations. While ethnic aspirations are very often targeted against nations and nation-states, they share with them the common aspiration for being territorial and having a homeland of their own. The author proposes to describe it as the mimicry by an ethnic community of the territoriality of the adversarial nation. If it is mimicry, it also entails subversion. For, while mimicking the nation-state, it also challenges it and contests the territoriality of the nation-state (Das in Bajpai & Mallavarappu eds. 2004: 284-313). Territoriality contains anarchy that is built into it. It may be likened to the process of peeling an onion that only ends with the end of the onion itself. The logic of territoriality cannot be extended so far as to mock at itself and its destruction can be arrested only by fixing and freezing the already existing territorialities – that is to say, by turning its logic on its head. There is no end to the process of present-day territorialization.

More often than not, we tend to forget that the legal regime established since the colonial times is only too inadequate to address communities' contentious claims to land. What makes the claims contentious is the fact that they are made often on the same tract of land and neither of the communities involved in the conflict is prepared for making any compromise in this respect. The problem in other words is that the proposed homelands crisscross with each other. While there are considerable overlaps between them, each of the conflicting communities advances it in more or less uncompromising terms. In this part of the paper, we propose to examine some of the reasons that are advanced by the communities while justifying their contending claims to homeland: First, there is what may be called the chronological justification. The claim to homeland is buttressed by an argument of historical precedence. The principle on which the claim is based is that one will have a rightful entitlement to land provided one can establish that one has settled in it before the arrival of others. 'Who came first (?)' becomes the most important question in this regard. But there are problems involved in the process. For one thing, often it becomes difficult to determine in any definitive manner, about who came first. In the absence of any mutually acceptable history, the claims are at times shrouded in origin myths and tribal and group-specific genealogies. Under these circumstances it becomes difficult—if not impossible to differentiate the history that 'stands the scientific test' from the history that is liable to be 'used as someone's political agenda'. Sometimes, the length of stay of the later-day settlers is too long to be dismissed and wished away. Secondly and as a corollary to the problem underlined above, there is the argument that the length of settlement of late-immigrants eventually gives them a right to live in the area they have been living for generations. The argument is not so much that they need to have a separate homeland of their own by way of evicting the early settlers. But the early settlers by way of invoking the logic of chronological precedence are reportedly out to evict them and lay siege over the land in a monopolistic manner. They even accuse the early settlers of having unleashed untold miseries and planned atrocities on the late-migrants. It is under these circumstances, they are forced to clutch on the demand for an exclusive homeland. It is like saying that notwithstanding their best endeavours, the early settlers are unwilling to accommodate them. But where will they go? Not chronology but a reasonable length of living in the same land becomes the basis of an argument. In the second kind of argument, chronology is not allowed to solely determine the *reasonableness* of the duration of living in the area. The claim to homeland is viewed as a rebound effect. Thirdly, the belief that the land one inhabits is the same where their ancestors too lived lends to it some sort of a ritual status. The land thus provides them with a source of collective memory, which as Agnes Heller points out is remembered through collective celebrations. Slightly rephrased, the third argument may be taken as a derivative from the second. For, the ritual status of the land lent to it by the ancestors often becomes the key to determine the rightfulness of the claim being made by them. But it is possible to decouple the argument from any frame of time sequence. Ancestry and heritage are not so much a function of chronological time as much as they acquire salience in a situation of politically contentious claims. Our collective memory is not benign - but is ignited by political conjuncture. Fourthly, the perceived history of isolation of a region or a community from the rest of India and its ability to successfully repel invasions from mainstream India is often cited as the justification of its claim to homeland. It is true that the British were able perhaps for the first time in their history to 'colonize' them. But the transfer of power by the British to the Indian rulers without consulting or taking them into confidence marked the continuation of the same 'colonial' legacy with the difference that this time the rule of New Delhi has replaced that of London. What we see is that each principle is distinct and is deployed in a manner that privileges a particular community as much as it disprivileges and censors the claims of others. Each one is sufficient by itself and rules out complementarities with others. It is this correlation between the desire on one hand and deployment of moral arguments and norms on the other that Kant sought to denounce in his famous *Critique of Practical Reason*. Violence under such circumstances becomes not only the inevitable outcome but also the crucial means of resolving conflicts. Such contentious claims to territorial rights are bound to and do spark off violence and are often responsible for violence and population displacement.

State and the Concrete Universality

We locate concrete universality not at the level of categorical imperatives a la Kant, but at the level of the local initiatives (we have already referred to mother's initiatives in the region), which involve certain crossing of the boundaries that keep one community from another and set off the conflicts. Concrete universality is not anathema to the question of identity and homeland claims made by the otherwise conflicting ethnic groups and communities of the region. But these initiatives instruct us to appreciate the value of peaceful social living and common existence notwithstanding such conflicting claims.

State's role vis-à-vis such village or local-level initiatives has been a bone of contention in recent years. We trace at least three divergent answers to the question of what could be the possible response of the state in normative terms: First, it has been argued that the issue of homeland has become totally incommensurate with the actual political economy of the region (Baruah 2005). The dynamics of actually existing political economy with informal systems of private ownership of land and the contributions made by the outsiders to region's agricultural development - whether by teaching the locals the art of wet rice cultivation and rendering land cultivable or by providing labour or a combination of both, have made it necessary for the state to confer legal recognition on them. It is only by derecognizing the homeland regime that necessary headway could be made for initiating comprehensive transformations in the society and politics of the region. This alternative poses the problem from the statist perspective. For, it views the state as the potential harbinger of such transformations while in actuality virtually nothing has changed in the state on the ground. What makes the state undertake the policy changes? This line of argument has no answer. Besides, it also takes the informal dynamics of actually existing political dynamics at their face value and conceives of the state as an entity that will have to make necessary changes while adapting it to the changes that have already taken place. Stated bluntly, this only smacks of a much criticized neo-liberal agenda.

Secondly and in contradistinction with the first, it is also argued that the state instead of taking on a maximal role should settle for a policy of complete neutrality. The objective of state neutrality is based on the twin principle of secularism and civic republicanism. As B. P. Misra puts it:

> The shared political culture and common civic identity may be kept separated from the traditionally given subcultures all of which have equal rights to coexistence within the polity. In other words, the state should remain neutral with respect to all pre-political forms of life by ... the decoupling of the majority culture from the political culture with which it was once focused. Cultural matters should better be left at the helms of the civil society to enjoy what might be a negative liberty for all of them (Misra 2007 mimeo: 20).

It is doubtful whether – given the kind of civil society that exists in the region, things will be better - if left to the realm of civil society. Civil society is not immune to the same cultural influences that also affect the state and many of the civil society institutions reflect the same cracks and fissures that lie at the root of interethnic conflicts and violence. If civil society is posited as a solution, then we certainly need to reform it. A plea for civil society must be coupled with an agenda for reforming it.

Thirdly, the state is also urged to be guided by 'normative concerns' while finding out 'just solutions' to the conflicts (Oinam & Thangjam in Biswas & Thomas eds. 2006). The paper does not give us any clue for how we might make the state find out 'just solutions' and ensure that it will be guided by such 'normative concerns'. Civil society obviously plays a role in making the state 'normative'.

REFERENCES

Baruah, Sanjib (2005), *Durable Disorder: Understanding the Politics of Northeast India*. Oxford University Press, New Delhi.

Chatterjee, Partha (1983), 'More on Modes of Power and the Peasantry', Ranajit Guha (ed.), *Subaltern Studies: Writings on South Asian History and Society*, Oxford University Press, Delhi.

Das, Samir Kumar (2004), 'Ethnic Sub-Territoriality and the Modern State: The Case of North-Eastern India', in Kanti Bajpai & Siddharth Mallavarapu (eds.), *International Relations in India: Theorising the Region and Nation*, Orient Longman, New Delhi.

——————— (2007), *Blisters on Their Feet: Tales of Internally Displaced Persons of India's Northeast*, Sage, New Delhi.

——————— (2007), *Conflicts and Peace: The Role of Civil Society in India's Northeast*, Policy Studies No.42. East-West Center, Washington D.C.

——————— (2007), 'Righting Governance or Governing Rights: Tripura (2000)' in Dipankar Sinha & Kaberi Chakrabarti (eds.), *Democratic Governance in India: Reflections and Refractions*, Kalpaz, New Delhi.

Heller, Agnes (2001), 'A Tentative Answer to the Question: Has Civil Society Cultural Memory?', *Social Research*, 68(4), Winter.

Kant, Immanuel (1966), *Critique of Practical Reason and Other Writings in Moral Philosophy*, Trans. and ed. with an intro by Lewis White Beck, The University of Chicago Press, Chicago.

Markus, Maria Renata (2001), 'Decent Society and/or Civil Society?', *Social Research*, V (4), Winter.

Misra, B.P. (2007), 'Democracy and Dialogue: Lessons for and Lessons from India's North-East' (mimeo).

Oinam, Bhagat & Homen Thangjam (2006): 'Indian 'Nation-state' and the Crisis of the Periphery' in Prasenjit Biswas & C. Joshua Thomas (eds.), *Peace in India's Northeast: Meaning, Metaphor and Method: Essays of Concern and Commitment*, Regency, New Delhi.

3

LAND AND INTER-ETHNIC CONFLICT IN INDIA'S NORTH-EAST:

Middle Grounds in a 'State of Exception'

—Prasenjit Biswas

Conceptualizing land related conflict has been an immense task, as the simple claims of belonging sours into territoriality and hegemony with the outcome that contests over 'belonging' turns into a conflict over 'owning'. There is a paradox of essentialization: 'belonging' versus 'owning' in a historical sense that constructs a 'we' versus 'them'. Democratic discourses of sharing and redistribution of land as a resource gets 'overdetermined' by such constructions of essential identities. The symbolic materiality of land takes precedence over distributive justice, which gets further problematized in moments of dispossession and displacement of a marginalized collective group that ironically marks a hegemonic possession over land. For the purpose of this paper, let us look into how categorization of land constitutes a discourse of identity that faces an unwarranted transformation in the hegemonic structuring of the paradox of 'belonging' and 'owning'. Cultural construction of identity centering territory takes an essentialist and reductionist form, it converts belonging into owning that acts as the 'limit' for the Other. In this context, the notion of community acts as a crucial determinant of how the discourse of identity centres itself on land.

I

SOCIAL BOUNDARIES AND LAND RIGHTS

Marx in his *Critique of Gotha Programme* talked about the possibilities of transformation of boundaries of the State under a modern political system that distinguishes between the 'pre-political' and 'political'.[1] The pre-political state remains ontologically different from the political state. In the pre-political state, boundaries of communities of productive labour remain unalterable. In case of India's Northeast, such unalterable limits imposed on ethnic forms of labour in relation to land acts as a paradigmatic force that enters into a dichotomy with extraneous processes of importing changes in the land relation. Operation of State and market in a political sense that tries to alter relationship between labour and land at the super structural level presents labour as universally mobile that can dissemble itself from land. Such a circumstantial over determination of the relation between labour and land by the operation of a political state in its conjunction with market or market forces has a latent telos of surpassing this relationship in the unilinear global flow of Capital. In the context of Northeastern peoples, the defining character of this relationship between land and labour lies in 'embeddedness' of communities in a marked social boundary. This social boundary is often transgressed by market forces in conjunction with the State. In defining a moment of embeddedness of 'communities' in India's Northeast, one can identify the situation of being embedded in the ensemble of relations within particular social boundary, *which also stands subverted* in the universalizing flows of Capital that converts labour into a commodity. As a result, the State and the market jointly act as an adversary to presumed social boundaries of communities. This formulation is in contrast to James C. Scott's generalized perspective on State-society relationship, where Scott raises the question, "why the state almost always been the enemy of the people who move around?"[2] He re-contextualizes the question by asking, "[W]hy has it been the project of nearly every state to concentrate and fix population in space?" In other words, the project of the State, according to Scott, has been to strive for permanent settlement of peoples in the valley to constitute the hills in Southeast Asia. In contrast to such a position by Scott, what needs to be re-emphasized is the relative autonomy of social boundaries of ethnic communities independent of the involvement of the State, which the state somehow intended to disembed and subvert. The question is, does the State support movement of peoples across social and cultural boundaries? It supports such movement only from the position of weakening social solidarities in order to bring the hill spaces under control. In order to do so, the State 'sees' the social boundaries in a relational sense, it is the mode of relation that the State has with the community in a moment of collaboration and conflict that determines how the State 'sees' such communities and their social boundaries. The State also attempts to 'read' these 'social boundaries' as 'alterable' by dint of its politics of management of resources and inter-community relations and 'reads' it from the perspective of emerging economic and political relations. The Statist interpretation of social boundaries is often 'borrowed' by dominant communities, who already have an entrenched place within the field of power within which the state and market operates. This borrowed perspective of the State can be termed as 'reading the way the State reads' following James C. Scott.[3] Reading the way the state reads essentially means a subversion of 'social boundaries' that would mean forcing the ethnic communities in question accept the 'values' attributed to their land in a globalized market. This stands in sharp contrast to ethnographically available 'authority of the social order' in determining 'values' within the ensemble of social relations by forces such as state and market. This undermining of community oriented values by extraneous forces is sometimes given the legal force to limit indigenous rights over land behind a veneer of land-reforms and agrarian reforms. This introduces a necessary conflict within the very system of holding land by way of generating a contradiction between 'land' and 'labour' reflected in the dichotomy between 'belonging' and 'owning'.

II

COMMUNITY AND THE LAND QUESTION

Does land belong to the community, or it is the other way round? This question has found ethnographic and ecological interpretation to a certain mode of use of land. Maurice Godelier identified land use in the hills as patterned after 'kinship relations' within the community in terms of its exchange and actual utility.[4] As far as inter-community relationship centring land is concerned, it also remains governed by a relationship of inclusion/exclusion. Therefore, the very notion of 'belonging' turns out to be an extended network of kinship relations within which land belongs to the 'community'. It becomes not just a material resource, but a symbolic domain that regulates social exchange, livelihood and political power. The social-symbolic value of land determines the material value. In the case of Northeastern India's communities, the material value of land is a 'reproduction' of the social-symbolic value that the logic of capital attempts to subvert with the help of an instrumentalist state that tries to alter the social boundaries. The political economy of a periphery bound capitalism also substitutes the infirmities of the accumulative processes by converting land into a 'property' by segregating communal labour from it. This segregation between land and labour apparently establishes a regime of individual ownership within the community that gives rise to an inevitable landless section. Further such segregation paves the way for employment of outside labourers in tilling the land that facilitates accumulation by the land-owning class within a community. The social-symbolic value of land as a community resource gets subverted by laws of economic returns and accumulation from the use of land creating a paradox of sort: land becomes a commodity in the sense of market relations and consequently remains open to sale to an able purchaser even from outside the community.

In the context of Northeast, Sixth schedule of the Indian Constitution does not allow purchase of land in the scheduled areas of Assam, Nagaland, Meghalaya, Mizoram, Tripura, Manipur by anyone other than 'tribes' listed in the schedule. One of the unwarranted effects of the Sixth schedule is the emergence of landed gentry that goes in contradiction to community based 'sharing' of land on the basis of 'filiation', 'descent' and 'alliances'[5] that open up 'logical possibilities' of sharing and exchange within the community. Given that the logical possibility is not closed in the case of business and economic transactions between community owners and an outside agency/person/source, the Sixth Schedule recognized local customary rights to regulate outsider's access to land and related resources belonging to a community or tribe, as defined by the Sixth Schedule of the Indian Constitution. Increasing operation of the market economy with the arrival and availability a large number of consumer goods and services for the hill communities has altered the perception of 'social boundary' with the increasing mobility of tribes outside their community habitat.

Apart from this rapid interaction and exposure to the outside world, the tribal communities of Northeast region are also subjected to inter-ethnic clashes and inter-tribal feuds. Such clashes emanate from mutually conflicting claims over a territory. Such conflicting claims are made on the basis of delegitimizing the presence of the other in one's own so called 'homeland'. Such a strategy of de-legitimization is not necessarily complemented by one's sovereign claim over the homeland; rather it is an act of negation that affirms an epistemic claim over a territory. Land figures as a "metaphor" within the epistemic limits of homeland claim. Homeland claims affirm unique first-person knowledge over a community and its resources in such a manner that knowing it is a mode of belonging, which acts as the operative principle for someone else's non-knowledge. The social-symbolic domain of value is an abstraction from first-personal experience to the collective forms of 'articulation' and 'sense-making' intended over concrete events of 'belonging' to a 'territory' with a reference to an area of land. The point can be exemplified in several ways.

In the height of Kuki-Naga clashes in Manipur, issues such as influx, claims of separate homeland and constitution of a separate revenue district centered upon 'owning' land areas spread over Churachandpur, Ukhrul, Tameilong, Chandel and Senapati districts of Manipur. The goal of establishing insulated and secured-from-others kind of homeland moved into turning others into a 'minority' by way of violent attacks leading to displacement and refugee-hood.[6] This kind of delegitimization of Others in the territorial claims of 'belonging' is the hallmark of ethnic exclusivism centring land. The justificatory force of curbing others from belonging to the same land draws its ominous inspiration from a desire to remain as majority and dominant in one's own locale. Attacks of all forms, especially attacks on women and children of the other community in the forms of killing, rape and maiming had spread a holocaust scenario among the smaller ethnic and tribal communities in States such as Manipur, Tripura and Assam.[7] The growing number of casualties inflicted on ethnic minorities, smaller tribes and women and children not only among the displaced and refugee-ed peoples, but also on the neighbourly communities living together peacefully for decades has been rampant in Manipur and Assam—two states emerging as 'slaughterhouse' of minorities.

III

MINORITIES AND MAJORITARIAN HOMELANDS

The panoramic and ghastly scenario of inter-ethnic clashes declaring each other as 'illegitimate' with the proliferation of 'medium and small arms' attempt to settle 'right to life and livelihood' within a liberal democracy into a theatre of violence and counter-violence that keep fuelling each other. It is a malevolent spirit of self-determination that produces a voyeuristic justifications for genocides, ethnocides and rapes, all used as instruments of 'rejecting' other peoples claims. In a majoritarian homeland claim, minorities necessarily are excluded. So, the question becomes imminent, *can there be a notion of homeland that includes others in a liberal-democratic sense?* Especially in the ploy-ethnic context of Northeast India, where each ethnic community and group 'belongs' in a liberal democratic sense with all their specificities and comparative advances in material and cultural terms, it is difficult to have an ethnically homogeneous homeland without violating liberal principles of citizenship. Homeland claims made at the behest of communities in terms of settlement in a territory and in terms of strength of population gain their legitimacy from the condition that such a territorialization is consistent with equal claims made by others too. But this assumption behind 'homeland claims' undergoes a 'performative contradiction' as it negates the very basis of making such a claim by negating others from within such a conceived homeland. The most interesting aspect of such a discourse of exclusion lies in the manner in which a justification is produced as a reason for exclusion of 'Others'. One or two examples suffice here: the case of Bodos excluded from the mainstream Assamese nationalism can be treated as an exclusion of the 'internal minority', as the Bodos took a different route of articulating their historical identity. The case of proving Assamese as the largest majority in the state of Assam resulted into a bitter linguistic jingoism that delegitimized all non-Assamese speakers as 'outsiders' and 'foreigners'. One can observe the rise of a fragmented discourse of citizenship that treats differently various groups of people depending on whether they belong to the majority linguistic group or not. Such a fragmented discourse had proliferated ethnic hatred, fear of the Other and a narrow notion of self-determination. One can also note that a discourse of difference that initially based itself on territorial belonging turns into a discourse of authenticity in matters of citizenship. It is a movement from the domain of livelihood and cultural belonging to the domain of an abstract notion of political subjectivity that throws up the criterion for determining land-related right claims.

Another interesting aspect of framing a criterion of belonging is an unmediated reciprocal differentiation between contiguous identities, which are connected by a strange kind of mutual relationality. Several such cases can be catalogued here such as Immigrant Muslim peasantry and the Assamese in lower Assam, Naga-Kuki, Bodo-Santhal relationship to name only a few among many. In such relationships, the notion of mutual need purely from a pragmatic consideration that acts as the cause of settlement goes wrong in moments of distrust resulting into a claim of first entitlement and be of the early settlers. The present mode of settlement is regressed to an arbitrarily chosen past as dictated by the dominant social groups that settle the matters of difference through physical force, which can be justified by referring to forms of cultural differences. For example, in the history of Assamese-immigrant relationship post-1930, there has been several and contradictory attempts at discovering 'common grounds' with Muslims by classifying them in different cultural categories such as 'indigenous Assamese Muslims', 'Mymmensing Muslims or 'neo-Assamese Muslims' and many other such factions. The distinction drawn between 'indigenous Assamese Muslims' and 'East Bengal Muslims' on the basis of linguistic difference intended to de-assimilate non-Assamese Muslims from their Neo-Assamese status. The result of such a micro-distinction in terms of difference has been an alienation of Muslim peasantry from land and instead it gave rise to a more middle class construction of Muslim identity that grows in parallel with dominant Assamese identity. One can surmise that the emergence of greater differentiation in terms of specificity within a historically bound and 'territorialized' community produces a sense of a comparable other, who is unmediated and represented in the mainstream. Land as a factor of production and livelihood finds an altered significance in such an shift of internal differentiation of linguistic and cultural identity that instantiates a kind of pluralism away from 'territorial bounds', while differentiated entities still remain within the bounds of a delimited cultural zone. A similar process can be located even within Manipur. One can quote an eloquent explanation,

> Instead of sloganeering land as 'economic capital', the 'right of the peoples and nations to sovereignty over their natural wealth and resources' (...) has been projected as the starting point for political campaign. Though this projection is close to realizing land as 'economic capital', the two are not synonymous either. So far, claims seem to confine to its political overtone. Projecting 'possession of native land' as an inalienable right not only unifies tribes under pan-Naga identity

> because of the common practical interest of inheritance of each tribe, but this strategy also serves as good ground for wiping out the enemy. This is a case of implicit 'use' of land as 'political capital'.[8]

The delimited cultural zone emerges as the 'political capital' in the course of unifying and consolidating a 'national' identity. The case of Pan-Naga national identity in relation to the state of Manipur has become a contentious matter of dispute that draws a vertical line between Naga and others in the claim for a unified Nagalim. One needs to raise a question here, 'why is it so difficult to cultivate the moral motive?'[9] Advocacy of unification of all Naga dominated areas from the hill districts of Manipur heavily wields a sense of justice, when an explanation is given in this manner that Naga inhabited areas have been forcefully divided and Naga families have been dispersed from each other by a crooked method of administration during colonial and post-colonial times. Such an explanation questions the normative basis of creating 'imaginary boundaries' within the very Naga community and evokes a counter-imagery of living freely in their own territory.[10] The moral motive of 'breaking artificial boundaries' between one's own community is juxtaposed against the administrative necessity of not breaking the existing boundaries of various states of Northeast India. Further such a project of redrawing the boundaries undercuts the imperative of living together in a peaceful manner between oneself and other. This is a situation of 'moral dilemma' complicated by the politics of 'land as capital' that often overshadow the choices of an autonomous ethical consideration.

If we think about such an ethical dilemma in political terms, one needs to answer the question of 'belonging' in a truthful and reasonable manner. As the idea of 'belonging' cannot just be within a singular cultural domain, therefore, one needs to widen the notion of 'belonging' and 'unifying' not merely as a political project of 'legitimate' social identity, but by evolving a different notion of non-ethnocentric positioning of identity-politics. Such a possible non-ethnocentric positioning within the public and shared space amidst others might address the question of homeland and social boundary in a manner different from the current articulation of 'territorial identities'. The manner of belonging within a group-identity does not in-itself give rise to a 'sensibility' to a different and alternate conception of legitimacy, but it merely confines itself to a mere 'sensitivity' about one's own cultural past and future ambitions. Probably one needs to cultivate a greater sensitivity towards the 'other' in order to overcome ethical dilemmas that arise out of a political goal of a secure self-identity,

> Sensitivity seems to me to be far more infused with the aura of the ego and self-involvement to be of use here. Sensibility on the other hand, seems to point precisely to the possibility of overcoming of such egoistic (cultural or personal) preoccupations. 'A rich enough conception of sensibility gathers together ideas of responsiveness and knowledge, motivation and cognition, the idea of "reading" and acting in its light as well as the idea of false readings, misrepresentation, delusion and ignorance'.(...) It is this kind of sensibility which enables one to avoid the arrogance of false superiority, honour autonomy, and resist the desire to appropriate.[11]

Such a sensibility in place of sensitivity can restore an ethical paradigm in the resolution of land-related conflicts in the shaping of a 'territorial identity'. The conflict between claims of boundaries and between territorial identities can be broken into ethical sensibilities towards aspirations of each other in a dialogic conversation between the so-called rivals and enemies. This may help reducing paradigmatic forms of majoritarian conflicts not by way of assimilation and surrender but by way of a free play of sensibilities that are constrained by narrow slogans of political and cultural boundaries.

IV

BIOPOLITICAL ORDERING OF THE SELF-OTHER DIALECTIC

Construction of identities in the sway of political projects is no longer free from the dichotomy of 'constituting' and 'being constituted by'. The agency of self-identity lacks the founding 'sovereignty' that usually gives it an existential ground of affirmation. As a consequence, defiance of the 'middle ground' between the State and the non-State constitutes the very affirmation of identity. This affects a lack of middle ground as well as creates an in-distinction between law and life, the State and the non-State. Carl Schmitt called this indistinction a suspension of both autonomy and norm[12], while Agamben went a step further to call this 'state of exception'.[13] Within such constitution of an identity without a middle ground, a distinction between 'life' and 'law' is only an a-*poria* (literally without a road). In such a situation of necessary and originary suspension of the distinction, collective life finds its 'closure' in claims of 'authenticity' and 'belonging' as an idea of 'indigenous sovereignty', which in effect, bases itself on a suspension of 'rights of others', which is inclusive of the State as well as other groups/communities differentiated in the space between the State and the non-State. While the differentiation is based on 'drawing a line' between the Self and Other, the notion of authenticity/belonging makes the Subject forget the suspension of middle ground between life and law that necessarily lies in the in-between space between 'we' and 'them'. One can concretely look at how this 'middle ground' is explored post-conflict between the parties of land-based conflict. Let us take an extract from Kuki-Naga conflict, where Kukis were 'victims' in their own account from a press release by Kuki National Organization (KNO):

Imphal, June 15, 2007: The KNO in a release today said it lauds the gesture of friendship by the NSCN (IM) but added it must first of all relent and acknowledge mistake in its Kuki genocide campaign in the 1990s.

The KNO was reacting to the NSCN (IM) statement on the Moreh incidents "as a responsible neutral observer".

On the claim that 'Kukis in Nagaland are very much Nagas and within the Naga fold', the KNO said in the statement that the Kukis in Nagaland are recognized as one of the indigenous tribes of Nagaland, and not as a Naga tribe, as suggested in the NSCN (IM) statement.

The Kuki people's status of being a true indigenous tribe is manifested in their participation in the Naga independence movement, of which history and records are the witness. The late Lengjang Kuki, (one of the founding fathers of Naga Club), was a signatory to the Simon Commission on January 10, 1929, representing the Kukis of Nagaland, the statement further said.

In addition, late Seikhohen Kuki and Jangkhosei Kuki were also elected as members of the Naga National Council in 1946 representing the Kuki tribe, it said adding that indeed the late Sekhohen Kuki was one of the members of the constitution drafting committee of NNC and also a member of the first Naga delegation to Delhi to meet the then Prime Minister of India on the issue of Naga independence.

Besides these leaders, other Kukis, such as late Onpao Kuki (then president of Kuki union), late Paochung Kuki, late Dr Lenzalal Kuki along with the rest of the Kukis of Nagaland put their finger printers in favour of Naga independence in the Naga voluntary plebiscite on May 16, 1951, it said.

Since then, there is no going back and at no point of time have they deviated from this course. The Kukis of Nagaland have been given equal rights, opportunities, and protection as bona fide denizens of the land, with the freedom to uphold their Kuki identity, it said.

However, since 1990s, in Nagaland more than 150 Kukis of all ages have been killed and 14 villages have been burnt down mainly due to outside influences. All this inhuman treatment occurred although the Kuki Inpi in Nagaland time and again clarified that the Kukis of Nagaland neither subscribe nor extend moral support to the Kuki movement outside Nagaland, it said.

The KNO appreciates and respects the political stand of the Kukis of Nagaland and wish and hope that their brethren Nagas of Nagaland will continue to extend the same treatment. The KNO also hereby state that any/all Naga tribes living within Kuki ancestral territory, Zalengam, will be accorded equal status, rights, opportunity, and protection as any Kuki tribe with the freedom to preserve their Naga identity, it said.

The relationship between the Kuki and Naga people has been characterized by historical affinity, mutual respect, understanding, and not only peaceful but also cooperative co-existence, it said adding that the NSCN (IM) by launching Kuki genocide from the beginning of 1992, attempted to destroy such harmony.

The KNO as also the Kuki people abhor and oppose such divisive and parochial moves by the NSCN (IM), it said adding that the KNO harbours no ill-will towards the Naga people. Further, the KNO appeals to the NSCN (IM) to henceforth discard the parochial ideology it has been pursuing, it said.

> *Today, if the NSCN (IM) relents and gives up its claim on Kuki ancestral lands as forming part of Nagalim, they should issue an unconditional apology over their misguided actions of killing more than 900 innocent Kuki villagers and displacing tens of thousands of others, and proactively advocate and facilitate the resettlement of the Kuki villagers displaced by their genocidal campaign, it said adding that the KNO for the love of peace and progress, is ready to forgive them*

> *and shall keep the doors open for future cooperation in the twin struggles to redeem the right to self-determination and self-rule for the Kuki and Naga people.*[14]

Although Kuki articulation of land-based rights of citizenship and equality has a strong liberal content that gives a criterion of 'justice' in the context of claims of authenticity, the attempt to 'write back' to NSCN (IM) is couched with an exploration of the middle ground between Nagas and Kukis. This is a self-other dialectic that arises post-conflict that begins with a denial of the rights of the Other ends up in a quandary or dilemma of settling the correctness of one's own perspective, which the Other shall continue to reject. The only alternative to such a quandary is to return to a self-other dialectic that explores the middle ground and recognizes the sovereignty and autonomy of each of the sides. While it is possible to return to a middle ground, it is not possible to return to claims of authenticity in the post-conflict scenario, as such claims suspend the 'middle ground' that both the sides attempt to construct. A sensibility towards the claims of the other makes a reciprocation or response possible. So, a responsive discourse by a minority from an experience of victimhood and displacement can provide a starting point for a return to the exploration for middle grounds that establishes a kind of harmony. What Schmitt and Agamben point out about modern forms of power-relations is the impossibility of subjection and subjugation that produces a large aporia between life and law. The consequence of such an aporia is that there is a compulsion about finding the 'middle ground' by way of responding to the Other, as power-relations would have to simultaneously delineate self-other dialectic and suspend it by the 'biopower' produced by a conflict.[15] Land is just one component of this power, which in a dialectic between self and other and its suspension gets constituted into a social boundary that is undermined by an 'over determined value' assigned to it by the territorialized sense of community. This also results into a resistance to the 'blurring effect' of a biopolitical functioning of the State in conjunction with the market forces that often pits a community against the 'minorities'. The majoritarian fear of the Other contributes to the blurring of the middle ground that can only be retrieved in the after-effect of a conflict.

V

COMPLEX NEGOTIATIONS OF LAND RIGHTS

In post-conflict scenario, there is an experience of shift in matters of land rights and distribution of land to whom it legitimately belongs to. In the context of Manipur, *Manipur Land Revenue and Land Reforms Act, 1960* (MLR&LR) and its subsequent amendment allows the intervention of government in the allotment and distribution of land in the hill areas, where land traditionally belong to the tribes. In a scenario of land-related conflicts, such an intervention in matters of settlement, regulation and distribution of land in hill areas leaves open the scope of settlement of other non-tribal communities in hill districts of Manipur. This increases the possibility of communal conflicts over issues of settlement in hill areas. Provisions of such an act stands in conflict with Sixth schedule provision extended to the tribes of Northeast whereby tribal land cannot be transferred to others. MLR&LR may give rise to conflicting claims over land between tribal population and others and therefore, such a possibility needs to be reduced by way of a complex negotiation. The point of negotiation could be accessibility to a certain portion of land in both plain and hill areas on the basis of need that won't restrict no permanent resident of the state of Manipur from acquiring such 'open access land'. Adequate care should be taken for regulating the use and utility of such land on the basis of an agreed upon modality between a tribe and the government. Primarily the right of tribes over their own land be recognized along with the provision of 'open access land system' on some portion of the territory so that a greater social cohesion is possible in a land-constrained state such as Manipur. A democratic negotiation by moving beyond both the MLR &LR and Sixth Schedule may pave the way for a mutually beneficial and reciprocal sharing of land between tribes and non-tribes in Manipur.

The Sixth Schedule of the Constitution is now supplemented by "The Scheduled Tribes and Other Traditional Forest Dwellers (Recognition of Forest Rights) Act,2006". The conjunction between the two constitutional provisions complicates matters related to owning forest land by tribes and its proper utilization. The Recognition of Forest Rights act, 2006 speaks of the symbiotic relationship between tribes and ecosystems, but reduces this relationship to a framework for 'recognition' and 'recording' of 'forest rights' and identification of 'evidences' that can provide sustainable basis to 'conservation regimes'. The law remains ambivalent about the specificity of forest habitats lived by generations of tribes, records of which are available only in 'oral traditions' and not much in legal testimonials, except those 'recorded' by colonial masters. The talk about 'conservation of biodiversity and maintenance of ecological balance' in terms of 'conservation regimes' is an interpolation of a 'scientific authority' that merely takes forests and forest dwellers as 'responsible' for conservation.[16] The legislation is a condensed statement of a stereotypical response of the collaboration between 'conservationists' and 'lawmakers', who shelve the embedded notions of ethical responsibility towards nature, as available in a rich variety of the notions of 'sacred' in tribal worldviews of India's Northeast. In the case of land rights in hill areas, such a notion of sacred assumes a central importance even in determining which part of the land should be placed under an 'open access system'.

The idea of 'survival and sustainability of forest ecosystem' and the access to such forest resources by forest dwelling communities, as mooted in the Forest act dangerously assumes such rights to be given to the 'primitive tribal groups and pre-agricultural communities', 'nomadic groups' and other such communities, who are dependent on forest resources for eking out a livelihood. Such rights are vested in terms of 'pattas' and 'tenures' and thereby it subtly brings forest land and resources into a form of 'ownership'. This has a historical consequence: the forested territories dwelt by tribes and communities shall now be defined in terms of tenures as no one can bank anymore on the memory of settling on a piece of land, which is only constitutive of a genre of folklore! The social and economic consequence of it shall be commercialization of land structured by ownership and utility functions. This idea of a tenure based habitat as introduced in the Act shall completely spoil the possibility of conservation of animals, flora and fauna, as all such resources can be sold under one's ownership. The larger picture that arises is a complete degradation of tribal habitats by tribes themselves as everybody will be driven by an urge to make quick buck without any ethical qualms. The idea of the sacred shall be overthrown by the idea of ownership, which has hitherto lay in the domain of values as embodied in beliefs. This immemorial 'value' of the habitat and dwelling is reduced to 'cash value' by this bill of patta rights.

Given this emergent scenario, the environmental and cultural good of the hill areas of Manipur possibly lie in a transformative self-construction outside the narrow notion of territoriality as defined by imagined 'social boundaries'. Land being the subject of the bio-political in which un-inspiring ironies of mutual annihilation are written over, it is necessary to re-consider the co-constructing character of cultural and political identities, not just in clashes, but in an ethical co-partnership in mutually sharing the land space of

Manipur between the tribes and plains. The colonial binary between the landscapes now need to be converted into a 'cultural intimacy'. If 'rice' from the plains symbolizes the survival of plain populace and if the 'rice' from the hills signifies the survival of the tribesman, it is possible that the twain 'symbols' shall meet in an overlap between 'homelands' of survival and affinity.[17] Such a meeting shall be an effective antidote to ambiguities of hegemony that attempts to break human relations by assimilating the marginal and the small. In the context of all the Northeastern States, strong bias against each other's cultural and political plans often result into breaking implicit moral norms of inter-cultural behaviour. Therefore, co-constructing other's identity as a partner in terms of sharing the resource base could be a solution not only to the problem of turning land into a material and symbolic capital, but also to attempts at crossing the 'picket line' of ethical behaviour. One has to also get rid of a repressive notion of outsider and insider that all the time quarrel along the moral picket line. *Defense against an Other in symbolic and real terms should not just be across a piece of land, but it should involve a proper ethical response to the Other without annulling the Other.*

NOTES

1. Karl Marx, *Critique of Gotha Programme*, Foreign Language Press, Peking, 1976, pp.25-6.
2. James C.Scott, "Freedom and Freehold: Space, People and State Simplification" David Kelly and Anthony Reid, (eds) in *Asian Freedoms*, Cambridge University Press, Cambridge, 1998,pp.37-64.
3. James C. Scott, *Seeing Like a State: How Certain Schemes to Improve the Human Condition have Failed*, Yale University Press, New Haven, 2001, pp.7-8.
4. Maurice Godelier, *Me´tamorphoses de la parente*, Fayard, Paris, 2004, pp.34-7, 89.
5. Rodney Needham, "Alliance" in *Oceania* vol.56, no.3,1986,pp. 165–80.

6. An estimated 8800 families are still affected due to Naga-Kuki clashes, who are still displaced in various places in five hill districts and in various relief camps.
7. Notable holocausts can be listed here. Massacre of Kukis and Nagas during 1992-93, Nellie massacre of 1983 etc.
8. Bhagat Oinam and Homen Thangjam, " Indian 'Nation State' and Crisis of the 'Periphery' " in Prasenjit Biswas and C.J.Thomas (eds.), *Peace in India's North-East: Meaning, Metaphor and Method*, Regency Publications, New Delhi,2006,p.67.
9. This question is raised by Mrinal Miri in the context of moral constitution of self and its relation to other. As Politics, in true sense, is an expansion on moral motives, such a question might indicate the 'ethical' basis of a certain political action.
10. A Lanunungsang Ao, "Indo-Naga Politcal Conflict" in Prasenjit Biswas et.al.(ed.) op.cit., p.398-99.
11. Mrinal Miri, "Plurality of Cultures and Multiculturalism" in *Identity and Moral Life*, Oxford University Press, New Delhi,2003,p.87.
12. Carl Schmitt, *Political Theology*, tr.George Schwab, MIT Press, Cambridge,1985,pp.135-37.
13. Girogio Agamben, *State of Exception*, tr, Kevin Attell, University of Chicago Press, Chicago,2005,p.32.
14. I cite this whole reportage the represent a kind of 'writing back' to the aggressors by the victims that aim to establish a middle ground that remained suspended during the conflict.
15. Prasenjit Biswas and Chandan Suklabaidya, *Ethnic Life-World in North-East India: An Analysis*, SAGE, New Delhi, 2008, p.270.
16. Indeed such an authority is also assumed by MLR&LR in sec 13 (B) of the amended act that empowers the government in regulating migratory cultivation for protection of environment.
17. Suzan Ilcan, *Longing in Belonging: The Cultural Politics of Settlement*. Praeger, Westport, CT, 2002.

REFERENCES

Agamben, Girogio, (2005), *State of Exception*, Trans., Kevin Attell, University of Chicago Press, Chicago, p.32.

Ao, A. Lanunungsang, (2006) 'Indo-Naga Politcal Conflict', Prasenjit Biswas et.al.(eds.), *Peace in India's North-East: Meaning, Metaphor and Method*, Regency Publications, New Delhi.

Biswas, Prasenjit and Chandan Suklabaidya (2008), *Ethnic Life-World in North-East India: An Analysis*, SAGE, New Delhi, p.270.

Godelier, Maurice (2004), *Me´tamorphoses de la parente*, Fayard, Paris, pp.34-7, 89.

Ilcan, Suzan (2002), *Longing in Belonging: The Cultural Politics of Settlement*. Praeger, Westport, CT.

Marx, Karl (1976), *Critique of Gotha Programme*, Foreign Language Press, Peking, pp.25-6.

Miri, Mrinal, (2003) 'Plurality of Cultures and Multiculturalism', *Identity and Moral Life*, Oxford University Press, New Delhi, p.87.

Needham, Rodney (1986), 'Alliance', Oceania vol.56, no.3, pp. 165–80.

Oinam, Bhagat and Homen Thangjam (2006), "Indian 'Nation State' and Crisis of the 'Periphery' ", Prasenjit Biswas and C.J.Thomas (eds.), *Peace in India's North-East: Meaning, Metaphor and Method*, Regency Publications, New Delhi, p.67.

Schmitt, Carl (1985), *Political Theology*, tr.George Schwab, MIT Press, Cambridge, pp.135-37.

Scott, James C.(1998), 'Freedom and Freehold: Space, People and State Simplification', David Kelly and Anthony Reid, (eds.), *Asian Freedoms*, Cambridge University Press, Cambridge, pp.37-64.

——— (2001), *Seeing Like a State: How Certain Schemes to Improve the Human Condition have Failed*, Yale University Press, New Haven, pp.7-8.

4

FRAGMENTED CIVIL SOCIETY: Problems and Prospects

—Pradip Phanjoubam

Introduction: War by other means

The debate over who or what should constitute the rather ethereal notion of "civil society" gets all the more intriguing in a conflict situation, such in Manipur. The question is, should "civil society" have a normative definition and be treated as constituting of the occupants of a space earmarked between the State and vested interests represented variously by the private sector and other power players, such as the militant challengers to the State's authority and legitimacy, or else between mutually feuding non-state combatants. While this definition of "civil society" may not be everything, it is a convenient one. The trouble is, when there is a normative definition of this space, this space invariably becomes hotly contested, and often readily transforms into an extension of the conflict zones they are supposed to be standing in between and arbitrating. Rather than be peace agents, they thus often come to fight, what Sanjib Baruah calls, "war by other means".

Manipur is familiar with this phenomenon. There can be no argument that the "civil society" space has been deeply fissured on sectarian lines. The result is, wars by other means are fought on practically every issue involving any two or more communities of the state's multitude of communities. This sectarian division is also seen along other broader lines such as between the hill districts and valley districts, between the tribals and non-tribals etc. It is not uncommon to even hear of self-proclaimed human rights organisations speaking two different and mutually hostile languages on many issues. It is as if there is nothing universal about such supposedly shared values as the powerful notion of human rights. How can any meaningful, problem solving discourse ever happen under the circumstance, is the ignored question.

The technical ear-marking of a so called "civil society" space leads to another familiar problematic situation. The conflicting parties themselves begin actually to contest for this space by putting up their "civil society" proxies, having realized how powerful these bodies can be in force multiplying their agenda through precisely the "wars by other means". Again this is a phenomenon not unfamiliar to Manipur at all. The result is not only a complication of the conflicts themselves, but also a discrediting of this very same "civil society" space, ultimately tarnishing the image of the "civil society" movement itself.

There is also a fierce contest amongst conflicting parties to absorb even students' movements to become part of their networks of organs. Some even float their own "civil society" bodies, and this is not difficult against the context of the definition of "civil society" as merely a matter of an organization positioned within a certain given space. As for instance, the minute a civil rights campaign body is formed, or students' body is constituted, it is assumed that they automatically qualify to be classified as "civil society" regardless of whether they have any interest in civility. This makes the notion of "civil society" become vulnerable to be reduced to the status of mere tools of conflict. Must this not be considered a corruption of the popular understanding of the notion of "civil society"? The need then is for a rethink on what "civil society" ideally should constitute of.

Moral constituent: As a thumb rule civil society should have some qualitative elements over and above just the quantitative. The issue must be made to become a moral one as well. Only such an approach can make the discourses generated within this space have a vision beyond just the immediate or community interest. Otherwise, it would be forsaking its exalted objective position of being impartial arbiters wherever conflicts of interests arise, and instead become another means to "war by other means."

If such a definition is agreed upon, then the ambit of the space called "civil society" would become broadened considerably. It can and would then include many more people in other walks of life other than the organized "civil society" bodies, or professional members of the "civil society" acting as the watchdog of the establishment and society at large. Professions such as the journalism, whose credibility equally depends on neutrality, and who too draws its succor from its image as watchdogs of the society, would definitely come to be included. But the dangers of the larger civil society being drawn into the "war by other means" would remain, and in fact has proven to do so in many instances. Media reporting of the aftermaths of the Naga ceasefire extension beyond territorial limits in June 2001, by newspapers in Nagaland and Manipur for instance, many media observers now point out, were starkly different. The facts were the same, but the way the stories were told, displayed or nuanced, conjured up totally different pictures of the same incidents altogether. Unwittingly, the media too was drawn into the conflict and fought the same "wars by other means." The challenge then is once again to restructure our notion of the contentious "civil space" so as to distinguish the tools of war from those of peace unambiguously.

Reconstructing Civil Society

In this conflict theatre, it is almost an axiom that the civil society is not always civil. Civil society vigilantes sponsored blockades, bandhs, strikes and many other disruptive activities, are more often than not for very sectarian causes. Civil society in the entire northeast is badly fractured and ethnically fissured and may not be quite what the term is generally understood to be. The term civil society presupposed certain shared values and qualities regardless of religious and community affiliations and these values are what have been relegated into the background in our context.

Hence when we talk of students' community or youth or women, in more ideal situations, there ought not to be any need for prefixing these understandings with community and religion specific qualifications. This however has been far from the truth in the northeast, and Manipur has been no exception in the regard. There is hence very little prospect of generalizing the problems. A few examples will illustrate this point. When we say students or youth or women communities, the nomenclatures themselves ought to have been self explanatory. The reality is quite different in the northeast, where every ethnic community forms its own students, youth, women organizations, etc, each with very different and more often than not sectarian agendas to pursue. Often again these pursuits of the different "civil society", work at cross purposes, accentuating, rather than solving problems. In Manipur such clashes of sectarian agendas are all too often. The almost entirely different objectives of organization such as the United Naga Council, the United Committee Manipur, All Manipur United Clubs Organisation, the Kuki Inpi Manipur etc, to name just a few, should suffice to make this point clear.

The scenario would virtually be the same if we were to list the various students' organizations, or women's organizations existing in the state. Under the circumstance ,there can be no general understanding of the term "civil society", as all institutions formed in this important sector of the society are always and necessarily coloured by ethnic tints. The general understanding of the term becomes split into numerous smaller ethnic specific organizations. Contrast these with organizations on the other extreme of the civil society panorama such as the International Red Cross Society, Reporters Without Frontiers, Amnesty International, Rainbow Warriors etc, just to have an idea of the direction civil society organizations in our own midst are heading.

While it may not be desirable to advocate for a total generalization of the energy of peculiar nature of civil society bodies in the Northeast, as it is also true that there are indeed area and ethnic specific problems to be tackled, it would also be as short sighted to totally ignore the commonality that must run in all such organizations the world over. Hence when we say youth problem, there must be a general thread that binds it to the more broad-based understanding of the problem. Our youth must be able to identify, empathize and sympathize with the national and international youth movements. Only when this happens can a reverse flow of the same sentiments will become possible. The need of the hour then is for an effort to reconstruct Manipur's civil society. Its civil society movements must be put back on track that will integrate the place to the mainstream of humanity.

Ethnic identity upsurge being what it is, this is not going to be by any standard, easy to go about doing this, but it is one of those very vital and urgent issues at hand, the place cannot shy away from. It is also the only way it can make its civil society civil in the true sense of the words.

Rule by People

Should democracy mean a rule by the people? The issue is of utmost relevance and importance because so many in the ethnic world seem to think that direct rule by the people would amount to a purer democracy. Our experience has been that it is it prone to degenerate into "mobocracy"?

Karl Popper, has some very interesting things to say on the matter in his new book, "All Life is Problem Solving." (Routledge 1999; distributed in India by Seagull). In the preface to the book, the author says for instance that there has never been anything as a 'democracy' in the sense of 'rule by the people' and when it has, it always degenerated and paved the way for an arbitrary and unaccountable dictatorship. He on the other hand believes that true democracy can vests only in the representative, democratically elected and constitutional form of government. For in the end, only a representative democracy can be accountable.

Accountable first to its electorate and ultimately to the wider constituency of humanity. The word accountability, we are also in total agreement, holds the key to responsible governance and justice. Only when this is ensured, can there be true democracy. In the cases of rule by the "people's court", or mob justice, as it is increasingly becoming, we are at a loss to discover who can be held accountable. In a representative government this can be and must be.

Democracy's Chink

An article by Fareed Zakaria, on a fundamental problem of democracy is interesting in that it's ill effects are quite pronouncely felt in Manipur. The article takes the example of newly formed democracies in the former Communist Bloc of Europe, as illustrations of the contention. The thrust is that a tradition of liberal thoughts and tolerance is essential for democracies as a system to work in any given society. In the absence of this liberal tradition, merely adopting a democratic system can accentuate divisive faultlines of ethnic nationalism within the society. This becomes dangerous in multi-ethnic societies as the brutal ethnic cleansing wars witnessed in recent history in the Balkans demonstrated. In Manipur things have not been as bad but nevertheless, these faultlines have become very prominent, as a consequence of electoral multiparty politics, the chief instruments in our case, of actualising democracy in the system.

The state's experience has been, for different communities and ethnic groups to crystalise into ethnic based electoral vote banks. That is to say, empowerment through the ballot has meant contest for power between these various ethnic groupings. Among the many adverse consequences has been the total exclusion of many marginal ethnic communities from the democratic process. As for instance today, there can be little or no hope for the Taraos or Kharams, to return a legislator to the 60-member Manipur Legislative Assembly.

For that matter, if the days of electoral boycott calls by various influential Naga organisation come to an end, there can be little hope of a Kuki or a non-Naga winning the Outer Manipur Parliamentary seat, as the Nagas are in the majority here. The only way the results can go against the Nagas is when there is a multiple division amongst their voters on account of there being too many Naga candidates. The same logic would apply to a tribal candidate wishing to contest from one of the non-reserved valley constituencies. In today's atmosphere of ethnic animosity, he or she will have no chance whatsoever.

These inherent tensions continue even after a government has been formed. This cannot be in the true spirit of democracy and democratic empowerment of the people. For a democracy to work, a certain degree of liberalism that is able to cut across the confines of ethnic and other vested interests amongst its most fundamental constituents, the voters, is essential. Political parties will also have to have similar broad-based and liberal philosophies, and elections have to be fought on issues bigger than ethnic interests.

Chain Reactions

The spiral of numerous ethnic insurrections in Manipur, often with one literally dove-tailing the other is evidence to the complicated nature of the issue in hand. It is not too rare to read reports by journalists and commentators from outside the state telling the story with patronising bewilderment that Manipur is witness to 30 and odd different insurgencies at one time. The number 30 is never accurately spelled out, giving the impression that they have lost count, and that these dime-a-dozen insurgencies have very little significance left. Often these stories also imply, in the same tone of condescension, that these insurgencies are floated as if they were cottage industries by people who want a little quick buck. A lot of these perceptions are understandable and even may hold some water, but when they are presented as the total picture, it betrays either intellectual dishonesty, or more probably, an abject failure to grasp the picture in its entirety. The broad brush, any painter will testify, is a tool often used to shroud and mystify a subject so as to disguise and give credence to ignorance of the inner dynamics of the subject.

And so, in the portrayal of insurgency in not just Manipur but the entire northeast region, the popular resort has been to rely on images of primitive clannish tribal loyalties, mutual and irreconcilable atavistic hostilities amongst tribal groups, primordial xenophobia reminiscent of the days of savagery, etc. This approach leaves little room for a resolution apart from keeping the warring parties separated from each other (just as the instinctually determined hostility between cats and dogs is resolved by keeping them apart). This approach is quite unlike in the case of other deadly conflicts, such as was seen in Punjab. In these situations, the same analysts would forward economic and political causes and consequently profoundly actionable economic and political solutions. One is reminded of the outburst of one of literature's most famous characters, Shylock: "If you prick us do we not bleed." The

Jewish blood and the Christian blood are both red, so why different standards in assessing them.

But if the portrayal of the phenomenon of the multiplication of ethnic insurrections as wild assertions of primeval loyalties is to be treated as only a smokescreen to hide abject inability to comprehend the deeper currents, what then are the real issues? What then has led to this phenomenal proliferation of ethnic insurgencies? Observing just the last decade of the multi-pronged conflicts in Manipur should provide some clues. A prominent historical landmark in this regard would be the Naga-Kuki feud in the early 1990s. Before this cataclysmic development, militancy amongst the Kukis was barely heard of. It was only after this period that Kuki militant groups began spawning, and the existing ones began reorganising themselves into much more potent fighting forces than they previously were. But the culprit, rather than the supposed instinctual animosity that so many have, and still rely on, always was in our opinion, aggressive sectarian nationalism against the backdrop of a weak administration, morally de-legitimised by corruption and inefficiency.

Such brands of nationalisms, always manage to alienate those either excluded or else in the margin of it, and the state institution being virtually absent, these marginal groups have nowhere else to look for security or succor than to raise their own militias. And there is no gainsaying that the early 1990s were the heydays of overbearing Naga nationalism with the NSCN(IM) emerging as the predominant Naga insurgent group, pushing the agenda of Nagalim (Greater Nagaland) with unprecedented aggression. But if aggressive Naga nationalism led to the consolidation of militant Kuki nationalism, this in turn made other communities at its fringe insecure. The confounding feud between kindred tribes, the Kukis and the Paites almost in the immediate wake of the Kuki-Naga feuds, may be thus explained. The truce document ultimately signed between these latter tribes spelled out these underlying causes pretty succinctly. The spiral however does not end here. There are also other parallel spirals. As for instance, aggressive Meitei nationalism is also having similar responses. Hence, even the origin of militancy amongst the Meitei-Pangals may be explained within this frame. The vehemence with the Meitei Mayek is being opposed in the hill districts etc, may also be part of this same phenomenon. Plenty of lessons here, but who is willing to learn, is the big question.

Laws and Diktats

In any discussion on Manipur at this juncture, be it development, culture, capital investment, ethnic tensions, education, trade and commerce, youth unrest and for that matter practically every area of activity in the state, including the fine art of statecraft, one overwhelming question remains the common denominator – the law and order situation. This question looms over every other issue and more often than not, its presence freezes all other discussions, making them redundant. We are reminded of the rather cynical little parable of the mice community making big plans and suddenly realizing that before any of their plans can be executed, the cat in the house will have to be belled. All jaws drop, expressions go blank, and the overwhelming question that eliminates all other questions is, who will bell the cat? The question itself then becomes the answer, and the awful realization is articulated eloquently in just one unspoken word – nobody. Such is the magnitude of the problem, and its effect can be felt and understood fully only by those who live in the state under the shadow of this awesome question. Casual onlookers and armchair highbrows in distant Delhi and elsewhere, often misunderstand this general silence on the question, and misinterpret it variously, including as a public complicity in the tumult or vested interest in perpetuating the problem etc.. No generalization can be further from the truth. People yearn for peace and normalcy, but these are qualities of life that have gone beyond their easy control for a long time now. The recent spate of kidnapping and killings has made the matter worse, and it does seem a critical point has been reached. Our civil society is becoming more and more assertive in speaking out its minds. After all, who wouldn't be tired of a perpetual state of chaos? The fallouts of the political turbulence that we know as insurgency, apart from the problems it itself directly causes, are increasingly being demonstrated to be far reaching. In the resultant absolute discipline vacuum, we now even have student's organizations dictating what the educational curriculum should be, likening the vital and onerous agenda of education to something like placing an order in a restaurant frequented by juveniles. It is extremely frustrating that the government remains a mute spectator even as many of our venerated institutions are falling apart right before our very eyes.

The conclusion then is, peace is a must for any rational discourse on the way our civil society wants to conduct its business of living life, to bear fruits. The government, in an ideal democratic situation, must also be a reflection of these discourses in the civil society. We do believe that the government to people relationship must be symbiotic in nature and a political system that guarantees this symbiosis is democracy. Either must shape and mould the other – a spirit far removed from what has become our staple of authoritarian diktats and bans. Authoritarianism may be able to ensure a regimented, military discipline, but when such discipline is allowed to spill outside the boundaries of military organizations, the casualty is the spirit of freedom which has been the fountainhead of human creativity in free societies through history. Authoritarian diktats, however well intended, also totally undermine the civil society's intelligence and ability to judge for themselves. While a law is an arbitration between different and often overlapping guarantees of freedoms, a diktat is a straitjacket.

No Space for Dissent

It is rather ironic, but speaks volumes of the mindset of our society today that the only institution against which anybody and everybody can raise a dissenting voice, or even stage disruptive protests without the mortal fear of losing life or limb, is the government. Nobody today would dare even think of raising similar banners of protest against any other non government power centres. The outcome of such an eventuality is predictable. If lucky the brave soul would end up only in bandages, if not it may be her or his last act on earth. One thing is crystal clear. The structure of the democratic polity indeed is liberal, and for this reason, everybody who feel they have a stake in nurturing a culture of liberalism in our society must contribute their mite to make this system work. The structure and execution can vary considerably according to the historical experience and culture of a place, but there can be no doubt whatsoever that there is no alternative to democracy to guarantee a flourishing liberal spirit. This spirit is encapsulated in a much quoted angry retort of an American president to a stabbing, and unfair according to many, criticism of his policy by an opponent: I totally disagree with whatever you are saying but I will defend to the last your right to make that criticism.

Our society today is heading the opposite direction. There are too many who so presumptuously claim to be the representatives of not only the interest of the people at large, but their undivided will as well. There is a distinction between the two. A child may have a will but it is unlikely she would know how to act in the larger interest of the will or for that matter her own wellbeing. This is why she needs the counsel of parents and schools. In like manner, a people may have the a united will, but as a collective, it is unlikely they would be clear on how to act in the interest of promoting this same will. Identifying the latter plan of action ought to be left to the policy makers, ably assisted by experts trained in economics, political science etc, and we may add the intelligentsia which is the bridge between the policy framers and the people. Our proliferating number of self-appointed moral local guardians in their hubris have assumed omniscience in these extremely complicated matters, and expect everybody to fall in line with whatever they prescribe is the greater common good, not tolerating in the process even the semblance of a free debate much less dissenting voices. Hence, we have the unabated book burning spree, although it is clear the disagreement is only in the time frame of the switchover of scripts; we have others threatening to shut down schools whose children are not allowed to join street protests; still others would hold the entire people to ransom by resorting to highway blockades and "statewide" bandhs and "public curfews" either to arm-twist the government or to silence dissents. Amusingly, these agitations are also self-labeled as "democratic". Amusingly again, these public turmoil rage even as the government blissfully continues to fiddle, or should it be, because the government is continuing to fiddle not bothering to do anything. What is also true is, amidst all the din, even the more profound question of the insurrection in the land is diluted unrecognizably in the minds of the people.

There are dissenting voices in plenty, although petrified into murmurs only. Those who care to put their ears close enough to the ground would have felt the pulse, and those willing to read the writings on the wall would have read the same message. The people are tired of being dictated and decreed to do the biddings of a few who claim omniscience on public good. They want a more participatory approach to chalking out the routes their society takes. Plebiscites and referendums are a good idea but the spirit of gauging public mood and aspirations in shaping public policies must be made to exist at every level of decision making. As for instance, the people must be free to debate and decide on issues like which school their children go or what dress they wear or what music they listen to. Not the least, boycotts and protests must be voluntary acts to be entitled to be classified as democratic.

Eat You Last

In Homer's "Odyssey" the great seafaring Greek warrior and king of Ithaca, Ulysses, who along with his men, got lost in the sea for ten years while returning after the war in Troy over the "abduction", or "elopement" if you prefer, of the famed Hellen from Sparta, once docked at a very interesting island where lived Cyclops and his tribe of one-eyed, man-eating giants. Ulysses and his men become the captives of Cyclops and the giant begins feeding on them one by one at every meal. Ulysses hatches a plot and feeds the giant with the wine from his ship, and pleased at this gesture, Cyclops awards him with a great favour and promises to eat him last of all his men. This is a theme that has occurred in many fables from all over the world in all cultures: A giant arrives at a village and demands to be fed with a villager a day. In the village every family is made to supply the giant's human fodder in turn, and this goes on until the village is either wiped off, or in the case of a very lucky few, a giant-killer in shining armour arrives and offers himself to be the giant's food for the day, meets the giant and then kills him. Everybody lives happily ever after. In real life, everything is not so simple.

But Cyclops' promise to Ulysses is interesting. It is such a peculiarly tragic irony to be promised life and death at the same time. It is a promise of life because Ulysses would not be killed immediately, but it is also a promise of death because he would be ultimately killed in a very finite period of time. One can almost sense the claustrophobia of a closed space and time that define a terrible certainty – the certainty of death. The helplessness in avoiding the fate is simply nightmarish. But nimble Ulysses overcomes Cyclops' terrible sentence, and it is his iron will and quicksilver wit which get him out of situations such as this that have endeared this literary figure to humanity through the ages, ever since Homer created him. He is even more endearing because the challenges before him were the challenges everybody in this world faces in his or her own way in every age. It is another story that not everybody is able to live up to the challenge.

Manipur's predicament today provokes thoughts of Ulysses and the Cyclops' promise. Our fates seem sealed and there seem to be to be no easy way out. Moreover everybody has either lost the courage to speak his or her mind, or have convinced themselves that there is nothing as independent thinking, all out of a state of petrification resulting directly out of the establishment's abject inability to guarantee a sense of security to them. Everybody's immediate concern today is to literally buy themselves their private peace even though each one understands it fully well that it is just a matter of pleading to be eaten last. It is not a question of tolerance either, which in reality is a facade we hide our impotence behind, for only a fool will not know that the present lawlessness that has enveloped the entire state will ultimately consume us all. And so we end up with our lives dictated at every turn – by the students who have no interest in studying, by the civic organizations which have no civic senses, by law-keepers who break the law, by lawbreakers who claim to be the law, by street-fighters with self-assumed peacekeeping missions, by leaders who would rather follow..... Most atrociously, all these roles are self-proclaimed in the name of public interest. Nobody wants to confront the situation although it is everybody's knowledge that taking the bull by the horns is our only salvation today. Nobody wants to confront it because in his silent panic, he has convinced himself that it is a great favour to be eaten last.

Brutal Justice

The best adjectives that describe Manipur today are

increasingly oxymoronic in nature – brutal justice, deafening silence, terrible beauty, street-fighters' law etc... to name just a few. There are too many situations occurring at unnerving frequently these days where such radically opposed senses, juxtaposed together, best describes Manipur's experience. The abundant mix of passion, energy, frustration, hopelessness, creativity etc, is resulting in a curious concoction that is life in the state. Too often for comfort, the mix is becoming dangerously explosive. A drug addict murdered a child in the neighbourhood to rob the child's gold earrings, and killer of the child was nabbed the next day and executed by an underground organisation. More than the atrocities involved in the murder of the child, it was the news of brutal retribution that everybody wanted to shout aloud from their rooftops. The news bannered across all the local dailies the following morning, and on the local cable television, for practically the whole afternoon and evening, at every bulletin, the news screamed. A brutal crime meeting with an equally brutal and swift justice, not surprisingly was greeted with such a palpable sense of social catharsis, but the manner and extent to which violence has come to be internalised in the Manipur society is, to say the least, disturbing. In an academic sense, it is also interesting to note how distinctly calibrated violence is on everybody's moral scale. Hence, the violence involved in the murder of the child was obnoxious, but the execution of the murderer was justice. It is as if our society is in such a passionate state of confused emotions, induced by the violence all around for so many decades, that often the only safety valve its unfortunate denizens are privileged to, is to scream blood and vengeance every now and then.

The moral calibration of violence however is layered in other ways too. If suppose the execution of the child murderer had been by the police, would the catharsis at justice delivered have remained the same. Perhaps, but the sense probably would not have been so overwhelming or durable. For at the back of the mind, the dangers associated with the counter violence would already have become much more pronounced. This doubt, in many ways would also have been a reaffirmation of the society's intuitive, though subdued, belief in institutionalised justice delivery mechanisms. An arm of the law breaking these institutionalised channels even to get after the devil, spells great danger for the society at large in the long run, as Sir Thomas More told us so convincingly in Robert Bolt's play *A Man for All Seasons*. Hence, much as we are appalled by the despicable crime of a drug addict murdering an innocent child, and much as we feel the murderer deserved the death sentence he received, we can only give two cheers to the conclusion of the case. We will reserve the third cheer till such a time as the justice delivery mechanism, be it those of the underground or overground governent, abandons all arbitrary elements and becomes an edified institution built by the collective wisdom of the people through refined and democratic means. Shouldn't we recall that one of the strongest objections against the Armed Forces Special Powers Act, for instance, was on the ground that it departs from institutions and strays into the arbitrary domain, and the dangers thereof?

The episode also perhaps tells another familiar story – the breakdown of institutions in the establishment. For whatever the reason the kind of catharsis witnessed after justice was meted out to the child murderer has come to be far beyond the scope of the establishment. The erosion of the moral authority of the establishment over its subjects is near total, and there are today very few who still fully believe that the establishment, rather those in charge of it, are capable of doing any good, leave aside deliver justice. What else can be expected, when murderers and known thieves are allowed to walk scot-free? Highways are being cut through established institutions to allow corrupt ways. Look at the ways government job recruitments are done. Look at the wealth that accumulates in the hands of those given the rein of the state, and their cronies. The chaos in our society must indeed be directly proportional to the abuse, keepers of the establishment heap on the establishment continually.

New Epoch, New Issues

One of the most overwhelming hurdles before the Manipur civil society today is a missing sense of time amongst its people. Its politics, its debates and in fact much of life in the state are still confined within yesterday's slogans, yesterday's manifestos, yesterday's outlook and yesterday's ego. For some reason or the other, the state seems simply unable to see or interpret its present reality with the idioms and paradigms thrown up by the greatly altered new world order. It seems caught up in a peculiar time warp of its own. This can have tragic consequences even in the not so distant future. The first bitter pill that it has to swallow is the acknowledgement that it no longer lives in a closed world. The kingdoms and principalities, as well as tribes and communities, that were once perceived as powers in the once insular universe have now to be placed in a much greater perspective.

The time has come for the civil society to ask itself where the state stands exactly on this new geography of power and economics. Failing to do this would make the difference between failure as a people and success to join the mainstream of the new world.

As of now, luck is not on its side, and its location on the globe, seen in conjunction with the turn of modern history is nothing enviable. Not just Manipur, but the entire northeast India and northwest Myanmar, have little significance on this new geopolitical map, and this is a reality. One example will illustrate. In the information age that the 21st Century is described as, it is hard to sell Manipur and the northeast to the rest of the world. Why the rest of the world, it is difficult to sell the region even to the rest of India. The national and international media literally blank out news of the northeast, but the implicit message in the phenomenon has to be realised. The media houses in the rest of the country, driven as they invariably are by commercial interests, would not have dared resorting to a strategy if there were buyers for these same news in their markets. The glut of northeast news that so many national dailies that reach the northeast carry, is only illusory in nature, for they are carried only in the editions that are circulated within the northeast and nowhere else. It is indeed difficult to sell the northeast outside the northeast. The same would be true on the question of the inflow of investment, national as well as foreign.

The region has to expand its vision and see the bigger chess board on which it is placed at a great disadvantage. As we see it, the region's brightest hope for a shift in the present geopolitics to lift us out of the current blind spot of the world, is a political and economic ferment in neighbouring Myanmar. The northeast's location then, as a bridge between the huge South Asian market and the South East Asian market, will give it back its significance.

Critical Masses

An essay "Insurgency and the Disintegration of Civil Society" (*Faultlines* Vol 13) by Samir Kumar Das, which seeks to represent the United Liberation Front of Asom, ULFA, as a political critique of Assam's historical experience, and indeed as an articulation of an intense discourse within the Assamese civil society, throws light on the insurgency situation in the northeast by both the strengths of the arguments as well as their weaknesses. Das' essay even goes to the extent of saying that the ULFA's relevance as well as integrity depend on its ability to continue to be this critique. Forming the foundation of this critique is the identity question. The ULFA, (and because it represents a vital part of the soul of the discourse within the Assamese society) the Assamese civil society, perceive their history and identity as fundamentally different from that of India. He cites the near parallel in the degeneration of the ULFA and that of the discourse within the Assamese civil society almost as if to say each is mutually the cause of the other. This is a powerful argument and if its strengths provide insights, its weaknesses unintendedly, in our opinion, also show ways to negotiate this vexed problem.

Das looks at the ULFA as an intellectual construct, or at least as a phenomenon in which its intellectual architecture has primacy over its physical manifestation, and because of this, in our opinion again, the theory is heavily tilted towards intellectual romanticism. Very much like *Hulk* the loveable comic strip monster, and now a movie, who is basically a materialization of excessive intellectual energy, Das' interpretation of the phenomenon of insurgency in the northeast is not altogether new in Manipur although it has never been argued out as cohesively as he has done. Here too, insurgency has been intellectualised (as opposed to empty propaganda) as an "enterprise" at its inception (Th Tarunkumar at the media seminar on the theme "Untying the Bind" organized jointly by the Institute of Conflict Management, New Delhi and the Imphal Free Press (IFP) in Imphal) that rose out of the rubbles of history. Insurgency in this interpretation, represents a strong will of the people amongst which it sprang up, to "re-people" and salvage lost dignity from a barren spiritual and moral landscape left behind after devastations by unfavourable but powerful historical circumstances.

Although the symmetry of this theory is strongly manifest in the continued sympathy insurgency enjoys (sometimes unreserved and sometimes grudging), amongst a good section of the people, (Das points this out), Das's theory, like many such intellectual constructs, is exposed to the danger of being weakened by its tendency to forget the contextual background against which alone it can exist and have a relevance. Adding to this vulnerability is the fact that the background is not constant, but a continually shifting one. As for instance, the very argument that the Assamese identity and history is different, assumes the rigidity of two entities – the Assamese identity and more importantly the Indian identity. What if one or the other, or both, shifts? Even if a shift in the Assamese identity to come in line with the bigger Indian identity is seen to amount to an "engulf and devour" phenomenon, and hence objectionable, the question is, what if the bigger identity itself softens and transforms and becomes more accommodative? The challenging question before all today is has this kind of a shift not been happening with the deepening of representative democracy? If not, then does not making this happen provide hope for a solution? We for one feel it is time for all of us to reassess our historical circumstances, after all nothing has remaineof what they were yesterday, and nothing will remain what they are today, tomorrow.

Violence as Language

One of the biggest factors that is throwing the state into total atrophy is the fact that increasingly the idea of violence as a language is being given legitimacy precisely by the lack of effective and credible governance. This is especially true in matters of communication between various interests groups and the government. Practically everybody today has come to believe, and reasonably too, however undesirable it may be, that they will only be heard if they resort to speaking the language of violence – violence in the extreme involving bloodshed, as well as in many other different shades and degrees of severity. Hence the spread of the culture of bandhs, highway blockades, ceasework strikes, boycotts, "public curfews", office picketing etc. Nobody will deny how irritating these can be, particularly when the causes behind them are as trifling as the service matters of sections of government employees. It really is an atrocious assault on public intelligence and sensibility, when each of these issues that have no relevance to the general welfare at all, are sought to be projected as public issues, and their pursuit to be in the interest of the public. It is also amazing how all of us, the lay public, can take such blatant abuses committed in our names lying down.

The desirability of these forms of protest apart, the moot question is, how has these disruptive activities come to gain so much currency? What has allowed violence to become the potent language that it is today? The answers to these questions are important and we are of the opinion the finger of accusation must first point at the style of governance that the state has been exposed to all these years. A combination of deliberate appeasement and weak-kneed governance must be held as the prime culprit. For we do believe that a government that believes in its own policies must not be too willing to capitulate in the face of arm-twisting opposition, as has been the case all along. This does not however mean that there must be no room for amendments to policy matters, but these must be through legitimate democratic channels of public discourse, and we add, by keeping an ear and eye open always to gauge public needs and mood. This is also why a vibrant media is essential. In years that have gone by, strikers have not only had their way, but also with the bonus of not being penalised for the days of no work. For too many times have the government announced the no work no pay clause to strikers only to withdraw it in the end, sending out in the process, the wrong messages to other putative strikers. Even if in the end concessions to the original demands have to be made, we see absolutely no reason why government employees should be paid for the days of no work from the public exchequer. That is, even if concessions are made, the penalties for neglecting work must remain, if not as a courtesy to the taxpayers then as an affirmative assertion that strikes are not absolutely penalty free. Today, strikes and bandhs have become very much a knee-jerk response. This unproductive conditioning must be de-conditioned. There are two things before the government to make this a reality. First, it must clean up its acts. It must ensure that the opportunities and benefits of the government reach out to all its parts equally. Justice thus ensured to the best within its capacity, it must not take any nonsense from the habitual strikers.

Secularism as Civic Agenda

If men were good, there would be no need for governments, James Madison, the third President of the United States of America, and one of the founding fathers of the country's constitution famously said in charting out the philosophy by which the American constitution was to be written. The innate suspicion of man's basic nature may be contrary to the idealistic teachings of religions, but it has nonetheless proven to be an effective mantra for governance. Madison's prescription for America definitely would cure a lot of the ills of any government anywhere in the world. The Manipur administration too could use some of it much to its benefit. If it had understood the significance of the statement in its letter and spirit, it might have been able not only to anticipate but also draw up effective administrative measures to prevent what happened at Tentha , whereby Hindu villagers burnt down a church built in the village by Christian converts amongst them. No, we are not talking about preventing conflict situations by beefing up security or through other intimidatory shows of state power, but through un-intrusive social engineering that takes into consideration that differences in faith, ethnicity etc, can easily translate into social friction and even conflicts.

Given the administrative foresight, we believe that most, if not all religious or ethnic frictions do not have to be much more than mere civic problems, well within the power of the civil administration to handle. In fact we believe that it is the duty of a secular government not to allow any of its social problems to escalate beyond the civic. What we are also saying is, it is a limitation of imagination that makes us see secularism only in terms of the doctrine of tolerance. The term tolerance itself implies putting up with something one is not altogether too pleased with. Rather than this, secularism as we see it, should be more about good impartial and farsighted administration that keeps in mind that men are not angels or saints. How do we apply this thought to the Tentha incident then? Allow us to answer this with another question. Supposing the government had earlier on, enacted a legislation restricting the building of public places of worship, be it a temple, church, mosque or synagogue in residential areas and opening it only to government approved sites, would the problem have taken the ugly shape it has? One might not have anything against living next door to a Hindu, Christian, Muslim or a Jew, even if he keeps a private place of worship in his house, but if he decides to convert his house into a public temple or church the next day and have congregations singing *bhajan* or performing midnight masses, it is likely to rub many other neighbours the wrong way. The Manipur government, and so too a large section of the public, in their obtuse sense of secularism, have been ignoring this particular dynamics behind conflicts of the Tentha variety. Mark our words, given the rapidity with which public places of worship are sprouting, if the administration does not take care to rectify this oversight, condemnable as the case was, Tentha will not be the last arena of religious friction in the state, not necessarily Hindus pitted against Christians, but in any permutation or combination of the religions practised in the state. After all, as Madison implied, men are not angels, and it is a senseless conflict resolution strategy to simply curse that men are not angels.

The word friction is appropriate in describing the situation. Literally, it implies that when two surfaces which are not smooth come into contact and rub against each other, heat would be the result. The obvious deduction is, in a non-ideal situation, no two surfaces which are not smooth should be allowed to rub against each other. We are not in any way prescribing total segregation. We are only saying that the government should apply its mind to identify the spheres where socialization between religions, ethnic groups and communities can be smooth, as for instance in the neutral grounds of work places, markets etc, and where they are likely to cause friction, and frame administrative policies that are fit for the purpose.

How Unbroken is Progress

While the postmodern theory of "deconstruction" cannot be a complete and rounded system philosophy as such, there can be little serious doubts about the irrefutability of the cautions it flagged against many presumptions of traditional thinking, especially in the fields of humanities and arts. Take the case of the popular understanding of progress – of history, arts etc. While history cannot be simply "one damn thing after another", how far can we be justified in saying it has followed a linear or even a traceable multi-directional locus. In the world of art, the ridiculous nature of the query was pointed out quite eloquently by someone considered one of the greatest historians of ideas and a scholar of world renown in his own right – Isaiah Berlin. He demolished the unquestioned presumption that art too has always "progressed" with one era dovetailing the other and because of the advantage of hindsight, the latest era coming out on top at the end of this continuous progression. Since art has to do with human aspirations and inner urges, it should follow from the progress theory that what a great master like Rembrandt aspired to be, would be to a great extent what Picasso represented centuries later, and that his own achievement was lower down on the ladder of that same universal quest. Or Homer's epics "Odyssey" and "Iliad" were incomplete expressions of the writer's aspiration to achieve what John Milton in "Paradise Lost" achieved two thousand years later. This obviously could not have been the case could it? For all they are worth, a Rembrandt may be a greater work of art than a Picasso, or Homer's artistic talent may be way ahead of Milton's. Or, alternatively, and more plausibly, there are no perfect scales on which these expressions in art can be measured and compared. Epochal achievements in these fields are definitely related and certain elements are definitely passed down generation to generation, but it is absurd to even imagine that a progression works in the manner that popular presumptions in social sciences have led most to believe. Human aspirations and creativity are inextricably linked to the contextual backgrounds they spawned in, and often they cannot cross the boundaries of these backgrounds. Hence in all likelihood, epics of the Homerian proportion cannot ever be written again, as in all likelihood the creativity and imagination that gave it birth belonged in that epoch only. The proposition, we imagine, will have to be true of all other social sciences as well, including history. Even history cannot be characterized as a simple progression of one building block piling atop another in endless successions. As in quantum mechanics in physics, we imagine huge elements in this social progression that are unquantifiable.

This thought of postmodern "deconstruction" is often evoked when confronted with the question, sometimes posed provocatively and at other times honestly, during seminars and symposiums outside the state, as to what the nature of the presumably ancient "imagining" called Manipur is all about. How could it ever qualify to be a "nation" or even a polity before the modern times? Where are the proofs that the Kabaw Valley ever belonged to Manipur etc? We sense a similar flawed presumption of historical progression in these questions. Who says a nation has always to have hard boundaries with boundary pillars, fenced off by barbed wires, guarded zealously by professional soldiers etc. The pre-colonial world outside of Europe did not understand nations and territory this way. Rather than national boundaries, there would have been frontiers only too. In the Hindu epic "*Ramayana*" there was a particular ceremony Rama performed to demarcate the domain of his kingdom, whereby he released a white stallion and let it run free. If anybody stood in the way of the free run of the horse, he would have to face the might of the king and if he managed to stop the king that would be where the former's kingdom was deemed ended. Such and similar alternate understandings would be more applicable in say the contested ownership of the uninhabited Kabaw Valley of the time between the kingdoms of Ava and Manipur. For that matter the very frontiers of Ava or Manipur or other Southeast Asian kingdoms, and indeed the rest of the non-European world would have been determined by such principles. If a king stuck his flag on the bank of a certain river and nobody dared oppose him, that point would become the extent of his kingdom, and so on. These understandings cannot simply be forced into the 19th Century European paradigm of nationhood with justice as too many attempt to naively.

Dwarfed States

One other very serious fallout of the fruitless prolongation of the peace talks between the Government of India and the NSCN(IM) is the dwarfing of the state authorities both in Nagaland as well as in Manipur. The latest incident in which the NSCN(IM) took into custody the suspects in the murder of two school children in Senapati, Moheni Martin and Hriinii Hubert, and the state governments in Manipur as well as Nagaland helplessly watching (and fuming in the case of Manipur), is a case in point. Ostensibly at the behest of the Ministry of Home Affairs, (MHA) Government of India, the Manipur government had ordered the arrest of certain

NSCN(IM) leaders who were holding the suspects, and as per the protocol prescribed by Indian laws, had requested the Nagaland government to execute the order and hand over those named. Nobody, not even lay readers of newspapers, took the news seriously, precisely because it was not meant to be taken seriously. And today, the order has been reduced to a farce as it was expected to. Maybe it was not intentional on the part of the Union government to humiliate the government authorities of the two states, all the same they were humiliated. And this has been carrying on for over a decade now. But this humiliation was evident in the very foundation of the talks modalities itself. For reasons best known to themselves, those who conceived it thought it fit to totally ignore the state governments, and keep it as a bilateral affair between the Union and the NSCN(IM).

So when the two NSCN factions engaged in open warfare in Zunheboto town, terrorising the population, the Nagaland government could do nothing to even provide a sense of security to its subjects other than appeal to the Union to do something, as there was a peace talks going on. In Manipur the NSCN(IM) was openly running a jail in Ukhrul, and like in Nagaland, the Manipur government could do nothing until the Assam Rifles, which is under the MHA decided to intervene. When these governments are so deliberately projected as powerless in the manner, what exactly is the esteem they are expected to command over their own subjects? We do hope the Union government realises the damages done and addresses the issue seriously.

One way of doing this is to overhaul the ceasefire ground rules, and enforce its terms strictly. Let the peace talks carry on peacefully, but without dwarfing the authority of the states involved. Even if the states are considered as excess weights in the progress of the talks, they should at least continue to have the powers to act in accordance to the law if the law is broken within their respective jurisdictions, precisely by not making those involved in the talks immune to the law. In Manipur another atrocious development has made matters more complicated. The Army has entered into a ceasefire with several Kuki underground organisations without first reaching an understanding with the state's civil authorities. The question is, just what are the state's own forces to do in the event of a breach of law in the state by any of the parties in this tentative peace arrangement with the Army? As in the case of the Naga peace talks, is it expected to simply watch? It is unlikely the Army can resort to what it has without the prior approval of the Union government, so the question once again is, is there a school of thought within the Union government that believes in playing out a larger game-plan to make the authority of not just Manipur but the other insurgency prone states of the northeast weak and insecure, stymied by a parasitic mentality in all spheres of economic and political activities, always looking timidly to the Union's charity for survival? Why cannot the Union government trust its northeastern states a little more, and have a little more faith in them that even if they become powerful and confident, their loyalty to the Union will not sway? Perhaps this is a grey area of the national psyche that the mandarins of the Union government will do well to explore and resolve. If tomorrow the Union government was to enter into peace talks with Naxalites in Andhra Pradesh, would it think it necessary to sideline the state government there? More pertinently, would it dare?

Virtual Governments

The urgency of issues on the home front still fails to bother those in charge of the government. A crisis prevented at Moreh seems to have been taken to mean time to relax, as if there are no other issues of governance left to be tackled. And so practically all of the government's top executives are currently camped in New Delhi to have the Congress central leaders settle what the bickering politicians have repeatedly referred to as the state Congress' family quarrel. Perhaps it would save plenty of time and public money if the Manipur Bhavan in New Delhi were to be made the second administrative headquarters for the state. Jokes aside, the reality on the ground is, in government's virtual absence, various NGOs and "civil society" bodies have taken virtual charge of day to day governance, beginning from excise control, education monitoring, moral policing, and for that matter even normal crime policing. Democratic governance they say is also about a public-private partnership, and perhaps in a skewed interpretation of this understanding, the government has decided to leave governance to private parties, so that those in government can concentrate full time to portfolio angling, contract distribution, lucrative transfers and postings of officers and so on. What a pity.

Can the ruling party leave aside their differences and get down seriously to the job for which they were given the mandate by the Manipur electorate. For, as much as the elected government has been reduced to a virtual government, there are also a mushrooming number of other varieties of virtual governments. That is to say, if the government is reduced to a virtual status for a lack of initiative, these other virtual governments have emerged precisely as an alternative mechanism to fill in this initiative vacuum. And we are not even referring to the underground governments, which have all along been parallel governments by their very ideological positions and the power they wield over public affairs. Instead, we are referring to a multiplying number of "civil society" organisations, pushing various social agendas as per their vision of what an ideal society should be. While we appreciate these private initiatives at streamlining deviant social mores, we are disturbed, indeed perturbed by the almost total absence of the government in this overt social engineering process, for this role reversal ultimately will be dangerous for the society. This especially because the vacuum left by the government's absence is also a hotly contested space between many "civil society" organisations. Surely even friendly matches can deteriorate into chaos if there are no rules or a referee, to monitor these rules are adhered to.

If citizen's policing which is becoming an increasingly arresting reality in Manipur today is within the government's scheme of things, then it must evolve the rules for the game, put strictures, and be the referee as well. As yet we haven't heard the government spell out it has taken private partners in the governance process, but we do see ministers and MLAs flagging off many of these private governance campaigns. Does this mean these campaigns have the government's blessing? This conflicting message also becomes all the more pronounced on the liquor question against the background of the government actually stating on a couple of occasions, even on the floor of the Assembly, that it plans to lift its more than a decade-and-half long ban on liquor sale and consumption in the state to augment its revenue. Needless to say this government ban has also been one which was far from effective, having only managed to drive liquor vending underground. But now, even though its stated policy intent is to allow liquor again, the government is seen participating, or at least pretending not to notice the significance of the aggressive drives for total abolishing of liquor by various organisations. Can the government come out with something clear cut on the matter? Whichever way it decides, either to continue with the ban or to lift it, let it be the one that leads and not follow the campaigns. Believe us, this is one effective way for it not to self destruct its own credibility before the eyes of the public.

Wonderland Revisited

Imagine a land where there is no law. If that is possible, you are either in the amazing dream world of Lewis Carroll's

Alice in Wonderland, which we all have read either in the original or else as abridged texts, or more likely in illustrated comic books. Or else you are in the other wonderland called Manipur. It is quite a parallel too. In Carroll's wonderland, the characters make law as and when they need it – so too in Manipur. There is supposed to be something as an established constitutional law in force, but that law today has receded into the background, thanks to its keepers who have either lost interest in it or else have become a law unto themselves. Instead, what are actually and most tangibly at work are on the spot laws, un-edified and untenable in any court of law, and made by any and everybody as and when they please. Leave aside the underground organisations which are pretty straightforward in their stand, claiming to be challengers of the established law as such. But other than them, the law and its enforcement have become a free for all agenda. What is absolutely confounding is, the government seems not to mind this at all when it should actually have been treating the matter as an insult to its authority. Reams after reams of commentary have been written on this and yet, not a single word or idea seems to have registered, and things continue as they always were, spiralling deeper and deeper into the abyss. What exactly is it that the government wants, can it please spell it out so that the people at least would know what to expect from it? Not that they expect much anyway, for proof of this the government just needs to look at the advertisement spaces of vernacular dailies and discover who the people are looking up with awe in matters of crime and punishment.

There are also people getting summarily executed practically every day of the week. Sometimes the guilt of these unfortunate victims are pronounced after they are dead and gone. Like in the haunting command line of the Queen in *Alice in Wonderland* "Off With His Head", pronounced every now and then, with no apparent forethought or afterthought, and said as if by rote absolutely at random, it probably occurred to somebody somewhere that somebody else was guilty and passed a verdict in one of the on-the-spot piece of legislation. If the government needs any reminder it should feel guilty for these incidents, it should look at the helpless and muted protests on the streets against these atrocities. Elsewhere, school buildings are being razed, hospitals are being stoned, bans are being imposed, "taxes" are being levied, shops are being shut down and the list of woes can carry on endlessly. All these are perpetrated by known and unknown players, but seldom ever named even if known. And the government still continues to turn the other way, pretending it has no eyes, ears or mouth. It does however, with zest, climb the podium at every opportunity, talking of the virtues of democracy and democratic rule. What a miserable irony. It is bewildering and frustrating to know that all complaints and cries of lament have seldom made a difference, or is hardly likely to fall on attentive ears of those who can make the difference.

Despite all this, the people however still want to believe in the established institutions of constitutional law with clearly prescribed and edified procedures, as opposed to arbitrary decrees. The Manipur government needs to get its acts together. While it is evolving a peace policy on the issue of insurgency, the government has to take control of the home front and ensure things do not descend into complete madness. For this, it must first of all establish its presence and prove its credibility. Let its focus come back to good governance. Let ministership become an important and powerful tool of governance, and not the goal itself, as has so long been. Let it lead by example and not merely appeal to the people to be law abiding and diligent. And most important of all, let it clearly demarcate what portion of law keeping is its sole prerogative and what areas it can share or outsource to private parties, if at all this is proper or essential. Failing this, it cannot blame anybody else but itself for the resultant chaos.

5

ETHNICITY, IDENTITY AND LAND IN TRIBAL MANIPUR

—Gangmumei Kamei

There is a popular assumption in the mind of the tribal people of Manipur that the introduction of any law or legislation for the land tenure in the hill areas will lead to the destruction of their land ownership system based on the age old customs and traditions. Such a law will erode the traditional polity; alienate them from their ownership and possession of the land held by community, clan, individuals or the chiefs. It will open the floodgate for the entry of the non-tribal immigrants who will swamp their mountain country and occupy the lands and forests. It will also lead to the demographic scaling up of the tribal communities the mainland India, reducing the indigenous sons of the soil into minorities. This will ultimately lead to the loss of their ethnic identity. There is a strong belief that their land or territory is the vanguard of their sustenance and livelihood as a community. Their identity binds them to their lands. The land is the greatest security for the preservation of their identity and survival. The issues of ethnicity, identity and land ownership are built into the psyche of the tribal people.

Is this fear genuine or justified? This paper is an attempt to explain why such a mindset has been imbibed among the tribal people affecting their political, economic and social development. It is also a plea that the tribal people have to respond to the call of the changing times.

Identity and Ethnicity

Identity is a psycho-social phenomenon. It is the state of remaining the same under varying circumstances. Identity is the sense or feeling of sameness and continuity of an individual or group. We talk of social identity, ethnic or cultural identity of a community in this sense. The identity of a group includes their common past or history, cultural heritage, linguistic heritage, linguistic affinity, their shared experiences struggles and sufferings with a strong sense of belonging to each other and or identification within an ethnic space, with an ideology and belief in the common future.

Ethnicity has been explained in the sense of ethnic consciousness. Ethnicity is regarded as the "primordial consciousness" of an ethnic group. This is the feeling of belonging of an ethnic group to their ancient roots and their ancestral heritage. Like identity, ethnicity is also a psycho-social phenomenon which persists in all societies in all times. Ethnicity is the motive force of identity assertion. Ultimately, ethnicity is the basis of the identity of an ethnic group or community. The economic basis of the tribal identity is the tribal mode of production and the nature of the ownership of the resources of the community. A tribal community enjoys the prerogative (it may be historical or social) over the sharing of the common resources. These are the hills, lands and forests. A membership of a person in a tribal community through blood relation and kinship, entitles him to get access to the resources of the community. His membership of a clan is an important status or criteria for getting access to the resources of the village.

It is in this context that ethnicity, identity and land ownership are inextricably interlinked in the tribal world of Manipur.

Demographic Features

The state of Manipur has a total area of 22.327 sq. km. and the valley covers an area of 2238 sq. km. According to the census of 2001, the total population was 22,93,896 (excluding the population of the sub-divisions of Mao-Maram, Paomata and Purul of Senapati district) the population of the hill districts was 8,82,130 and the scheduled tribal population was 7,41,142 out of which the ST population of the valley districts was 56,247 and the urban dwellers were 28,058 only.

The ST population constitutes 34.2 per cent of the total population of Manipur. The total number of villages in the state is 2391 according to the census of 2001. And 1901 are villages in the hill areas and 490 are villages of the valley. The tribal villages increased from 1402 (1971) to 1547 (1981), 1727 (1991) and 1901 (2001). These hill villages are mostly inhabited by the 33 Scheduled Tribes.

According to the tribe wise population, the Thadou is the largest tribe with 182.594 (24.5%) followed by the Tangkhuls with 1,46,075 (19.7%), the Kabui with 82,386 (11.1%), the Paite with 49,271 (6.6%), the Hmar with 42,933 (5.8%) the Kacha Naga with 42,013 (5.7%), the Vaiphei with 38,262 (5.2%), the Maring with 23, 288 (3.1%) and the Anal with 21, 242 (2.9%).

The Tribal Land System

The tribal land system assumes a great importance due to the economic development sweeping the tribal and hill areas of Manipur. The natural resources of the state, especially the vast lands in the mountains, which constitute ten – eleventh of the total areas of the state, the forests, the rivers and their basins are in the tribal areas. The process of privatization of tribal lands along with the alienation of the land is going on for the development of wet rice cultivation, terrace cultivation, horticulture, forest plantations, development projects, road making and establishment of the administrative centers.

Despite the absence of any land law, the tribal land law continues to operate. The tribes, both the Nagas and the Kuki-Chins had developed their traditional polity which did not grow beyond the village level. It did not develop into a tribe polity formation. The village is the autonomous political, social and economic unit. There are two types of polity formed on ethnic lines, the Naga and the Kuki-Chin. There is a sort of democratic type of political system among the Nagas. And chiefship exists among the Kuki –Chins. Their polity is based on customs and traditions which have the force of law. The traditional polity has a clear cut boundary of a village; there is a well regulated land ownership, a judicial system and social institutions. The polity is based on the village and the land holding system.

The studies on tribal land holding system are fewer than are references to land holding system in the ethnographic accounts of the tribes. Recently several work on the land system which are research works from Manipur University have been published. Yet intensive studies are lacking and we have the gap in our knowledge of the tribal land system.

Ethnicity is again reflected in the broad nature of land system among the two ethnic groups. The Naga land system covers the community land, the clan land and the individual land. There is a strong community ethos behind the system. The Kuki-Chin system is based on the ownership of land or the whole village vested in the chief, who is a hereditary functionary. The traditional polity was recognized by the Meitei state during the pre-colonial period. The Kings of

Manipur did not impose the direct administration over the hill villages. They imposed only political control on the villages in the foot hills and on the trade routes. The land ownership in the tribal villages was not interfered into by the Kings. There was a friendly relation between the Kings and the headmen or chiefs of Naga villages who paid homage to the Kings.

When the Kuki immigration occurred in the 19th Century, the Kings and the British Political Agents gave them settlements in the hills of Manipur. And the Kuki chiefs were allowed to practice their polity and feudalistic land system. The Chiefs were the owners of the village and its resources; the villagers became his tenants. The state did not interfere in the internal affairs.

In the colonial period, the British did not impose any land tax on the tribal lands. They imposed the hill house tax of rupees three per household. Like the rulers of Manipur. They also did not interfere in the tribal polity and their land system. They conferred themselves to the keeping of law and order, adjudication of disputes and collection of house tax.

In the post-independence period, the government of Manipur introduced the Manipur Hill People's Regulation Act, 1947 which provided for the administration of justice through the village authorities. The institution of the Village Authority was created by this Regulation. In 1956, the Government of India introduced the Manipur (Hill Areas) Village Authorities Act, 1956 for the administration of the hill villages. While these two legislations diluted the traditional polity, they did not affect the land holding system. The concept of a hill village recognized under the Act of 1956 emerged in contrast to the revenue village. The tribal hill village was recognized as a statutory unit of administration.

The Manipur Land Revenue and Land Reform Act, 1960

The greatest fear and apprehension in the minds of the

tribal people with the land and revenue administration was the introduction of the Manipur Land Revenue and Land Reform Act (MLR&LR), 1960. The preamble of the Act says that it extends to the whole of Manipur except the hill areas. What is meant by 'hill areas' in this Act? It differs from the terms like tribal area or tribal district. It means the topographically "hill" area in contrast to "plain" area. This Act shall operate in the plain areas of Manipur, either hill districts or tribal areas. The framers of this legislation wanted this law to be confined to the valley areas where there was a land revenue system since the colonial period. But this Act is extended to the plain areas of the hill districts. The Act had been extended.

The Act was extended in the Chandel district (Maha river and Chakpi river basin and Moreh), the Khuga valley of churachandpur district, Khaupum valley of Tamenglong district, Imphal river basin of Senapati district. In these areas, the lands were surveyed by the Settlement Department; the records of land rights were prepared, pattas were issued to the tribal land owners, revenues were assessed and collected. This Act disrupted the traditional land system, in both the Nagas and the Kuki-Chins areas.

The Acquisition of Chiefs Rights Act 1967

A fall out of the MLR and LR Act was the attempt made by the Government of Manipur to introduce land reform in the hill areas. The Territorial Assembly under the Chief ministership of M. Koireng Singh passed the Acquisition of Chiefs Rights Act in 1967. The legislation was perhaps inspired by the Acquisition of Chiefs Rights Act on Mizo Hills District. The Act provided for the following:

i. Abolition of Chiefship among the Kuki-Chins

ii. Payment of compensation to the Chiefs for the loss of their rights and their ownership of the land

iii. It visualizes the introduction of the MLR and LR Act

M Koireng Singh, the man behind the Act wanted to abolish the undemocratic Zamindari like feudal system. But the law was not appreciated by the Kuki-Chin people who took it as infringement on their rights, customs and tradition. There was a strong resistance against the Act. So it could not be implemented.

The protest against the Act of 1967 was also directed against the MLR and LR Act of 1960. More than two decades latter, in 1989, a serious attempt was made by the Government of Manipur under the Chief Ministership of R. K. Jaichandra said to introduce the MLR and LR Act through its 6th Amendment bill of 1989. One cannot understand how this Act could be imposed with the approval of the Hill Areas Committee of the Assembly. Due to the strong opposition from the tribal people and the constitutional objection of the Hill Areas Committee, was rejected and withdrawn. The then Chief Minister R K Jaichandra was condemned by the tribal people. And a great mistrust was imbibed in the mind of the tribal people. Any talk on MLR and LR Act reminded the people of the fiasco of 1989.

Fall out of the Opposition of the MLR&LR Act, 1960

As a consequence of the failure of the introduction of the Act of 1960 through the Assembly, there emerged a debate in the politics of the Manipur. Those who were the supporters of the Act belonged to the political parties based in Manipur valley. There are pressure groups, mostly students unions of the valley. They raised a demand for the introduction of the Act in the hill areas. They also spread a propaganda that it was not justified that while the tribals were allowed to settle in the valley, the non-tribals, particularly the Meiteis were not allowed to settle in the hills. There was equally strong opposition of the tribals to the Act.

The tribal spokesmen replied that this Act does not prevent the plainsmen from settling in the hill areas. The non-tribals like the Nepali, Tamils and Meiteis are found in Senapati, Choubal and Churachanpur districts. The famous Meitei village of Kwatha is in Eastern Chandel District. For the transfer of land from the tribal to the non-tribal, the permission of the Deputy Commissioner of the districts and the concerned district council is necessary.

Now, the heat of the debate has gone down due to the informal discussion on the issue among the scholars and opinion leaders. There is a realization that the demand for the introduction of the Act without modification to suit the tribal situation is unjustified. The tribals do not object to the extension of the Act in the plain areas of the hill districts. A consensus has emerged that there is a need for a legislation for tribal land tenure in the hill areas.

Who Owns the Land in the Hill Areas?

There is another dimension to the question of land in the hill areas. Who owns the land in the tribal areas, The State or the Tribals? To whom is vested the ownership of the lands?

In those villages which are settled with the permission of the state, either the Maharaja in the pre-colonial period or the colonial authorities or the succeeding state governments the ownership of the land was granted by the state to the village in its collectivity. The Chief is the head of the collectivity. This is the case of the Kuki-Chin villages settled in Manipur since 19th century onwards.

But in those villages which have been in existence for centuries, before the conquest of the hills by the Meitei rulers of Manipur, or "from times immemorial", the lands were owned by them and it was not granted by any authority. They were like "small republics" as observed by William McCulloch in 1859. These villages are Naga villages in which there are three categories of land: community land, clan land and individual.

The fact that the village community represented by the head of the village or the village council of a village is the owner of the land has been incorporated by a few judicial pronouncements: the decree of the Judicial Commissioner of Manipur and the Gauhati High Court.

This position is not accepted by the state revenue department. But several government departments, both central government and state, are paying compensation to the tribal owners whose lands are acquired for road making, construction of dams and other development projects.

This upholds the view that the tribals have proprietary rights over the lands in the villages.

The nineteenth century documents show that the King of Manipur was the "absolute proprietor of the soil" based on the assumption that "lands belong to the Raja". The state of Manipur holds the view that the state is the owner of the lands within its boundary.

There is a perception entertained by the tribal people that the MLR&LR Act of 1960 was meant for the valley areas where there was a revenue system since the colonial period. And the Revenue Department extended the valley areas to the plain areas of hill district bringing the tribal lands under the purview of the Act. The fear of the tribal people that this Act, if implemented in the hill areas, will make the tribals landless, requires to be examined.

The Act provides for the survey of the land in a particular area. The Act mentions the cadastral survey which is meant for the plain areas. The survey of the hill lands cannot be done by this method.

Once the survey of the particular area is made, the land owners or possessors who are in the actual possession of the particular plots shall be recorded as the possessors of the lands and they are given the record of rights, like Dag Chitha and Jamabandi.

The mountains are vast. The hill tribal people practice shifting cultivation which is carried on by rotation. Of the total forest area of a village, a small portion (an average of 2 acres per family) is used for shifting cultivation. In case a survey is carried out at a given time, the plots of shifting cultivation in the possession of the cultivator will be recorded as being possessed by the cultivators.

As the big chunk of the forest lands are not cultivated at the time of survey, the unpossessed lands will be declared as wasteland or Khasland. According to the Act, all Khaslands should belong to the state. So the tribal shifting cultivators will not be entitled to cultivate the state owned Khaslands. So the fear of the tribes of being landless is genuine and justified, for the jhum lands.

The fear of losing one's identity when he loses his land exists. The transfer of the lands from the tribal to the non-tribal is not allowed except on the permission of the Deputy Commissioner and the District Council. At the same time there is the usual protection given to the Scheduled Tribes. There is conscious efforts made by the tribes themselves to preserve their identity, there should not be any fear of losing one's identity.

Land as the Key to Development : A Land Law

Land is the key factor of production. Land in the hill areas should be an instrument of the institutional finance for investment in development. One notices a change in the tribal mindset among the intellectuals. There is a talk of the need for the introduction of an appropriate land law for the tribal hill areas. The progressive community leaders are raising the issue as they require bank loans for various enterprises.

We have seen that the MLR&LR Act of 1960 in its present form is not applicable. Either a separate law is framed or a separate schedule dealing with tribal tenure may be added to the existing Act.

Who will advice the state to frame the appropriate law? There is a strong prejudice in the minds of the officials of the Revenue and Settlement Department. The tribal people have a mistrust of the Revenue Department.

This is an opinion that the government may appoint an expert committee presided over by a High Court judge to examine the crucial issue and recommend the appropriate law. The government has to get the endorsement of the Hill Areas Committee of the Assembly. The proposed law shall regulate the land system, taking into consideration the tribal traditions and democratic ethos of the constitution. The legislation should prevent alienation and exploitation of tribal lands by the rich planters and businessmen. Such a law should ensure that every tribal farmer, the tiller of the land, should get access to the land. Time is ripe for such a regulation in the hills of Manipur.

6

LAND, DEVELOPMENT AND IDENTITY: Agrarian Transition and Social Issues in Manipur

—Ch. Priyoranjan Singh

Introduction

The problem of utilization of land for productive purposes has to be looked at as a historically evolved phenomenon and also as having material and non material components. In a complex society like India, there are different modes of productive organization that give rise to differing rights, duties and obligation, leading to particular patterns of property rights. In the Asian context, Gunnar Myrdal had inferred that the most important basis for inequality is the distribution of land, with which leisure, enjoyment of status and authority are associated. In the transitionary economy and society of Manipur, issues of land, development and identity have in recent times become contentious, in the hill regions as well as in the valley, though differing in content, dimensions and ramification. Alarmingly, historical, non-material and territorial politics have sidelined fundamental issues of livelihood, poverty and inequality, which in any case, underpins most contestations. The material, the human and the universal, have a historical tendency to abruptly terminate grand designs of social and political engineering, progressive or retrograde, that are marginally rooted in the ecological and social reality of a given context.

This paper seeks to highlight the nature of agrarian transition that is taking place at the micro level in the villages of the valley and the hills, delineate social issues that are vital to our understanding of the complex discourses and contestations that have been lately shaping up in the political economy of the state.

The state of Manipur has two distinct physiographic divisions within which two different land systems and productive organization of economic activities have historically emerged. The valley region, right in the middle of the state, constituting barely ten percent of the state, is the habitat of the majority ethnic group, the Meities, mostly Hindus by religion. The hill region, constituting ninety percent of the land, is inhabited by the Kukis and the Naga tribes. Historically, the state polity emerged under the rule of the Ningthouja dynasty and monarchy, in the valley region. The more advanced civilization in the valley, having its own script and literate tradition, coinage and foreign trade with its neighbouring countries and beyond with China, having more organized administration and military and other institutions of the state, evolved land systems and productive organizations that were capable of producing huge surpluses based on much more organized and equitable distribution of land[1]. On the other hand, the hill regions, though politically under the suzerainty and the control of the valley monarchy, was given high degrees of freedom in the matter of economic organization of land, village polity and social dynamics. Each tribal village were thus defined as autonomous republics of their own. As a result, though the broad contours of the land systems of the two tribal groups of the Nagas and the Kukis are similar, the details widely vary from village to village to such a high degree that the exceptions sometimes seem to be the rule[1].

In the valley region, a rich tradition of wet rice cultivation based upon the meticulous and elaborate crop husbandry practices and technologies of the wider south-east Asian rice cultures, resulted in an agrarian economy that rarely experienced food security problems[2]. Efficient land utilization thus formed the basis upon which the Monarchy in the valley consolidated its regime within the state and throughout history, fought political as well as territorial wars with neighbouring kingdoms. In the valley region, the linkage between land and identity did not arise in the pre-independence period. It is only a post independence phenomenon that the issue of land and identity are assuming alarming proportions among the majority population, in the face of tribal sub-nationalism movements that apparently and avowedly draws their ideological sustenance from the vital linkages between land and identity in the peculiar ecological as well as historical context of tribal history in Manipur. Pre-colonial and colonial Manipur was a political entity that was firmly anchored in the bedrock of a historically evolved plural and multi-ethnic society. Tribal nationalism in the Northeast, and latter on in the state, is infringing upon and threatening this shared history, polity and identity. Thus unwillingly and unwittingly, the Meities of the valley region are drawn into the vortex of the issue of land, identity and territoriality conflicts in the hill regions. The majority community has become the favourite whipping boy for almost all problems in the hill regions including land problems, development issues as well as identity consciousness.

In the hill regions however, the issues of land identity and development has indeed become a heady mix that has intoxicated a many, and blurred considered and measured debates for tribal development and social change. Land as a means of production and livelihood is much more vital in the hill economy than in the valley region. Absolute lack of general development, especially in the interiors, and negligible growth of non-farm economic activities, has made land, so much more precious. Land and land systems are therefore sought to be sacrosanct and inalienable, in fact traditional land rights and tanure systems are construed to be the vary basis of tribal village polity and identities. The reality however is that the traditional land rights and tannurial systems had started breaking down since the colonial days and in fact in the present context the traditional system exists in largely corrupted forms among the Nagas and the Kukis, so much so that internal contradictions are pulling down the system itself and tribal themselves are crying out for change.

Tribal villages in Manipur were established by clans and the dominant clan became the chief of the village. Within the vast village boundary of hill faces, river valleys and forests, land was apportioned among the clans. Some non-clan common village lands are earmarked also. Within the clans, the clan head has the major hand in intra clan land distribution. Theoretically, however, the chief and his village council have the ultimate authority over all village land and its distribution among the villagers, including clan land. Land in the pristine traditional consciousness, was the village commons, to be enjoyed by all, inclusively as well as equitably. It was the property of non but the property of all, to be defended for, to be looked after and to be sustainably exploited for the welfare of the villagers. The authority of the chief and village council and the intra-clan distribution power of the clan head, were but institutional details for the smooth functioning of the land system which was fundamentally based on 'community ownership" rather than "private ownership". In an ecological and moral environment of low population, vast lands, subsistence and non-monetized village subsistence economy, far removed from the forces of markets and profits, private property consciousness and accumulation, the system worked not only equitably but also morally. In fact the "strong chief" and the common property foundation of the land system was a necessity to maximise or maintain common welfare[3].

With the advent of colonial rule and collection of monetary house tax, monetization and intrusion into village polity of modern state institutional norms, private property and accumulative consciousness, inevitably cut at the moral foundations of the tribal land systems. Imagine the powerful clan heads are also the members of the village council, as is in most village councils. Imagine also that populations are growing and the jhum cycles are shortening so that land has become scarce to the extent of the emergence of landless households in villages. These were the right conditions for the emergence of a village elite, the emergence of a land market, the birth of private property in land and albeit new colonization of land, preferably in the non-traditional, non-jhum, river valleys, beyond the control of the chief or clan heads. In the contemporary tribal villages, a new political economy is slowly enveloping remnants of a cherished and remembered tribal land system, towards privatization of land, land alienation, land hunger and differentiation among the villagers[4]. And yet the elite is harking for the pristine traditional land system and community ownerships of land, that does not in any case, exist today[5].

The groundswell of dissent against the corrupted tribal land systems that are turning into exploitative and inequitable tannurial structures, especially among the Kukis, is finding currency not only among the educated new generation of tribal opinion makers, but also among a minority section of the tribal elite. This is the reason why the extension of the Manipur Land Revenue and Land Reforms Act 1960, in a suitable way for the hill region, is now generally accepted, even though the fundamental basis of the act is to get the hill regions cadastrally surveyed, and private ownership of land introduced in the hill areas.

The muted voices in seminars (mostly in the valley), Ph.D. thesises and a few books have not been yet able to catalyze into a popular demand at the state level. The reasons are quite obvious. Firstly it has been convenient for the political elite to raise the bogey of the conceived attempt of the majority community to extend the MLR Act to the hill regions to compromise their ethnic identity which has been largely built around their land system. Secondly, by keeping anti majority feelings on the burner, the political elite have been able to largely ward off criticisms of their own part in the underdevelopment of the hill regions. Thirdly the proponents of land reforms have not been able to come up with acceptable alternatives to the MLR Act. Fourthly the economic conditions of the common tribal villagers are too precarious to openly challenge the stranglehold of the political elites over their livelihood sources.

Given the inter tribal conflicts as well as the intra-village power equations, concrete proposals for land reforms are unlikely to emerge from the tribals themselves, at least in the short run. Meanwhile the ordinary tribal villagers are likely to be trapped in the time warp of a land system that has gone out of step with the demands of a modern economy, a system that is increasingly becoming parasitic of the natural resources and ecosystems of the hill regions.

In the valley region, development has taken place in a distorted fashion, and the economy is hurtling down the path of tertiarisation. The absence of a healthy manufacturing sector, employment and income are getting increasingly marginalized and casualised. The impact on land and the agrarian sector development has been retrograde, and the signs of a commercial agriculture led growth are being retarded by the nature of the emerging political economy and agrarian structure. What then are the social issues that are being thrown up in the state, both in the hills as well as in the valley. The following two sections provide us glimpses of the economic and social realities in village Manipur.

Land and Agrarian Transition in the Valley

The people of the valley had mastered the art of dredging rivers and digging new courses in the first century AD and the peasantry had become a solid aspect of life. By the fifth century, wet rice cultivation through irrigation system of dams and canals known as Ethei Loukhong complex were being carried out. The developed culture of crop husbandry, especially for rice, led to the abundance of rice production in the valley and stability of the food economy. Brown reported paddy yields of 2700 kgs per hectare on the worst land and 4320 to 5400 kgs of paddy per hectare on the best land. The yield rates are not much below the yield rates in the post-green revolution valley of Manipur.

By the fifteenth century, state formation was completed and when the British set foot in the 1830s and colonized in 1891, a systematic and rigid land system was firmly in place. All land was considered state land and was distributed by the king. There was no private property in land and land distributed by the king would in general, return to the king, after the lifetime of the grantee. The basis for land distribution was administrative, martial, social, religious or feudal. The nobility received land grants in lieu of remuneration. The Sepoys, Brahmins, Temples, Awardees, Queen, Royal family and the King himself, all had land granted to them. There was a unique land grant known as the Touna Lou. Newly colonized land was termed as Taona Lou and had a quasi private property character, in that the king could not deprive the peasant of this type of land. This type of land was perhaps an incentive to the peasantry to colonize land to counter population growth.

The landed gentry, constituting of the royal family, the nobility and the awardees, on an average held 15, 10 and 6.4 hectares of land per household respectively. This small class of some 488 households, in 1891, had little room for direct economic exploitation of the produce of the land, partly because rent was customarily and legally fixed at low levels (1 to 6 percent on the best land and 2 to 12 percent on the worst land) and partly because a market for rice was almost non-existent in the valley. The demand for rice in the tertiary sector hardly amounted to requirements for 5 to 6 thousand people, requiring the produce of barely 1.5 percent of cultivated land in the valley. The gentry and the landlords had therefore vary little inventive to reduce the general peasantry to feudal penury or misery through the extraction of the produce of the land.

From a broader perspective, one could look at agrarian structure as consisting of two principal classes, the class of the non-cultivating gentry and landlords and the class of the cultivating peasantry. The common rented peasants, the sepoys and the Touna Lou holders who had land grants, constituted the common peasantry upon whom the exploitative burdens of feudalism could have fallen. However, as there was surplus land and every household had more or less, some land grants, as the rents were but nominal, except for the class of the cultivating slaves, as there hardly existed any significant market for surplus rise, feudalistic exploitation was largely non-economic and much less severe than those prevailing in the rest of India. Thus before the advent of colonial rule, in the absence of private property in land, land relations were benign and uncomplicated.

Colonial Commercialization of Agriculture

The Rayatwari system of land tenure was introduced in Manipur. Private property in land and taxation in money, started the process of monetization and marketization of the economy and commercialization of agriculture. The private property effect of the land system was such that area under rice increased from 26500 hectares in1891 to 75370 hectares in 1941. During the period, population increased by 153 percent as against the increase in cultivated area by 184 percent. The estimated rice surplus in the state rose to 34 percent during the colonial rule. Thus a closed agrarian society was opened up and the introduction of an export sector, led to the commercialization of agriculture and the economy in general.

The emergence of big land lords was effectively stopped by a Manipur State Darbar resolution of 1925, prohibiting the acquisition of more than 10 hectares of land. De-industrialization and population growth during the colonial period led to expansion and colonization of new land, further thwarting tendencies towards differentiation and landlordism. The census of India 1951 reveals that landlords constituted only 2.5 percent of the agricultural population, against this, 85.5 percent wholly or mainly owned their own land and 12 percent wholly or mainly un-owned their land. Agricultural labour was insignificant at 0.3 percent. Low levels of tenancy and agricultural labour were further depressors of differentiation and landlordism in the state's agriculture.

The monetized and marketized economy and open agrarianism were the basic character of the economy. The productive base of agriculture in the state had tremendously expanded and it was on this base that the impact of planned development would shape new agrarian relations and the structure of the economy.

Agriculture in the Post-Colonial Era

Manipur is one of the states in the Northeast which has achieved commendable success in agricultural modernization and production and productivity growth, especially in the valley region. Area under paddy has more or less stabilized around 1,62,000 hectares of land since the 1960s, though population has increased from 7.8 lakh persons to 22.9 lakh persons during 1991-2001. Agricultural modernization has been the key factor behind keeping food grains gaps within manageable levels in the face of near three folds increase in population but fixity of land under cultivation. Yield of rice was 2382 kg/hectares in the state during 2004-05 and the advent of mechanization has created situations of bullock scarcity in large areas of the valley regions. Compound growth rates of rice were 2.75 percent during 1990-91 and 2000-01 and 2.36 percent during the period 1960-61 and 2000-01. Double cropping is practiced in 6.8 percent of area and of the created irrigation capacity of 55,000 hectares in the valley, hardly 15,000 hectares receive irrigation. Food grains gap was 16 percent in 2004-05.

The impact of population growth on fixed land supplies and modernization of agriculture, are visible on the structure of landholdings in the state. During 1971-1991, marginal holders (below 1 hectare) jumped from 51.56 percent to 72.49 percent, small holders (1 to 2 hectares) dropped from 35.53 percent to 19.66 percent, medium and large holders virtually disappeared. The average size of the biggest farms is only 4 hectares, even ignoring high degrees of parcelization and 92.15 percent of all operational holdings are below 2 hectares. Up to the 1991 Census, 70 percent of labour force was absorbed by agriculture. In the face of non-industrialization and tertiarisation of the economy and high population growth, the state's agrarian sector exhibits all signs of marginalization and stagnation. It was within these structural dimensions that land and production relations in Manipur's agrarian sector are shaping.

Land and Development in the Village

The village that we have chosen as the context for the illustration of land and development in the valley region of

Manipur lies in the Kakching settlement of the district of Thoubal. Kakching settlement is known as one of the most agriculturally advanced region of the valley. This is a settlement that has been at the fore front of adoption of technologies and innovations, whenever these set foot in the state. Population pressures are also high in this settlement and tertiary sector activities are also growing at a high pace. A small but vibrant township has emerged right in the middle of the settlement. The village would serve as a fine example of how tertiarisation of the economy along with population growth and fixity of land combine together to have telling effects on agrarian structure, land relations and agrarian development.

The land holding pattern in the village exhibits a high degree of marginalization and absence of any farm that could function at any significant levels of commercialization. In this village of 325 cultivating households, the largest operational holdings are only of 5 acres and there are only five households in the village operating in the size class. Over 63 percent of the operational holdings are below 1.5 acres and in fact, 93.54 percent of the holdings are below a hectare.

Given the historically determined pattern of ownership and holdings distribution of land, agrarian relations in land are essentially set by the structure of land rights as reflected in the tenure conditions and tenure types. Fixed rent tenure is the main tenure form and share cropping and mortgaged tanures are of recent origin, though they are on the rise. Rents are 25 percent of the produce in the state but in this village, rents have gone all the way up to 33 percent. This is no surprise as only 37.25 of cultivating households are owner cultivators and the rest of the cultivators are lessees. All size classes of the land owners are leasing in and leasing out land, there is heterogeneity within the lessees as well as lessons. There is no class of big landlords having monopolistic tenure powers.

Population pressure on land has been the main reason for the majority of the holdings being below subsistence levels. High levels of occupational diversifications into the tertiary sectors to supplement farm income, was observed. However as tertiary sector employment are also limited, there was a high tendency for the households to fall back upon, on their small pieces of land or to lease in small parcels of land at hunger rents, at least to insure the minimum cereal needs. This is the main reason for the existence of a large and highly competitive lease market. The high levels of rent, along with high costs of cultivation, are making it more convenient and economic for the better off land owners to rent out land and resort to usury (debt levels reached 72 percent in the lowest size classes and 62.15 percent for all cultivators). The net result is that tenants and non-land owning households are seeing their positions weakened as land hunger is driving up rents and tenures are becoming more insecure. Households in the village who own some land and are also government employees, teachers, shopkeepers, business men or are rich, are the class of the economically strong who are seeing their positions strengthened. These owners lease out land and at convenience revert to cultivation at will, creating high levels of insecurity of income for the tenants. The village is thus getting increasingly polarised into the economically strong and the economically weak. Land relations in the village are exploitative of the non-land owning tenants but in general land relations are not pre-capitalist, nor is it progressive.

The analysis of the production relations and the structures of the land, labour, product and credit market in village agriculture, points to an agrarian structure in the village that is in the transitional phase. There is a largely free labour market where labour has acquired the character of a commodity with the bigger farms realising more surplus value. Commercialization led by demand is fairly high and the comparatively larger farms sell bulk of their produce in the market. All farms make fairly high levels of investment in the new seed- fertilizer technology and have achieved high yield rates. However there is no effort on the part of the bigger farmers to reinvest their profits in farm capital or land improvements, though they invest in the purchase of land, mainly to lease out. Polarisation in concentration of land holdings and farm equipments and capital, seems to have been largely arrested. Thus surplus values are not changing the organic composition of capital or leading to a continuous process of technological advancement. On the other hand many features of pre-capitalist structures are alive and persisting. Usury and indebtedness is having a strong hold on the peasantry giving rise to forced commerce in agriculture and market involvements, rising of obligatory debt labour, though low in volume, and a rising preference for landowners to lease out at high rents. The Kautsky-Lenin limits to capitalist agriculture seem to have set in early in the village.[6]

Fixed land, persistence of non-viable farms, peasant's readiness to pay hunger rent, and land owner's preference to lease out small parcels of land, have led to a high level of rigidity in the land market, that is not favourable to the consolidation of holdings for capitalist enterprises. Labour shortages are being created by the voluntary unemployment of highly educated younger generations and others, who are showing marked preferences for tertiary sector employment opportunities. The multiplication of marginal indebted tenants has become the vested interest of the economically strong and landowners, and to that extent usury is becoming a limiting factor to the polarisation in landholdings and capitalist farming. The nature of development of production relations and class configurations and the existing levels of the development of forces of production seems to have brought in a state of comparative stagnation in the development of agriculture in the village, after having achieved a certain level of technological change. The essence of capitalism are manifested in many aspects of village agriculture but the dominant social group in the village, Rudra's "Big Landowners"[7], has managed to keep pre-capitalist structures in agriculture, functioning. The Mode of Production in the village is thus neither pre-capitalist nor capitalist; in Utsa Patnaik's term, it is Non-capitalist. Which mode of production would dominate in agriculture in the village, would depend among others, upon the changes that are likely to emerge in the very tertiarised structure of the state's economy.

Manipur, like all states in the Northeast, have not been able to industrialize in the post-colonial period. As such the development phase of the agricultural population moving away from agriculture to industry has thus been bypassed. The movement is from agriculture to the tertiary sector, in a state that is linked to the rest of the country but by one functional national highway across hilly terrain, restricting physical mobility to great extents. Thus the only options open to the growing population in the agrarian sector is, either farming on fixed land area and further marginalisation, involving agricultural involution, or branching off to the tertiary sector which has its own limited absorptive capacity. Given the tiny size of the state's economy with around 70 percent of labour force persistently tied to agriculture, its impact on agrarian structure in a tertiarised economy is quite predictable.

Hoards of professionally trained and highly educated youths, both from the farm sector and urban area, have migrated to the mainland for various job opportunities but are only a fraction of the incremental population growth (2.6 percent). With the virtual break down of the joint family system, the further fragmentation of holdings and marginalisation in agrarian structure seems quite inevitable in the agrarian sector of Manipur.

The settlement of Kakching within which our sample village lies, is the most urbanised rural area in the small

Manipur valley, with its agrarian structure experiencing the greatest impact of urbanisation and tertiarisation in the state's economy. Rural settlements in the valley along the state highways from Imphal are growing into townships like Kakching, having Municipal Councils and municipalities. These are the rural settlements mainly contribution to the agricultural products of the valley and the state. The type of production relations and agrarian structure we have observed in the village are likely to be already replicated or likely to be replicated in these urbanising valley settlements at various levels and degrees. Then the future trajectory of agriculture development would not suggest a progressive path. While we are not here, arguing for large-scale farms, the fact remains that unless non-farm rural economic activities are nurtured or the process of industrialisation hastened in the state, the state's economy as well as the agrarian sector is likely to regress into structural retrogression.

Land and Agrarian Transition in the Hills

Village Reality and of Things to Come

Siroy is a medium sized village in the Ukhrul district of Manipur and lies at a distance of 15 kilometres from the district headquarters. The village lies on national highway 150, also known as the Jessami road leading to Nagaland. Its inhabitants are the sturdy Tangkhul Nagas and the village is as old as antiquity. The village is well communicated as well as well incorporated into the hill political economy and further to that of the state's economy. Siroy village is therefore, a village that has experienced whatever development impulses the hill region of the state should have gone through, in the post independence period. The village should therefore represent a snap shot of a village in transition in the hill regions of the state and serve the larger purpose of addressing the issues of tribal Manipur, though it would not represent the entire gamut of tribal life in Manipur.

Siroy village has 153 households with a population of 831, consisting of 418 males and 413 females. The sex ratio is therefore nearly even. The village is highly educated. The literacy rate is 77.6 percent, that of males being 83.4 percent and that of females being73.8 percent. In fact the village has 4 PhDs, 9 post graduates and 37 graduates. The village has a private English medium school and the deserted and unmaned primary health centre is the only sign of government presence in this village.

National Highway 150, cuts right through the middle of the village, the original village is located on the upper face of the mountain and to the north of the highway and the rest of the village on the lower face of the mountain and south of the highway. The church and community centre are in the lower settlement and this lower settlement is a result of population growth. The lower settlement looks definitely more affluent and their political clout is visible in the way the village polity has been modified. All Naga villages have one chief and a village council but this village has two sub-chiefs representing the upper part and the lower part of the village under a weak common chief. The two sub-chiefs are elected, though the legal one is hereditary. The sub-chief of the lower part of the village, a retired army man obviously was the one who had the greater authority. For the better or for the worse, the village polity was definitely not of the pristine types so often discussed in formal platforms.

A high degree of occupational diversification is taking place in this village. Among male heads of households, only 61.5 percent were cultivators and 18.2 percent were government employees. Businessmen constituted 5.2 percent and woodcutters 3.5 percent. Other occupations included shop keeping, basket making, driver, nun, pastor, teachers etc. Almost half of the male heads of households (45.2 percent) had subsidiary occupations, indicating livelihood struggles through farm and non-farm employment strategies, for round the year employment. Of these multiple occupation heads of households, 48 percent considered cultivation as a subsidiary occupation and another 19.3 percent considered woodcutting as a subsidiary occupation. Three households claimed rice milling, saw milling and truck owning as subsidiary occupations (Based on time allocation?). Agricultural and casual labourers constituted 11.6 percent of household heads. This occupational profile of households clearly exhibit livelihood diversifications and movement away from agriculture. Why this is so is clearly visible from the structure of landholdings, production and types of cultivations.

Siroy village entirely changed over to wet rice cultivation on terraces and river valleys, only one household was cultivating on jhum land. The chief of the village pointed out to us, the barren face of hills that was once the jhum land of the village, which had no chance of re-generating itself in the face of population growth. Villagers are now compelled to etch out small terraces or colonize narrow strips of river valleys for cultivation. Ironically an ecological disaster and hunger is compelling more sensible crop husbandry.

The land holdings pattern shows that 76.63 percent of the cultivating households are below subsistence producers of rice. All size classes lease out land but only the highest size class own and also lease in land. Clearly a land market is emerging in the village and there are signs of cultivable land hunger in a region of land abundance. The land holdings distribution shows that only less than a quarter of the cultivators hold sufficient land to meet the rice requirements of the households. This is the main reason for the wide occupational diversification among the villagers. Given the fact that 18 percent of the households are government employees with comparatively high cash flows and the fact that over three fourths of the cultivating households are below subsistence holders of land, a high degree of indebtedness is therefore but inevitable. Over 68 percent of the households in the village are indebted and the average debt per household range between Rs 15547 and Rs 38142, in the three size classes. Among the indebted households, 7 percent are subsistence holders, 17 percent middle holders and 71 percent are upper holders. Education, consumption and health are the main reasons for debt, investment in agriculture accounting for barely 4.8 percent of total debt. The share of education in total debt is 46.9 percent, that of consumption 19.9 percent and that of health 16.1 percent. The two upper size classes borrow more for education (70 percent and 59 percent) than the subsistence class (37.64 percent), the subsistence class borrow more for consumption and illness. The interest rate is extremely high in the village, ranging from 4 percent to 10 percent per mansum, that is 48 to 120 percent per annum. Organized money lending called "Societies" account for 66 percent of lending and about 20 percent are accounted for by money lenders.

The village also has a fairly large livestock and poultry base. Bovine population is 123 and there are 85 pigs and 787 poultry stock. Besides, three households had three fisheries. The village also has garden and farm horticulture, which, besides providing subsistence, generated a total market surplus of Rs 65 thousand. The brief sketch of the economic base of Siroy village suggests a number of social and economic transitions that are underway in a relatively advanced tribal village. We list them as under.

1. Agriculture, even on terraces and river valley, is no longer a viable livelihood option for over 75 percent of the households, as the produce of the land is not sufficient to meet the subsistence needs of the family. Smallness of wet rice cultivation holdings, mono-cropping and the non use of HYV seeds and fertilizers are the main cause of food deficits in the village. No villagers used the two vital inputs in the village.

2. Horticulture and livestock activities on tiny homestead scales are the vital secondary economic activities of a diversifying livelihood strategy. Casual labour in state construction works and the tertiary activities in the nearby township, are also meagre employment options for the large number of under employed in the village. Institutions like communal and exchange labour are giving way to paid and hired labour forms, in spite of the prevalence of high levels of surplus labour in the village. Rice shortage, increasing cash needs, emergence of non cultivating land holders and the high opportunity costs of tertiary sector casual labour are the main reasons for this paradox of high labour costs in the face of large labour surplus in the village.

3. Industrial activities are almost non-existent in the village and handicraft and even handloom, are only subsistence activities for a few households.

4. Tertiary sector activities are almost absent. Only three tiny shops were found and there is no market in the village.

5. There are 24 government employees and six businessmen in the village, Credit Societies are the parking space for surplus funds for these village elites.

6. A highly educated new generation is less willing to venture into agriculture as a first option. Compelled ones are venturing into horticulture, vegeculture and livestocks and fishery, but are yet to make a head way.

7. Unorganized and heterogeneous small time marketing is a main cause for weak supply response of agriculture in spite of good communication and markets.

8. Population growth is having a negative effect of village homestead and farm land. The village formerly lay on the ascending hill face on the north of the highway. The village has spread on the descending hill face south of the highway. There are now two nominal village chiefs under a legal chief's household.

9. Tribal landholdings institutions based on community, village or clan ownership are fast giving way to de-facto individual ownerships, leading to emergence of land markets and new tannurial systems based on private property concepts.

10. New economic opportunities (private or state based) are fast eroding traditional village authorities, as control over land is becoming looser. However the concepts of the village commune with its institutional structures are still intake. The village chief and the elite are now concentrating on government funds and programme to maintain their stranglehold on the village political economy. Successful entrepreneurs migrate to greener pastures without a second thought on investing within the village economy. Those who are left behind are resigned to the structures of tribal life that imposes many restrictions on the working of the invisible hand.

If these are the dominant characteristics of advancing and luckier villages like Siroy, what would be the fate of remote villages in the hills that has to be approached by foot journeys lasting days. One can only say the obvious, that there are a mass of tribal villages in the state that have been largely left out of the development process and a minority of villages on the highways which are slowly being shaken up by development impulses. This development dichotomy within tribal societies, is one vital blind spots that policy planners as well as intellectuals have failed to address. What than are the limited lessons that Siroy village teaches us for tribal Manipur? We also list some of them below:

1. Unless the economic base of tribal villages are strengthened, institutional rigidities will continue to undermine development efforts.

2. The institutions development contradiction can largely be broken by using the institutions themselves to push through development programmes.

3. Any development strategy should have agriculture as the pivot around which other non agricultural programmes should revolve.

4. Agricultural development should be conditional upon research and development of suitable HYV seeds and its widespread introduction in the hill regions.

5. An appropriate market structure and mechanism has to be worked out that takes care of diseconomies of scale and transport cost disadvantages. This calls for clustering of villages with an appropriate private public participatory institutional mechanism.

6. There is a huge information failure at the level of the villages. This is feeding the politician-village elite nexus that brazenly siphoned off village development funds of which the villagers are mostly unaware of. High levels of education needs to be complemented with transparent information on development programmes and funds. This will cut at the roots of institutional rigidities as well as vested interests.

One could lengthen the list ad-nausem but these are on believes, the core issues. The tribes of Manipur are far more advanced than the tribes of mainland India, socially, economically and culturally. In the post-independence period, the building of roads, schools, health centres, and government offices etc, in the districts, have opened up the hill districts of the state. The district head quarters in the hills are developing into vibrant townships and are fast spreading development impulses into their hinterland villages. Politically, the hill regions return twenty of the sixty members of the state legislature, and as such, are an integral, as well as a critical part of the political decision making process in the state. Two tribal politicians had in fact risen to become the chief ministers of the state. Political, economic and social integration into the modern development process in the state, coupled with the high levels of education, has altered the mind sets and the value systems of the tribes irreversibly. The elite, the educated and especially the youths are well aware of the opportunities that are opening up in the modern times. Thousands of the state's tribals have spread out to mainland India and abroad in search of greener pastures and lucrative jobs, unlike many of the backward tribes of India. Within the state, reservation in government jobs, educations et al, have drawn them out from the isolated village republics of yore, driving huge wedges into their consciousness of their community, identity and future directions of change and development. However, the gains of development has hardly percolated down to the level of the remote villages, thereby creating a tragic dichotomy within tribal societies. The tribal doctor, engineer, contractor or the politician, settle down in the many densely populated tribal neighbourhoods in the valley, abandoning their villages, though they retain their land rights in their villages. There are many absentee tribal village chiefs settled in the valley. Tribal wealth is being accumulated in the valley or the district headquarters and the inevitable divide between the masses and the elite is glaringly visible in the state. The political economy spawned by this power and wealth dichotomy within tribal society is the lever that is jacking up many of the vexing issues of land identity and development in the state. While the tribal elite are not coming out themselves with workable development paradigms, any proposal from the state is lampooned and maximally milked for sectarian short term gains. It is here that the issues of identity, community and territory finds maximum currency, thereby even derailing discourses on positive development initiatives.

Tribal Manipur is ethnically divided and the emergence of consensus among the tribes, be it about land, identity or development, is still quite a long way to go. Political conflicts in a plural and multi-ethnic society are inevitable, especially where development has not taken place significantly. However the ruling elite and the political class needs to realize is that the humane, the universal and the material concerns of the masses cannot be ignored for too long. History has repeatedly shown that social engineering that are not rooted in the real concerns of the people have a tendency to be rejected by the people.

Coming back to the original issue of land, identity Tribalism and development, institutions are the framework within which cultures thrive and identities are formed. Just as the modes of production change over time and give birth to more efficient production processes, institutions have also to change and give birth to new cultures, cultures that strengthen our identities rather than destroy them, for after all fossilized identities belong to the dustbin of history and a living and growing identity is the stuff of the future. Sections of tribal political elite in collision with diehards are vehemently floating notions of timeless cultures and identities that they prescribe as uncompromisable, thereby intentionally erecting road blocks to development. One is hardly pleading for defacement of cultures and identities, especially of the tribes, but one needs to cry out for a considered debate on how to programme on acceptable escape from tribalism. Until we settle this issue, much of tribal north east is likely to pull on as tribals for quite some time.

NOTES

1. Insights into the variation and corruption of tribal land systems among the Rongmei Nagas are provided in the case studies by Gangmumei Kamei. The study reports 80 percent of village land *transfers* to seven individual *Rampous* or land owners, in Awangkhul village in the Tamenglong district. See Kamei in *Land Use System in Manipur*, N. Lokendro, (ed.), pp. 1-20.
2. Pemberton (1835), p.30, reported how the produce of the foot hill paddy fields surrounding the valley, was able to feed the population when the valley was almost entirely flooded.
3. Strong tribal chiefs enforcing rules, can internalize many external scale economies of tribal societies to increase each individual's welfare. Rigid rules however discourage investment and productivity. An excellent theoretical analysis is available in, Jeffrey B. Nuget, and Nicolas Sanchez, (1993).
4. In Phadang village of Ukhrul district, 20 percent households are landless, rent is 1/3 of produce and all agricultural land is private land and most forests are now under private control.
5. The concept of "Communal Land" among the tribes, has embedded in it, ideologies of private property, individual ownerships and land markets. Inevitably therefore, contemporary constructs of communal land systems tend to be ideologized models where the construct is often used for private or political advantages. Angela Cheater (1990), provides incisive case studies in Zimbabwe.
6. Limits to the development of capitalist and commercial agriculture are set by land market rigidity, workers shortages and usury. For a detailed analysis, see Ranjit Sau (1973).
7. Ashok Rudra argues that India's agricultural populations cannot be neatly fitted in the classical schema of class. There are a set of people who exploit others, the "Big Land Owners" and those who are exploited, what Alice Thorner calls, Rudra's "Drastic Dualism". See A. Rudra, (1992) p.376.

REFERENCES

Arambam, Lokendra (1996), 'Meitei Cultural History: Economy, Society and Ideology from Early Times to the Eighteenth Century A.D.', *Unpublished Ph.D. Thesis*, Manipur University, Imphal.

Cheater, Angela (1990), 'The Ideology of Communal Land Tenure in Zimbabwe', *Africa: Journal of the International African Institute,* Vol. 60, No. 2, pp. 188-206.

Bharadwaj, Krishna, and Das, P.K. (1975), 'Tenurial Conditions and Mode of Exploitations: S Study of Some Villages in Orissa,' *Economic and Political Weekly,* Annual Number, February, pp. 221-239.

Brown, R. (1873), *Statistical Account of Manipur,* Reprinted 1975, Sanskaran Prakashan, Delhi.

Dun, E. W.(1981), *Gazetteer of Manipur,* Vivek Publishing House, Delhi.

Devi, Binodini, P., (2006), *Tribal Land System in Manipur,* Akansa Publishing House, Delhi.

Howell, A.W. (1891), *A Short Account of Land Revenue in Manipur,* Assistant Political Officer, Manipur Political Agency.

Hudson, T.C. (1911), *The Naga Tribes of Manipur,* Low Price Publications, Delhi.

Nuget, Jeffrey, B. And Sanchez Nicolas (1993), 'Tribes, Chiefs, and Transhumance: A comparative Institutional Analysis', *Economic Development and Cultural Change,* Vol. 42.No. 1, pp. 87-113.

Pemberton, R.B. (1835), *The Eastern Frontier of India* , Reprinted 1979, Mittal Publications, Delhi.

Rudra, Ashok (1992), *Political Economy of Indian Agriculture,* Bagchi and Company, Calcutta.

Sau, Ranjit (1973), 'On The Essence and Manifestations of Capitalism in Indian Agriculture', *Economic and Political Weekly,* vol.8, no. 13, , pp. 27-30.

Singh, C.P.,(2005), 'Agrarian Structure and Production Relations in Manipur', *Unpublished Ph.D.Thesis,* Manipur University.

Singh, N., Lokendro (2004) (ed.), *Land Use System in Manipur Hills,* Rajesh Publications, Delhi.

SECTION II

HISTORY, POLITICS AND DEVELOPMENT

7

CONTESTING SPACE, COMPETING CLAIMS, SHAPING PLACES: Violent Conflicts and Development in Manipur

—Bhabananda Takhellambam

Manipur once so fondly described as the 'jewel of India', lay shattered, rocked by violent armed conflicts. The genesis of these armed conflicts can be dated to the early struggle against the British rule, which was carried forward after the merger of Manipur to the Indian union. Since then it had taken different turns and twist. In the early 90's, for the first time, Manipur witnessed a violent armed ethnic conflict between Naga and Kuki ethnic groups. Hundreds of people were killed, villages uprooted, people rendered homeless and still the memories of the atrocities committed on one another, haunts the people of Manipur. It has created a sense of insecurity among the ethnic communities that once live together under the composite Manipuri civilization.

This paper is an attempt to reflect the interethnic relation, their competing territorial claims, imagined/proposed territorial homelands and its impact on the development of Manipur. The struggle for an autonomous region, exclusive to Naga ethnic community, the form of (Greater Nagaland) Nagalim, within the Indian union, the demand for a Kuki Homeland and the endeavor to preserve the territorial integrity of the state of Manipur has fragmented and fractionalized the politics of the ethnic communities of the state.

Land, Ethnicity, Settlement and Dynamic Relations

The topography of Manipur comprises two distinct geographical regions, the valley and the surrounding hills, a total area of 22,327 sq. kms, (which is 1/149 of the total area of India). The total area of the hills comprises 20,089 sq. km i.e. 92 percent of the total area of the state while the valley is 2,238 sq. kms. i.e. 8 percent of the land. The total population of the state, according to 2001 Census, is 23,88,634. The density of the population (per sq. kms.) is 107.[1] However, there is a lot of variation in the land and population concentration ratio between the hills and valley. The hill population comprises only 29.88 percent of the total population of the state, while they occupy 92 percent of the total land. The valley which is only 8 percent of the total land accommodates 70.12 percent of the total population.

The hills are inhabited by different sub-ethnic groups (thirty-three plus unspecified groups) broadly categorized under the Naga and Chin-Kuki-Mizo (Chikim) ethnic groups. This does not mean that they reside only in the hills but are scattered in the valley too. Some localities in the capital city, Imphal, like Nagaram, Lambulane, Kakhulong, etc are their exclusive areas. Almost all the populations are followers of Christianity, except for Rongmei, Puram (of Kabui) and few others where there are traces of traditional religious practices.[2] Their total population is 7,13,813 i.e. 29.88% of the state population. The valley is predominantly inhabited by the Meitei, their estimated population is 13,61,521 which is 56.99%. Most of the Meiteis are followers of Gaudiya Vaishnavism, where there are also traces of followers of Snanmahi religion (traditional). The rest of the population, Meitei Pangal, believers of Islamic religion and others (Bengalis, Biharis, Jains, Nepalis, Sikhs, etc) comprised a total of 31,33,00 (13.1%).

The five districts namely Senapati, Churchandpur, Ukhrul, Chandel and Tamenglong are the Hill districts and the four districts of Imphal West and East, Thoubal and Bishnupur, the four comprise the valley districts. Senapati district is inhabited by thirteen ethnic groups scattered in different parts of the area, "the scheduled tribes" that constitute the major groups are Mao, Maram and Thadou. The minor groups are Kabui, Tangkhul, Maring, Chiru, Kom, Vaiphei, Kacha Naga, Sema and Koireng.[3]

In Churchandpur District the Chikim dominates over the Naga group. Here also there are "thirteen scheduled tribes" scattered, the major groups among them are Hmar, Paite and Thadou. The minor groups are Anal, Chothe, Kabui, Kom, Vaiphei, Zou, Mizo, Gangte, Simte and Ralte. The Naga groups dominate Ukhrul District, the major tribe is Tangkhul and the minor group is Thadou. In Chandel District, fourteen scheduled tribes inhabits the land, the major groups in the district are Anal, Maring and Thadou, whereas the minor groups comprises the Lamkang, Zou, Gangte, Myon, Monsang, Aimol, Chothe, Puram, Mizo, Thangkhul and Kom. In the four valley districts, the majority are Meitei, Meitei Pangal along with minor groups of the tribes living in small pockets.

The pattern of settlement in the hill districts are mixed among the Naga and Chikim ethnic groups. It is just the variation of one dominating the other in two districts and while in the other, three districts they are fairly balanced.

Thadou (1,15,045) the largest of the tribes in Manipur dominates the Churchandpur District, the special feature of the Thadou being that it is the only tribe who are found in thousands almost in every hill districts of Manipur. They also settle in Imphal in large numbers.[4] Tangkhuls (1,12,944) dominate the Ukhrul District. Sizable populations are also found in Senapati and Imphal districts. Mao (80,568) and Maram (10,510) tribes dominates the Senapati District with few numbers in the valley. Monsang (1,635) and Moyon (1,710) tribes are found concentrated in Chandel district. Purums (503) mainly inhabit the Senapati District. Sahte (3110) settles in Churchandpur District.

Maring (17,361), though concentrated in the Chandel District, they also inhabit the district of Senapati and in the valley too. The smallest of the tribes the Sema (25) live in Churchandpur and Tamenglong Districts. The Mizo/Lushai (10,520) dominate the Churchandpur District but are also found in the districts of Senapati and Chandel. Zhou (19,112) concentrate in Churchandpur District but are also found in Chandel District. Though most of the Paite (44,861) tribe are in Churandpur district, they are also found in all the districts. Even the Vaiphei (27,791), though concentrated in Churchandpur and Senapati Districts, also inhabit every hill districts in Manipur.[5]

Ethno-demographic composition and its influence in the politics play a very important role in the ethnic relation in a state. According to Prof. Gangmumei Kamei, "ethnicity was first introduced in the governance of Manipur during the colonial rule when they separated the administration of the hill tribes from that of Manipur valley."[6] The colonial rulers were also responsible for the nomenclature of Naga and Kuki ethnic communities, "the Nagas who are an indigenous community divided into several tribes" were "given a exogenous identity by the British colonial rulers through a generic name 'Naga' since the beginning of the nineteenth century and the Kuki Chin who migrated to Manipur in different periods of history" were "given another exogenous identity called 'Kuki.'"[7] Though it would be wrong to put the entire responsibility of the dynamic ethnic relations between the Naga and Kuki groups on the British rule, their rule up to a large extent played havoc on the interethnic relations, "...ethnicity was made an element of governance of the hill tribes. And it still continues in the post-independence period. Politicization of ethnicity was rooted in the colonial administrative system and it is continued even later on."[8] The divide and rule policy of the colonial rule is beyond doubt proven time and again, not only in Manipur but in the entire subcontinent. They exploited the existing inter-ethnic relations among the Kuki and Naga groups.

In the modern times, "the Kuki rebellion of 1917-19 and the Zeliangrong Revolt of 1930-32 affected the inter-ethnic relations."[9] But this is not to say that rivalry amongst the Naga and Kuki were absent in traditional times, but the relationship became more complex in the nineteenth century. The colonial policy of Kuki settlement and the motive behind also played a negative role in the interethnic relations, according to Prof. Lal Dena, "in 1840, McCulloch, the then Political Agent, purposively adopted the policy of allowing the settlement of Kukis on the frontlines and even among the Nagas. The double purpose of Kuki settlement in and on the frontiers of Manipur was that the war-like Kukis has to act as a buffer first against the Burmese and second against the recalcitrant Nagas and Lushai tribes."[10] Kukis and Nagas were used among one another by the British in subduing the other; this was the time when the seeds of ethnic animosity were sown that was to be flowered in the contemporary times.

The Kuki rebellion of 1917-19, which began in April 1917 against the British highhandedness, in the later stage, turned against the Nagas. "When the Kukis rose in revolt against British domination in 1917 the conflict spilled over into inter-tribal warfare between Kukis and Nagas with much bloodshed on both sides."[11] The cause of the Kuki rebellion, according to Prof La Dena, "was the objection of the Kuki chiefs to allow their subjects to be sent to war fronts with labour corps which had been raised for the second time."[12] However, "upto March 1918, the animosity of the rebels seemed to have directed solely against the British authority. But, by the end of April 1918 a series of brutal outrages were committed on their surrounding (Naga) villages by the rebels and in the next three months 19 villages were raided with the loss of 193 persons killed and 26 missing. The cause of some of these raids was old feuds."[13] Other reasons were, "the Kuki chiefs sought help and cooperation from the Zeliangrong villages in their rebellion against the British. However the latter did not co-operate. As they did not get help and cooperation from the Zeliangrong people the Kuki directed their offensive against them."[14]

Similar raids were also conducted on the other Naga villages, "in October 1918, 20 Kabui-Naga villages were raided and burned with a loss of more than 85 lives ... no wonder, the Kabui rebellion (Zeliangrong Revolt) in 1930 -32 was directed both against the British and Kukis". In these raids hundreds of people were killed many taken as slaves and few young beautiful girls were presented as gifts to the king of Samsok in Awa land. In a way the Kuki rebellion served as the foundation of Kuki nationalism and their aspiration for an exclusive homeland, "The Kuki rising of 1917-1919 serves as a foundation of Kuki nationalism. In present-day context, the Kuki country covered by the movement ranges broadly from the upper Chindwin, Burma, in the West; the hills in Manipur; and Aisan, Nagaland, in the East."[15]

The Zeliangrong Revolt of 1930-32 was an attempt on the part of founder leader Jadonang to unite the Zemei, Liangmei and Rongmei tribes collectively (Ze-liang-rong) of Tamenglong. "He (Jadonang) initiated a movement which had social, religious and political objectives. He aimed at the political integration of his people under a kingdom after the achievement of social unity through religion."[16] The main objective of the movement was to make war, first on the Kukis and secondly on the British Government. "J.P. Mills, after interviewing the headmen of several Kach Naga villages wrote that Jadonang narrated to his supporters that through his miraculous power, he came to know that the Kukis have captured two Naga girls. One of them was brutally murdered and the other was buried alive by Kukis during the (Kuki) rebellion."[17]

According to John Parratt and Saroj N. Arambam Parratt, "At any rate the movement moved swiftly to its final phase and took on an increasingly belligerent attitude towards both the Kukis and the British Administration in Manipur. Although it is well documented that the Kabuis did not adopt a 'strike first' strategy towards the Kukis, there can be little doubt that they were ready and eager to pay off old scores and that the prophetic propaganda machine was playing on their traditional animosity. In particular this was encouraged by the frequent references to Naga girls tortured and killed during the Kuki rebellion. The Kukis themselves were clearly frightened. Some villages had stopped working in their fields for fear of attack..."[18] The Zeliangrong Revolt founded Naga nationalism in Manipur.

Contesting Space, Competing Claims

The basis of the claims and counter claims for lebensraum of the expanding Kuki and Naga ethnic groups, though rooted in the historical process of migration and settlement, to a large extent was abetted by the antipathy of the government against these ethnic groups. After India got independence the program and policies of the state government created a sense of insecurity amongst the Kuki community regarding their land and settlement. They felt that they were threatened and they even feared the total annihilation of their ancestral land that resulted in a political demand for a Kuki homeland. In the course of the time the demand were carried forward by the Kuki insurgent groups. In the case of the Naga community, the central government decision to ban the Naga National Council that forced Phizo and his boys to go underground was a blunder on the part of the government. The birth of National Socialist Council of Nagalim (NSCN) was the turning point in the territorial claims of the Naga ethnic community. Both the groups began their demand on a fairly democratic ground, and the government response forced them to resort to armed struggle. In the course of time the territorial demands/claims became diametrically opposite, the territory/space became contested. The competing claim is between the Naga & Chikim ethnic groups and the five hill districts of the state are made their contesting space.

The anticipation of the British departure from the state encouraged many ethnic groups in Manipur to form their own social and political units. From the inceptions of these organizations it was, according to Gangmumei Kamei, the colonial rulers that encouraged the proliferation of these organizations based on their ethnicity, "Manipur remained a native State under the British paramountcy but the colonial rule encouraged the ethnic groups, the Nagas and Kukis to assert their separate ethnic identity. During the last years of the British rule, the tribal elites were encouraged to form their tribal organisations, Kabui Samiti (1934), Kabui Naga Association (1946), Zeliangrong Council (1947), Manipur Zeliangrong Union (1947), the Kuki National Assembly (KNA), Paite National Council, Tangkhul Long, Vaiphei National Union, Gangte Tribal Union, Hmar National Union, Khulmi Union etc. The tribes had asserted their ethnicity in social, economic and political formation. In such a plural society, conflict is inevitable."[19]

However, on the occasion of the Indian independence, Hijam Irabot knew the danger of these ethnic assertions and called for a meeting on November 1947 of the representative of ethnic communities of Manipur, hills and valley. The organizations present were, the Tangkhul Long, Kuki National Assembly, Kabui Association, Khul Union, Mizo Union, Manipur Praja Sabha, Manipur Krishak Sabha, Meitei Marup and Nongpok Apunba Marup. "This conference... decided to keep the territorial integrity of Manipur and form an United Front of Manipur. They sent good-will mission to Nagaland to talk to the leaders of Naga National Council."[20]

Meanwhile the interim Government of Manipur adopted the Manipur Constitution Act of 1947 and prepared for the election of 1948. The Act provided "for a limited constitutional monarchy... provided for a 53 member legislature."[21] However the striking feature of the constitution was not just the provision of representation of the hill people, but the inclusion of the representatives of the hill people in the constitution making body. "In the drafting of the Manipur State Constitution in 1947, the Maharaja appointed both the dominant Meitei leaders and representatives of the Naga and Kuki groups as member of the drafting committee. The Kabui Naga Association complained that no Kabui representative was appointed as a member of the committee. Later on, their representative was appointed after the completion of the drafting. During the work of the drafting committee, a Mao Naga leader, A. Daiho strongly argued that the hill tribes should have the right of secession from the State after five years. His proposal was rejected."[22]

The spirit and fabric of the inter-ethnic unity which was forged by the native people of the state was destroyed when Manipur merged to the Indian Union in October 1949. The election of 1948 and the short-lived government of the state saw the high watermark of inter-ethnic unity in Manipur.

"In the election of 1948, 18 seats were reserved for the hills but not on the basis of tribes, ... Democracy had provided the opportunity for participation in the governance of the state either as Ministers or members of the Assembly. Every community was represented except the Mao as there was no election due to political agitation. The election of 1948 was the endorsement of the state by the people of Manipur in a democratic way. There were 8 Naga MLAs - 5 Tangkhuls, 2 Zeliangrong and one Monshang, the other 9 were Kuki-Chins including Kom and Paite. The hill people accepted the Maharaja as the symbol of unity of the kingdom. This symbol was destroyed when the state was merged with the Dominion of India in October 1949."[23]

The birth of the demand for the Kuki homeland can be attributed to the passing of "the Manipur (Village Authorities in Hill Areas) Act 1956, which was published in the Extraordinary Gazzette of Manipur under Notification No. 1/15/54 dated 17th January 1957, Vol No. 6-E-4, Imphal Thursday April, 1957."[24] There was a strong opposition and a great deal of discontentment among the Chikim groups. They felt that it was an attempt to do away with the rights of the Chiefs over land. The initial opposition was brought in the Territorial Council by the Kuki members/representatives. "The apprehension, lest their land be snatched away from their hands with the Village Authority Act 1956, having been enforced, became stronger which could not be marginalized. The minds of the Kukis rest in fear of cornering them out from their habitation that might lead to complete extermination of Kukis in the backdrop of gradual steps taken up by the government over their right on land.. Thus, the insecurity looms large over their heads like 'Democle's Sword', the Kuki National Assembly decided to take political decision to demand a 'Kuki State in 1960."[25]

In order to materialize their demand the Kuki National Assembly submitted a representation to the then Prime

Minister of India, Jawaharlal Nehru, on March 24, 1960. It was basically the resolution passed at its General Assembly Meeting held at Thingkangphai (Manipur South District) which was held from January 19 to 22. The principal demand was for the creation of a Kuki state, within the Indian Union. Even after ten years of patient wait, when it failed to materialize, "the Kuki National Assembly, India, in their general meeting thereby resolved, while affirming its solidarity with the rest of the country, to make a just strong demand of the Government of India for immediate establishment of Kuki state for unification of all contiguous areas now under the inhabitation of Kukis in India and for pursuance of their demand to its final end in suppression of its earlier demand for establishment of a Kuki District.'[26]

In the meantime the All Manipur Students Association (AMSU) demanded for the state government to extend and enforce the Manipur Land Revenue and Reform Act, 1960 in the Hill areas of Manipur through a memorandum vide Memo No. CM -20/GS-M/MR & LR/89 dt. September 19, 1989. At this instance, "with a view to tackle such suppressive elements against the Kukis and to perpetuating political demand of the KNA, the Kuki National Front (KNF) was formed by late Nehlun Kipgen in 18th May 1988, to pursue creation of a Kuki Homeland (Kuki State), within the framework of Indian Constitution so as to fulfill aspiration of the Kukis as initiated in 1960 by the KNA."[27] Another objective of the KNF was to defend the Kukis from the atrocities and brutalities of the Naga activist. The Kuki land demanded by KNF consists of the districts of Churchandpur, Chandel, parts of Tamenglong, Ukhrul and parts of Senapati, Sadar Hills Autonomous District Council."[28] Another armed Kuki insurgent group, Kuki National Army claims these areas as the constituent of Zalengam (freedom of the people in their land) – or the Kuki nation.[29]

In the beginning of 1950's, Naga nationalism gained momentum under the leadership of A. Z. Phizo as the president of Naga National Council. The Nagas under the banner of Naga National Council raised their rights to self determine their future by declaring their independence. "They did not participate in the Constituent Assembly nor did they accept the Indian Constitution. The NNC conducted a plebiscite on May 16, 1951, to express their support for an independent Nagaland,"[30] "in which it was claimed that 99.9% of the Nagas voted for independence. The plebiscite emotionally integrated the various Naga tribes and boosted the morale of the movement."[31] However, the Nagas of Manipur did not participate in the process.

The Naga National Council was declared as an illegal organization and restrictions were imposed on the activities of the organization and arrest warrants were issued on the heads in 1952. The leaders went underground. The ban was a blunder on the part of the government of India. However, there was still a chance to reconcile the difference that could have stopped the Naga insurgency in 1953, when the then Prime Minister of India Jawaharlal Nehru and his counterpart of Burma U Nu visited Kohima on March 1930. "But the then Deputy Commissioner of Kohima, for reasons best known to him, did not allow the Nagas to submit a memorandum to the visiting Prime Ministers. The several thousand Nagas gathered at the venue to receive the VIPs, turned and left the ground enmass when they learned that they were not to make themselves heard before the Prime Ministers"[32], "...they hit their bottoms. And they walked away... He (Nehru) addressed them (a few Nepalis and Indians of Kohima). He thought it was an insult to him. I think that incident was the beginning of the trouble in Nagaland."[33] NNC revolted in 1956 at the expiry of the ten year tenure of the 9-Point Agreement between the NNC and Governor of Assam.

The genesis of the unified Nagalim or Greater Nagalim was born in 1959. According to Prof. Gangmumei Kamei, "the ethnic 'Irridentist Movement' reflected in the Naga integration and Mizo integration are co-terminus with the ethnic nationalist movement. It was the demand for the integration of 'contiguous Naga areas' raised by the Naga People Convention in their Sixteen Point Memorandum (1959) which was subsequently recorded in the 16-Point Agreement of 1960 and the creation of Nagaland State in 1963 that gave encouragement to the Naga leaders of Manipur to start the Naga Irridentist Movement in the years before the granting of Statehood to Manipur by the Government of India in 1972. ... this was reinforced by the Indo-Naga Ceasefire of 1964 which was extended to three sub-divisions (Ukhrul, Mao-Maram and Tamenglong) of Manipur which gave legitimization of the claimed 'ethnic theory' of the Nagas."[34] The Shillong Agreement of November 11, 1975 could not bring a lasting solution to Naga aspiration and it finally led to the birth of Nationalist Socialist Council of Nagalim in 1980. It was the turning point in the history of Naga insurgency in Manipur. NSCN's (IM) territorial claims include Ukhrul, Senapati, Tamenglong, and Chandel District.

Shaping Places

The Nationalist Socialist Council of Nagalim (IM) feels that the Chikim inhabiting in their proposed/claimed areas of the state are 'intruders', so the NSCN (IM) imposed tax on the Chikim ethnic groups in these areas, " the NSCN (IM) imposed all sorts of taxes over the Kukis as a source of revenue. The Kukis refused to comply with such imposition, on the maxim, 'Pay to Caesar what belongs to Caesar', said the Kukis, 'They have paid to the Government whatever was due to be paid". Ultimately NSCN (IM) served 'Quit Notice' to the Chikim ethnic groups to quit from their claimed territory, "Thus, an atmosphere of 'ethnic tension' was formed with the result the NSCN (IM) served 'quit notice' to the Kukis to leave their villages as issued on November, 22, 1992 (to be precise) by the United Naga Council (overground wing of NSCN (IM), as per secret documentation, probably official, entitled, "Does Violence get a mandate", p. 25, under the caption, "NSCN (IM) intolerance to Kuki tribe."[35]

The problem in shaping or drawing the territorial claims of Nagalim or Chikim Land on the ground, posed a difficult problem. From the demographic compositions and settlement pattern of these ethnic groups in various districts of Manipur, it is very clear that the issue is not just the integration of the contagious areas of one ethnic community but it also involves in uprooting of the other community from the proposed or the imagined land. The demographic compulsion and ethnic pluralism works against the theories of Nagalim of the Chikimland.

Violent Conflicts and Development

Ethnic group conflicts are always related to the demographic composition of the population in which ethnicity, religion and economic classes are politically played out. The government of Indian and the National Socialist Council of Nagalim, (Issac-Muivah) sees the creation of the Nagalim which include almost eighty percent of the territory of Manipur and other areas of the neighboring states of Nagaland, as the logical culmination of the protracted Naga struggle for the right to self determination. So in the early 1990 s there was an attempt to ethnic cleanse the Kuki community from the hill areas of Manipur so that the Naga community can claim the entire Hill range of Manipur as Naga dominated and Naga inhabited area. "One of the most ruthless activites in which NSCN (IM) is engaging in Manipur is the ruthless murder of Kuki group of tribes. This is a policy of ethnic cleansing."[36] There was a massive displacement of villages and a large number of people were killed, "in between 3 June 1992 and 31 December 1993, 336 persons were killed out of which 272 were Kuki, 62 were Naga and another 2 were Koms. Another 145 persons were seriously injured, out of which 76 were Kuki and the remaining 69 were Naga. Altogether 3569 houses were burnt down out of which 2115 belonged to Kuki, 1376 belonged to Aimols and Nepali respectively."[37]

The reaction to the aggressive Nagalim was met with the proliferation of the Kuki armed ethnic groups in the districts dominated by the Kuki community in Manipur. This was a logical outcome, when the state cannot protect an ethnic community they have to armed themselves to protect their own group. "When one ethnic group has its militia, a rival ethnic group sees it as a threat to its security. Since the state is not perceived as a reliable provider of security, the latter group forms its own ethnic militia and seeks security through self-help."[38] And in the course of time the Kuki insurgents raised the demand for a Kuki homeland in the state.

Today, these struggles are reflected in the various forms in the workings of the various organizations that supports the interest of their ethnic claims. Above all the statelessness of the administration has only added fuel to the engulfing fire of competing claims and ethnic insecurity. Manipur has become a 'playstation' of ethnic politics, and a fertile ground for exploitation taking advantage of the ground realities.

The fragmentation and fractionalization of the ethnic communities and their competing claims have created an environment of uncertainty. Total strikes, economic blockades, lockouts and burning of state institutions and properties have become the order of the day. These action and reaction of the ethnic communities have created havoc with the development of the state. The two resources, which are badly needed for the development of Manipur, the Human Resources and the Natural Resources lay in shambles. Able bodied men, the powerful human resources are engaged in fratricidal killings with guns in their hands, and the hindrances on exploitation of the rich natural resources of Manipur have only degraded the chart of development in Manipur.

Conclusion

The need of the hour is to foster the estranged ethnic relations between the communities of the state. But it is easier said than done. First, we must find the binding forces between the communities that existed in the state and how new ways could reinforce those bonds. Case studies could be conducted on how plural ethnic societies in Asia and Africa coexist in contemporary times and find out ways how it can be applied on the ground realities of Manipur. At the same time human resources (skilled and unskilled) and the vast reserve of natural resources; need to be gainfully exploited taking care of ecological consequences that might emerge as many of the reasons for the ethnic clashes are material in nature.

NOTES

1. *Statistical Handbook of Manipur 2002*, Directorate of Economics & Statistics, Government of Manipur, 2002.
2. Ahiebam Koireng Singh, *Ethnicity and Inter-community Conflicts: A Case of Kuki-Naga in Manipur*, Akansha publishing house, New Delhi, 2008, p.12.
3. *Ibid*, p.12.
4. All Manipur College Teachers' Association (ed), *Manipur Fact File 2001*, Bir Computer Printing Works, Imphal, 2001, p. 38.
5. *Ibid*, p. 38.
6. Prof. Gangmumei Kamei, *Ethnicity And Politics In Manipur*, http://www.manipuronline.com/features/December2003/ethnicityandpolitics21_1.htm
7. *Ibid*.

8. *Ibid*

9. Prof. Gangmumei Kamei, *Pluralism, Democracy and Ethnic Relations in Manipur – A critique,* Second Arambam Somendro Memorial Lecture, Imphal, June 10, 2007.

10. Lal Dena, Kuki-Naga Conflict: Juxtaposed in the colonial context, Cited in Ahiebam Koireng Singh, *Ethnicity and Inter-community Conflicts: A Case of Kuki-Naga in Manipur*, p.65.

11. John Parratt and Saroj N. Arambam Parratt, 'Kabui Messiah': The Jadonong Movement in Manipur, available at http://www.kanglaonline.com/index.php?template=kshow&kid=57&".

12. Lal Dena, Kuki Rebellion, 1917 – 1920, in Lal Dena (ed) *History of Manipur (1826-1949),* Orbit Publishes, New Delhi, 1991, p.126.

13. *Ibid*, p.126.

14. Dichamang Pamei, Liberty to Captives, cited in Ahiebam Koireng Singh, *Ethnicity and Inter-community Conflicts: A Case of Kuki-Naga in Manipur*, p.66-67.

15. Seilen Haokip, *The Kuki Rising, 1917-1919*, available at http://www.kukiforum.com/menu_files/Kuki_Rising_1917_1919.htm

16. Gangmumei Kamei, Zeliangrong Movement under Jadonang and Rani Gaidinliu 1930 – 1949 in Lal Dena (ed) *History of Manipur (1826-1949),* p.135-36

17. Letter of J. P. Mills, Deputy Commissioner of Naga Hills to the Commissioner Surma Valley and Hill Division, SIlchar, dt. 24 march 1931, cited in Ahiebam Koireng Singh, *Ethnicity and Inter-community Conflicts: A Case of Kuki-Naga in Manipur*, p.67.

18. John Parratt and Saroj N. Arambam Parratt, 'Kabui Messiah': The Jadonong Movement in Manipur, available at http://www.kanglaonline.com/index.php?template=kshow&kid=57&".

19. Gangmumei Kamei, *Ethnicity and Politics in Manipur*, *Imphal Free Press*, 8th Anniversary Special Supplement, 2004, p.36.

20. Gangmumei Kamei, Leftist Movement and Hijam Irabot Singh, in Lal Dena (ed) *History of Manipur (1826-1949)*,p.168.
21. *Ibid*,p.168.
22. Gangmumei Kamei, *Ethnicity and Politics in Manipur*, p.36.
23. *Ibid*, p.36.
24. Dr. Thangkhotinmang S. Gangte, *Land Problem and Ethnic Tension in Northeast India with special reference to Manipur*, a monograph.
25. *Ibid.*
26. *Ibid.*
27. *Ibid.*
28. Phanjoubam Tarapot, *Insurgency Movement in NE India*, Vikas Publishing House Pvt. Ltd, New Delhi, 1996, p. 216.
29. Ahiebam Koireng Singh, *Ethnicity and Inter-community Conflicts: A Case of Kuki-Naga in Manipur*, p.83.
30. Gangmumei Kamei, *Ethnicity and Politics in Manipur*, p.37.
31. Dr. Thangkhotinmang S. Gangte, *Land Problem and Ethnic Tension in Northeast India with Special Reference to Manipur*, a monograph.
32. *Ibid.*
33. Thinoselie M. Keyo, *The burden of history* in Civil Society Initiative on the Naga Peace process, Four Years of the Cease fire agreement, Other Media Communications, New Delhi, 2002, p. 75.
34. Gangmumei Kamei, *Ethnicity and Politics in Manipur*, p.37.
35. Dr. Thangkhotinmang S. Gangte, *Land Problem and Ethnic Tension in Northeast India with Special Reference to Manipur*, a monograph, p. 14.
36. All Manipur College Teachers' Association (ed), *Manipur Fact File 2001*, p. 25.
37. Ahiebam Koireng Singh, *Ethnicity and Inter-community Conflicts: A Case of Kuki-Naga in Manipur*, Akansha publishing house, New Delhi, 2008, p.103.

38. Sanjib Baruah, Durable disorder, *The Telegraph*, 22 September, 2003, p. 9.

REFERENCES

Ahiebam, Koireng Singh (2008), *Ethnicity and Inter-community Conflicts: A Case of Kuki-Naga in Manipur*, Akansha Publishing House, New Delhi, p.12.

All Manipur College Teachers' Association (2001) (ed), *Manipur Fact File 2001*, Bir Computer Printing Works, Imphal, p. 38.

Baruah, Sanjib (2003), 'Durable Disorder', *The Telegraph*, 22 September, p. 9.

Dena, Lal (1991), 'Kuki Rebellion, 1917 – 1920', Lal Dena (ed) *History of Manipur (1826-1949)*, Orbit Publishes, New Delhi, p. 126.

Gangte, Thangkhotinmang S. (n.d), 'Land Problem and Ethnic Tension in Northeast India with special reference to Manipur', *Monograph*.

Government of Manipur (2002), *Statistical Handbook of Manipur 2002*, Directorate of Economics & Statistics.

Kamei, Gangmumei (1991a), 'Zeliangrong Movement under Jadonang and Rani Gaidinliu 1930 – 1949', Lal Dena (ed) *History of Manipur (1826-1949)*, p. 135 36.

——— (1991b), 'Leftist Movement and Hijam Irabot Singh', Lal Dena (ed) *History of Manipur (1826-1949)*,p.168.

——— (2003), *Ethnicity And Politics In Manipur* . http://www.manipuronline.com/features/December2003/ethnicityandpolitics21_1.htm.

——— (2004), 'Ethnicity and Politics in Manipur', *Imphal Free Press, 8th Anniversary Special Supplement*, p.36.

——— (2007), 'Pluralism, Democracy and Ethnic Relations in Manipur – A Critique', *Second Arambam Somendro Memorial Lecture*, Imphal, June 10.

Keyo, Thinoselie M.(2002), 'The burden of history', *Civil Society Initiative on the Naga Peace process, Four Years of the Cease fire agreement*, Other Media Communications, New Delhi, , p. 75.

Parratt, John and Saroj N. Arambam Parratt, (n.d), *'Kabui Messiah': The Jadonong Movement in Manipur*, http://www.kanglaonline.com/index.php?template=kshow&kid=57&".

Phanjoubam Tarapot (1996), *Insurgency Movement in North-East India*, Vikas Publishing House Pvt. Ltd, New Delhi, p. 216.

Seilen Haokip, *The Kuki Rising, 1917-1919*, http://www.kukiforum.com/menu_files/Kuki_Rising_1917_1919.htm.

8

LAND, ETHNIC-RELATIONS AND THE 9th ASSEMBLY ELECTIONS IN THE HILLS OF MANIPUR

—*S. Mangi Singh*

Introduction

Land, it is said, is forever, and that it is the only thing worth fighting for. Contests for exclusive ownership rights over it are bound to result in serious conflict among the different contesting parties. The situation in the hills of Manipur serves as a lucid example of this. The age old relationship between the Kukis and the Nagas has always been neither purely friendly nor hostile to one another. Inter-dining has always been there between the two and both attended the social gatherings of each other. Inter-marriage, though not common, was not forbidden between the two. Yet, raids and reprisals among various villages belonging to the two communities and the British policy of divide and rule inevitably insured that an element of mutual distrust, animosity and hostility was not altogether absent in the traditional relationship between the two. Besides, cases of inter-village boundary disputes have also been there between villages of different tribes belonging to the two groups of people.

However, inter-ethnic relationship between the two got seriously disturbed with the emergence of contest for exclusive ownership rights over land during the second half of the last century. Indeed, such a contest for exclusive ownership rights over land has been on of the basic factors which led to the ethnic clashes between the two communities during the 1990s. The clashes were so severe that it claimed about 2000 lives and many more were injured. Many were also maimed for the rest of their lives. About 500 villages were attacked and about 7000 houses were burnt down to ashes. It also led to the displacement of about 15000 families and more than one lakh people.

The Contest for Land

The contest for exclusive ownership rights over land emerged as a serious issue with the emergence of aspirations for more or less ethnically exclusive homelands. According to the Kukis, the problem started with the demand for a sovereign Nagaland in the then Naga Hills (now Nagaland) and inclusion of Naga inhabited areas contiguous to the Naga Hills into it.[1] It was also described as an extension of the NSCN (IM)'s design for domination and the ethnic complexion injected to it by the leaders of both the communities to further their ends.[2] It was during the later part of 1956 that the spreading of secessionist movement of Nagaland into Manipur was felt conspicuously. It was first heard of in the Naga inhabited areas of in the then East, North and West Districts of the state.[3] Some of the Nagas of these areas secretly organized themselves into Naga Home Guards which later got changed into Naga Army. By 1960, the Naga undergrounds became very active in these areas and they had both civil and military setups.[4]

All these developments created lots of apprehension among the Kukis who were in the Naga dominates areas contiguous to the Naga Hills. Their apprehension was further heightened when a peace agreement signed between the Government of India and the Federal Government of Nagaland in 1964 was extended to Naga inhabited areas of Mao, Sadar Hills, Tamenglong and Ukhrul in Manipur. In fact, Mr. Paolun Haokip, the President of Kuki National Assembly, appealed to the public of Manipur to consider the situation before it was too late.[5] The situation got seriously aggravated from 1980 onwards. This was the year when the NSCN (IM) was established. With it, Naga inhabited areas of Manipur in general and the Tangkhul inhabited areas in particular, became the mainstay of underground Naga activities. In order to consolidate their claim over all the hill districts of the state except Churachandpur district, the Nagas allegedly started pressurizing the Kukis in these areas to leave or live as subordinates by demanding taxes from them or to assimilate themselves within the fold. P. S. Haokip alleges that as the Naga secessionist movement grew stronger, the Nagas became increasingly aggressive on the Kuki inhabitants of Ukhrul and Tamenglong districts, and that the Nagas were obsessed with the thought of uprooting the Kukis from their land by all means at their command.[6] Altogether, during the period from 1956 to 1987, the Kukis claim that 79 Kuki villages, 26 from Tamenglong, 46 from Ukhrul district, one from Tengnoupal and six from Senapati district, were uprooted by the Nagas.[7] As the Kuki Inpi Manipur (KIM) alleges, earlier 'there was only a threat to clear the Kukis from the northern tips of Manipur, the second stage was imposition of unauthorized taxes, restriction of movement to the Kukis and the last stage to drive the Kukis from their long established habitation is now in progress."[8]

The contention of the Nagas, on the other hand, is best exemplified in a resolution passed in an emergency meeting of the Executive Committee of the United Naga Council (UNC) held on 22 October 1992. It contended that the Kukis were nomads and due to their nomadic existence, they were but dependent on the Nagas who were the real land owners. In the process of their migration, the Kukis do not normally establish their ownership over the land just as they seldom settle down at any place for permanent occupation.[9] The meeting also decided that those Kukis who have settled before 1 July 1972 may continue to reside in that particular village, if they so desire, but on the condition that they give an undertaking to the original Naga village authorities with copies to the concern SDOs/DCs of that district to the effect that they will live with the next immediate Naga village by recognizing the sole ownership of the Nagas over the land and that they will not invite or allow any new settlers in their village. The Kukis were to furnish this undertaking to concerned authorities within the month of November 1992 failing which they must vacate their unauthorized occupation of the land and settlement in the village within the month of December 1992.[10]

The UNC further said that those Kukis who have settled after 1972 in Nagas areas must vacate their land and their settlement in the village by December 1992. Any Kuki who claim to have some specific reasons to continue their occupation in the Naga areas must report in writing giving explanation and justification to the Naga village authorities of that particular area for the latter's scrutiny and decision. Any Kuki person/family who fails to comply with the above conditions within the stipulated time was warned that they "will face dire consequences at their own risk."[11] The UNC also said that the Kukis demand for conversion of Sadar Hill Autonomous District into a full-fledged revenue district was another root cause of the clashes. It further alleged hat the Kuki National Army has always operated against the innocent Naga villagers at full connivance of paramilitary forces and civil authorities.[12] The NSCN (IM) also alleged that the Kukis as taking side with the "Indian occupation force" in the latter's efforts to root out the Naga freedom movement.[13] This was soon followed by reports of quit notices served in a number of Kuki villages in Senapati, Tamenglong, Ukhrul and Chandel districts. In Tamenglong district also, the Zeliangrong Nagas alleged that the Kukis are living in the land of the Zeliangrong people.[14]

The Naga Lim Guards further accused the Kukis of (i) demanding a greater Kuki land comprising Churachandpur District, Kamjong Sub-Division of Ukhrul district and Kuki inhabited areas of Myanmar; (ii) demanding a Kuki Homeland within Manipur; (iii) demanding a revenue district for the Kukis with parts of Ukhrul, Senapati and Tamenglong districts; and (iv) inviting Kuki refugees from Myanmar into India.[15] According to them, these were the main factors which led to the Kuki-Naga conflict, and the Kukis have to stop all these in order to solve the problem.

The Kukis, on the other hand, insist that the conflict is not of ethnic origin. "It originated with the independence of India. While the Kukis accepted the Indian Constitution, some of the Nagas in the present Nagaland did not do so. The Nagas observe their independence day on 14 August every year. In their claim of separate sovereignty, they launched their movement against the loyal citizens, their own Naga brethrens at first and the Kukis with whom they have lived together for centuries."[16] Herein lays the root cause of all troubles. They further say that ethnic problem was not the real issue. The conflict was between the disloyal and the loyal Kukis, loyal to the Government and the Constitution, and upholders of the territorial integrity of the entire country and Manipur.[17] As the KIM claims:"The Kuki Inpi, has been observing carefully the turbulent situation in the North-East and Manipur in Particular and unanimously came to the conclusion that the root cause of all the trouble in this is the NSCN (IM)'s claim of secessionist movement and its subsequent drive for the so-called 'ethnic cleansing'."[18] The

KIM further said that "till today, the Kukis have no intention, plans or preparation to wage war against the Nagas. It is only a section of the Naga tribes that has been waging war against the Kukis. It is only in consequence to that the Kukis have been caught unprepared, have had to organize themselves for and to protect kith and kin, hearth and homes."[19] They also accused the Nagas of falsely calling them nomads or gypsies and comparing them with flying birds in a concerted propaganda against the Kukis.[20]

The Kukis also blame the NSCN (IM) for perpetuating the worse kind of violence against them. The KSO, for instance, accuses the NSCN (IM) of instigating the Tangkhuls and their cohorts-hoodlums to harass and kill innocent Kuki villagers.[21] It also said that under the influence of the NSCN (IM) the village authorities, student organizations and the youth wings extended their policy of harassment to the Kukis and subsequently their armed intervention has claimed hundreds of deaths since 1992 till 8 June 1993, and hundreds of villages have been burnt down to ashes.[22] Claiming that they took active part in the INA/Azad Hind Fauz war efforts against the British imperialism and that they have never waged war against the Indian Government, the KIM said that it will be "incorrect" for the Government of India "to treat the Kukis and the secessionist Nagas on equal footing."[23] In fact, it asked the Government of India: "Whether the NSCN (IM) killed the Kukis as Kukis or citizens of India?"[24]

The relevance of Nagas' demand for a South Nagaland may also be mentioned here. Ukhrul, Senapati, Tamenglong, Chandel and Parts of Churachandpur districts are included in the map of the so-called proposed South Nagaland and the remaining parts are left out to be that of Manipur.[25] The Kukis are obviously against it as it affects all the Kukis in these districts. Regarding the issue of the Kuki Homeland demand, the KIM says that the Kukis have made this demand in view of the demand for political unification of Naga inhabited areas in the form of either merging "areas contiguous to Nagaland inhabited by the Nagas" into Nagaland or in the form of a South Nagaland which will comprise all the hill districts of Manipur except Churachandpur or in the form of a sovereign Naga Lim.[26] This, along with "the unbearable atrocities from the NSCN led movement such as imposition of Nagaland taxes, forcible eviction from their villages and the inability of the State Government to protect them" have led some Kukis to "raise the demand for Kuki Homeland in India where they can live with others in peace."[27]

Regarding the claim of the Nagas that the Kukis are in their land, the Kukis say that "There is no separate Kuki or Naga area in Manipur Hills. All the hill lands belong to the various tribal groups and each village has its own village boundaries which has withstood the test of time. His being the case, there is no question of Nagas' land being taken over by non-Nagas or vice-versa. This position should be accepted."[28] They further reiterate that "all the land in the respective possession of the people as on 15-8-47 was their own since they occupied the same for years prior to 15-8-47."[29]

The demand for a separate revenue district for Sadar Hills is also relevant here. This is an issue on which the Kukis and Nagas do not see eye to eye. There are at present five revenue districts in the hill areas of the state with six Autonomous District Councils which includes one for the Sadar Hills. The Kukis want the Sadar Hills to be converted into a full fledged revenue district for better administration. This is not to be called a Kuki district. But the Nagas opposed it believing that it will be a Kuki district for all practical purposes to be carved out of what they believe to be areas traditionally belonging to the Nagas. It may be remembered here that upgradation of the Sadar Hills into a full fledged revenue district has already been approved by the Jayal

Commission.[30] Besides, Rishang Keishing, himself a Naga, had also promised time and again, to inaugurate Sadar Hills as a full fledged district.[31] However, the state government has still yet to implement it. This irked the Kukis very much.

The Kukis had felt the need for converting Sadar Hills into a full fledged revenue district all the more urgently in view of the slogan for South Nagaland so militantly raised by the Naga insurgents at one time. It may be remembered here that though the Kukis are in minority in the entire district, they are in majority in the Sadar Hills Autonomous District Council Area. They also have felt the crucial disadvantage of having no access to the district headquarters as it was surrounded by Nagas. Such an aspiration of the Kukis drew serious attention from the Naga Students' Federation (NSF). Expressing its concern over a proposed bandh to press the demand, it said that it may cause untold hardships and miseries to many innocent public and further aggravate the situation. The Federation, while not objecting to the creation of any new district or state or Homeland for the Kukis, said that "Not an inch of Naga Traditional Land Should Be Carved Out While Creating Any New District or State or Homeland."[32] However, the Kukis maintain that the Nagas have turned the issue "not only into a communal one but also as means to further their covert intention of breaking Manipur."[33] They also argued that the UNC's objection to the demand has revealed the latter's "hollow cry for peace between the Kukis and the Nagas is shorn of any belief in co-existence."[34] The issue was further made complicated by the inapt handling on the part of the State Government which, by making tall promises, was simply indulging in bravado without any follow up action.[35]

There are also still many cases of inter village boundary disputes between the Kukis and the Nagas at present. For example, in Chandel district, Kangol Khunnou, a Maring village affected during the Kuki-Naga clashes, had boundary disputes with the neighboring Kuki village, Modenphai.[36] Another affected Kuki village of the district, K. Moljol, also had boundary disputes with Ngalan Naga Village.[37] Likewise, Harup Kuki Village which was affected during the clashes also had boundary disputes with Harup Naga and Thonglang Naga Villages.[38] In Senapati District also, an affected Kuki village, Gelnel, had conflict with Kadi Anal Village,[39] and T. Gojang, another Kuki village of Saikul, also had conflict with neighboring Naga village of Makeng on land questions.[40] Kekru Kuki, another erstwhile Kuki village at Saikul of Senapati district, also had similar disputes with the neighboring Kekru Naga village.[41] Bollen, another erstwhile Kuki village also had conflict with their neighboring Naga villages, Satin and Khongnem, on land questions. In Tamenglong district, Lasa, and affected Kuki village had conflict with the neighboring Naga village, Lamka, regarding land.[42] Joupi, another erstwhile Kuki village at Tamei sub-division of Tamenglong district, also had conflict with Lenglong, a neighboring Liangmai Naga village.[43] Similarly, in Ukhrul district, Toljang, an erstwhile Kuki village, had land disputes with the Tangkhul Nagas of the nearby villages.[44] Likewise, Pangjang, an affected Kuki village in Churachandpur district, also had differences with the neighboring Naga villages over land questions.[45]

Impact on the Inter-Ethnic Relationship Between the Two

The conflicting claims over land has not only strained the relationship between the Kukis and Nagas but also has greatly contributed to the outbreak of the Kuki-Naga clashes during the 1990s. At present, inter-dining between the two continues and both attend social gatherings of one another. In most of the villages, there is no restriction or threat on entering and free movement of different communities. However, inter-marriage has become rarer. Many villages attacked during the clashes remained deserted for long times, and some of them have been abandoned permanently. Even after the clashes have subsided, inter-tribal or inter-village relations continue to be strained on account of finding one's village occupied by others when they returned from their places of displacement, and were refused the return of their village to them. The clashes due to conflict over land have also affected ethnic affiliations of smaller tribes though the same cannot be said about the major tribes. There emerged for quite sometime a tendency on the part of these tribes to identify themselves with one of the groups in their bit to be secure during the clashes. There were also instances of villages of the same tribe claiming to belong to either Kuki or Naga group in accordance with the dominant community surrounding them or with whom they wee in proximity. A tendency to identify themselves by their individual tribal names also emerged. Social polarization of the Kukis and Nagas also has increased in recent times due to the conflict and clashes over land. It is evident in terms of socio-cultural organizations, civil society groups, human rights bodies, student organizations, etc. More disturbing is the fact that the basic view points of the Kukis and Nagas about land issues have not been properly reconciled. Both remained as sensitive as ever about any possible development which may give one an edge over the other. The issue of Sadar Hills is a most appropriate example here. Ethnic outfits acting as champions of the conflicting claims are also far from being disarmed. Instead, their interference in the day to day life of the people is increasing. Forget about the far flung villages, it is not rare for one to see their cadres in the district headquarters in broad daylight, and that too in full uniform. The grim reality of possible clashes among the ethnic outfits also persists. In fact, there was a serious clash on three September 2007 between the NSCN (IM) and the Kuki Liberation Army (KLA) which led to the killing of ten KLA cadres. Indeed, as the Peace declaration at Kangpokpi on 14 November 2003 says, the situation remains one of "potentially reversible amity".[46]

Impact on Electoral Politics in the Hills During the 9th State Assembly Election 2007

Coming to that of the impact of the contest for ownership of land, and the resultant strain in the two's relationship, on the electoral politics in the hills during the 9th Assembly Elections 2007, first it is essential to have a clear understanding of the Assembly Constituencies (AC) profiles of the hills of Manipur. The entire hill area of the state is divided into 20 ACs. Of the five districts in the hills, Chandel has two, Churachandpur six, Senapati six, Tamenglong three and Ukhrul two. 19 of these are reserved seats for the Scheduled Tribes. The remaining one viz. Kangpokpi AC in Senapati District is a General AC. Speaking in terms of the composition of the voters in these ACs, the six ACs in Ukhrul and Tamenglong are overwhelmingly dominated by the Nagas whereas the six ACs in Churachandpur District are overwhelmingly dominated by the Kukis. Regarding the six ACs in Senapati district, three are dominated by the Nagas and two by the Kukis and one (Kangpokpi AC) is keenly contested by both the Kukis and Nagas. The two ACs in Chandel district are also keenly contested by both the communities. This means, the representation of the Kukis and Nagas in the Legislative Assembly of the state has usually been a case of 1:10 or 11:9 or 12:8 unless the Kangpokpi AC goes to a Nepali. In other word, regarding their representation in the State Legislative Assembly, the six ACs in Ukhrul and Tamenglong districts (three each) always return Naga MLAs whereas the six ACs of Churachandpur district always return Kuki MLAs. In case of Senapati district, the six ACs are usually divided into three each between the Nagas and the Kukis unless the Kangpokpi AC goes to a Nepali. The two ACs of Chandel district are also usually divided into one each between the two. At present, the two have ten MLAs each in the State Legislative Assembly.

It is important, however, to note that none of the five hill districts are exclusively inhabited by one particular tribe or group of tribes. In fact, there are many Kuki villages in Ukhrul and Tamanglong districts, more so in case of the latter. There are also many Naga villages in Churachandpur district. In case of Chandel and Senapati districts, as already mentioned, both constitute two more or less equally effective communities there. Indeed, there was one Kuki candidate each in as many as five Naga dominated ACs (all the three ACs of Tamenglong district, Ukhrul AC of Ukhrul district and Karong AC of Senapati district).

As the elections approached, the UNC on January 11 directed all the naga political leaders and functionaries to resign from national and regional parties within two days in the interest of the Naga people. The UNC further directed all intending candidates to attend a meeting on January 16 at Senapati along with their family members and chief election agents. In the meeting, 60 intending candidates signed an eight point declaration. According to this declaration, the signatories agreed to accept those persons "determined by the Naga people as represented by the UNC as the consensus candidate." The signatories also agreed that they will steadfastly defend the interests of the Naga people for integration/unification of the Naga areas and that they "will resign from the legislature if called upon to do so by the Naga people as represented by the UNC." All theses steps were taken up with a view to uphold the Naga people to uphold the Naga people for integration of all Naga areas under one administration. The UNC ever appealed to other Naga candidates to withdraw their candidature or retire from the elections in the interest of the Naga people and extend support to the consensus candidates as decided by it. Ultimately, the UNC was able to find consensus candidates for 11 of the twelve ACs the Nagas contested in four of the hill districts of the state which accounts for 14 ACs.

Here, it has to be remembered that, except for Churachandpur district, all the other four hill districts of the state viz. Ukhrul, Tamenglong, Chandel and Senapati, are areas being claimed as Naga areas. Hence, these developments obviously concerned the territorial integrity of the state and drew the immediate attention of both the Meiteis in the valley and all the Kukis in all the five hill districts of the state. For the Kuki inhabited areas, the issue became overwhelmingly important as their own secure existence inside the state was very much at jeopardy. For the Meiteis in the valley, the hills and plains are two organic parts of the state never to be severed from one another, and all the basic unity and oneness of all the different communities inside the state are never to be destroyed. In Naga inhabited areas also, the issue became a crucial one as the credibility and reputation of the UNC was at stake. Indeed, at another level, the elections were a contest between parties who committed themselves to the protection of the territorial integrity of the state and the UNC working in close collaboration with the NSCN (IM) for unification of the Naga inhabited areas. And, with the possible exception of NNP, all the other 17 parties, national and state, contesting the elections stood for the protection of the territorial integrity of the state.

The development had serious effects on the democratic functioning of electoral politics in the hills in general and the Naga inhabited areas in particular. With their reputation at stake, the UNC and the NSCN (IM) went all the way to throw their combined weights in favor of the UNC sponsored candidates. Reports of their interference in the free exercise of the right to vote on the part of the people started pouring in, in the newspaper columns. The NSCN (K) criticized the NSCN (IM) for the coercive interference the latter made in the elections in the Tamenglong district.[47] As the day of elections approached nearer, there were protest rallies in the hills against encroachments into the right to freedom of choice of the people. On 19 February 2007, there was a protest rally in Chandel district headquarters where people joined the rally with placards reading "My Vote My Right".[48] There were also various reports of pressure being put on the voters of Tamenglong AC to cast their votes for the UNC sponsored candidate. In fact, on 17 February 2007, people took out a rally in Tamenglong also as one of the candidates in Tamenglong AC was kidnapped by the NSCN (IM).[49] It was even reported in the local dailies that candidates other than UNC sponsored ones feared to even hoist their flags, let alone go ahead with their election campaigns.[50] Lodging their serious concern about the involvement of the NSCN (IM) in the elections, the women of Nungba AC in Tamenglong district also organized another protest rally on 15 February 2007 shouting slogans like we want free and fair elections, we want peace, etc. They also condemned the threats given by the UNC to the voters there.[51] There were also complaints about political parties. For instance, there was the CPI, Manipur State Council, alleging that several candidates were fielded under the dictates of the NSCN (IM) in Naga dominated areas.[52] The party also alleged that two of its candidates, T. N. Haokip and Onjamang Haokip in Chandel and Tengnoupal ACs respectively were forced not to contest the elections by underground outfits there.[53] The withdrawal of the Congress candidate from Chandel AC after filing his nomination was also largely believed to be because of pressure from underground outfits.

Electoral politics on the lines of party competition also became a casualty in the Naga inhabited areas. There was a sharp decline in the number of political parties contesting the elections in the Naga dominated ACs. In fact, out of a total of 18 political; parties contesting the elections, only four parties among the Naga candidates. They were the Indian National Congress (INC), Manipur State Congress Party (MSCP), Samajwadi Party (SP) and Naga National Party (NNP). Together, they accounted for 13 candidates (INC four and the other three one each). This steep decline in the number of political parties among the Nagas was solely because of the dictate from the UNC. Correspondingly, there was an astounding increase in the number of independent candidates among the Nagas. In fact, out of a total of 46 Naga candidates contesting the elections, only 13 were party candidates and the remaining 33 were all independent candidates. All these developments meant that the freedom of choice to join a party of one's own choice, and contest the elections in a free and fair manner, was very much adversely affected among the Nagas. They also further meant that party politics, elections on line of party competition, etc. suddenly eroded from among the Nagas.

Contrast to it, one sees a multiplicity of political parties in the electoral politics of the Kukis. There were 12 political parties viz. the INC, Communist party of India (CPI), Bharatiya Janata Party (BJP), Natioanalist Congress Party (NCP), Rashtriya Janata Dal (RJD), Janata Dal (U) {JD (U)}, Lok Jana Shakti Party (LJSP), SP, Samata Party (SAP), Manipur People's Party (MPP), Nationalist People's Party (NPP) and Peoples' Democratic Alliance (PDA). Together they accounted for 53 candidates with LJSP putting up ten, Congress nine, RJD six, NCP five, BJP four, CPI four, NPP four, SP four, MPP three, SAP two, PDA one and JD (U) one. There were only six Independent candidates among the Kukis. This shows that there was far greater freedom in the Kuki dominated areas to contest the elections on the ticket of a party of one's own choice and that elections were very much on the lines of party competition.

Once the results were out, they revealed a number of significant things pertinent to the land conflict between the two. First of all, the UNC had sponsored 11 candidates and out these only six won. The ACs where they won were Tengnoupal in Chandel district, Tadubi in Senapati district, Tamei in Tamenglong district and all the all the three ACs in Ukhrul district viz. Chingai, Phungyar and Ukhrul. Here something more has to be said about the Naga interests as represented by the UNC. There should have been 12 Independent candidates at the most if everyone adhered to the dictate of the UNC because the Nagas have contested in 12 ACs in four of the five hill districts of the state. However, there were as many as 33 independent Naga candidates. This was in addition to the 13 Nagas who contested the elections as party candidates (Congress ten, SP one, MSCP one and NNP one). Besides, there was no UNC sponsored candidate in Kangpokpi AC which was also contested by the Nagas.

More glaring is the fact that the UNC won only one AC each in the other remaining three districts contested by the Nagas and these three districts accounts for a total of 11 ACs. The ACs where the UNC won were Tamei AC of Tamenglong District (having three ACs), Tadubi AC of Senapati district (having six ACs) and Tengnoupal AC of Chandel district (having two ACs). Only in Ukhrul district (having three ACs), it had a cent percent success winning all the three seats there. Another question is why the UNC sponsored Independent candidates failed in Karong (which went to Congress) and Mao (which went to a non-UNC independent candidate) in Senapati district and in Nungba (which went to Congress) and Tamenglong (which went to another non-UNC candidate) in Tamenglong district? Does it have anything to do with the aspirations of the Shepoumaramtha and Zeliangrong People? These are two sub-groups within the Naga umbrella. Within the Naga group, Mao (Se), Poumai, Maram and Thangal tribes are together known as Shepoumaramtha whereas the Kabui, Rongmei, Zemi and Liangmei tribes come within the Zeliangrong group. While Karong and Mao ACs are dominated by the former group, Nungba and Tamenglong ACs are dominated by the latter group. The failure of the UNC in these Naga areas hints that the Shepoumaramtha and Zeliangrong Nagas are not fully overwhelmed by the UNC and the NSCN (IM), and that they are not all too happy with the machinations of the two.

About the Naga interests as represented by the UNC, Ukhrul, Chandel, Tamenglong and Senapati are four hill districts which are being claimed as the land of the Nagas, and to be apart of a Naga country, independent or otherwise. These four districts account for 14 ACs. The Nagas contested in 12 of them and won in ten. The remaining four went to Kukis. Of the ten seats won by the Nagas, six went to the UNC supported Independents, two to the Congress and another two to non-UNC independents. Speaking district-wise, it had a cent percent success in Ukhrul District where it won all the three ACs there. But it won only three seats in the other three remaining districts i.e. Tamenglong, Chandel and Senapati districts which together accounts for 11 ACs. The remaining eight went to four Kukis (one NCP, one NPP, one RJD and one Independent) and four Nagas (two congressmen and two non-UNC Independents), and they all stood for protection of the territorial integrity of the state. In other words, leaving aside Ukhrul district, in the 11 ACs of the other three districts being claimed as land of Nagas, the Naga interests as represented by the UNC could translate itself into electoral success only in three ACs. All the remaining eight ACs went to Independent or party candidates who stood for the protection of the territorial integrity of the state. Losing sight of this fact while negotiating any issue which concerns ownership rights of land in one way or the other, and also the territorial integrity of the state, will be the height of lack of political far-sightedness.

NOTES

1. Minutes of Discussion of the Special Kuki Tribal Leaders' Meet held on 29 June 1993, signed by T. Kipgen as the Convenor of the Meet and the President of the Kuki Inpi Manipur.
2. No. GSM/LA 18/93, dated 5 October 1993, Governor of Manipur's Report to the President of India.

3. Proceedings of Security Co-ordination Meeting dated 13 December 1983, venue – Tamenglong, Part File Hills Section, Notes in Connection with Security Co-Ordination Meeting, w.e.f. 1983, CID Office, Government of Manipur.
4. *Ibid.*
5. *Prajatantra*, a Manipuri daily, Imphal, 5 July 1965, p. 1.
6. Memorandum submitted to the Chief Minister, government of Manipur, by the Consultative Committee of Kuki Leaders, Imphal, Manipur, dated 4 July 1987.
7. *Human Rights for whom?*, published by the Kuki People's Forum for Human Rights, Churachandpur, pp. 9-11.
8. Minutes of discussion of the Special Kuki Leaders' Meet, held on 29 June 1993, op. cit.
9. Abstract copy of the resolutions passed in the emergency meeting of the Executive Committee of The United Naga Council held on 22 October 1992, in the Souvenir of the Kuki Inpi Manipur, 1995-97, published by the Souvenir Committee on behalf of the Kuki Inpi Manipur, Imphal, 1997, pp. 19-21.
10. *Ibid.*
11. *Ibid.*
12. *Ibid.*
13. New Phase of Indian State Terrorism in Nagaland, Statement of the National Socialist Council of Nagaland on he Indian Backed Kuki and Naga Public Clash, 18 September 1983.
14. Kuki-Naga-Problem, a statement issued by T. Kipgen, President KIM, dated 23 November 1993.
15. SOLUTION, a press release issued by the Publicity Wing, Naga Lim Guards, dated 8 November 1993.
16. Memorandum submitted to the Home Minister, Government of India, by the KIM, for and on behalf of the Kukis of Manipur, dated 17 January 1994.
17. *Ibid.*
18. Traditional Policy and Standpoint of Kuki Inpi Manipur, signed by Holkhomang Haokip, President KIM, dated 1 September 1995.

19. *Ibid.*

20. *Ibid.*

21. *The Freedom*, a local English daily, 11 June 1993, p. 1.

22. *Ibid.*

23. Traditional Policy and Standpoint of the Kuki Inpi Manipur, op. cit.

24. Political Resolutions of the Second Kuki Inpi General Assembly, signed by Holkhomang Haokip and Honkholet Khongsai as President and Speaker of the KIM respectively.

25. Views of the Kuki Defence Force, released by the Commander, Kuki Defence Force, Manipur, appeared in *The Freedom*, 24 April 1993, p. 1.

26. Memorandum submitted to His Excellency, the Governor of Manipur, by KIM, signed by T. Kipgen, President, KIM, no date, produced in the Anniversary Souvenir of the KIM, 1994, published by The Souvenir Committee, KIM, 1994, pp. 21-23.

27. *Ibid.*

28. The Anniversary Souvenir of the KIM 1994, published by The Souvenir Committee, KIM, 1994, pp. 21-23.

29. Memorandum submitted to the Union Home Minister, Government of India, by the KIM for and on behalf of the Kukis of Manipur, *op. cit.*

30. Memorandum submitted to His Excellency, the Governor of Manipur, by the KIM, reproduced in the Anniversary Souvenir of the Kuki Inpi Manipur, 1994, op. cit.

31. Political Resolutions of the 2nd Kuki Inpi General Assembly held on 12th December 1996.

32. Atong Yanglem, General Secretary, Naga Students' Federation, Kohima, produced in *The Freedom*, 19 April 1993, p. 1.

33. Press release, not dated, and signed by Haokip Khaisei, Secretary, KIM.

34. No.GSM/LA 18/93 dated 5 October 1993, op. cit.

35. *Ibid.*

36. Yamthing, personal interview, 18 March, 2004.

37. Kaikholal Kipgen, Chairmen of K. Moljol Village Authority, personal interview, Senapati, 1 March 2004.

38. Haokip Seitam, personal interview, Kangpokpi, 23 March 2004.

39. James, personal interview, T. Waichong, Senapati, 23 April 2004.

40. Thongkhulen, personal interview, T. Gojang, Senapati, 10 February 2004.

41. Hourullung Rongmei, Village Chairmen of Kekru Naga Village, personal interview, Senapati, 22 June 2004.

42. Laiminlung, personal interview, Kangpokpi I. T. Road, Senapati, 23 March 2004.

43. Group interview with displace villagers of Joupi, Kangpokpi IT Road, 28 December 2003.

44. Seikhomang Chongloi, Village Chief of Toljang, personal interview, Churachandpur, 26 November 2003.

45. Ngamkhodei Haokip, personal interview, Churachandpur, 26 September 2003.

46. Declaration towards peaceful co-existence of Baptist Christians of Manipur State made on 14 November at Mission Compound, Kangpokpi, Manipur.

47. *Ireibak*, a local vernacular daily, 21 February 2007, p. 1.

48. *Ibid*, 20 January 2007, p. 1.

49. *Poknaphan*, a local vernacular daily, 18 February 2007, p. 1.

50. *Iriebak*, op. cit, 16 February 2007, p. 1.

51. *Ibid*, 16 February 2007, 0p. 1.

52. *The Imphal Free Press*, a local English daily, 22 January 2007, p. 1.

53. *Ireibak*, op. cit., 21 February 2007, p. 1.

REFERENCES

Declaration towards peaceful co-existence of Baptist Christians of Manipur State, 14 November, Mission Compound, Kangpokpi, Manipur.

Displace villagers of Joupi, Kangpokpi IT Road, Group interview, 28 December 2003.

Govt. of Manipur (1993), *No. GSM/LA 18/93, dated 5 October 1993*, Governor of Manipur's Report to the President of India.

Haokip Seitam, Personal interview, Kangpokpi, 23 March 2004.

Hourullung Rongmei, Village Chairmen of Kekru Naga Village, personal interview, Senapati, 22 June 2004.

Ireibak, a local vernacular daily, 20 January 2007, p. 1.

——— 16 February 2007, p. 1.

——— 21, February 2007, p. 1.

James, Personal interview, T. Waichong, Senapati, 23 April 2004.

Kaikholal Kipgen, Chairmen of K. Moljol Village Authority, personal interview, Senapati, 1 March 2004.

KIM (1994), *Anniversary Souvenir of the KIM*, The Souvenir Committee, KIM, pp. 21-23.

Kipgen, T. (1993), *Kuki-Naga-Problem*, 23 November.

Kuki People's Forum for Human Rights (n.d), *Human Rights for whom?*, Churachandpur, pp. 9-11.

Laiminlung, Personal interview, Kangpokpi I. T. Road, Senapati, 23 March 2004.

Memorandum submitted to the Chief Minister, Government of Manipur, Consultative Committee of Kuki Leaders, Imphal, Manipur, dated 4 July 1987.

Memorandum submitted to the Home Minister, Government of India, KIM, for and on behalf of the Kukis of Manipur, 17 January 1994.

Minutes of Discussion of the Special Kuki Tribal Leaders' Meet held on 29 June 1993, signed by T. Kipgen as the Convenor of the Meet and the President of the Kuki Inpi Manipur.

New Phase of Indian State Terrorism in Nagaland, Statement of the National Socialist Council of Nagaland on the Indian Backed Kuki and Naga Public Clash, 18 September 1983.

Ngamkhodei Haokip, Personal interview, Churachandpur, 26 September 2003.

Poknapham, a local vernacular daily, 18 February 2007, p. 1.

Political Resolutions of the 2nd Kuki Inpi General Assembly, 12th December 1996.

Prajatantra, a Manipuri daily, Imphal, 5 July 1965, p. 1.

Press Release (n.d), Haokip Khaisei, Secretary, KIM.

Seikhomang Chongloi, Village Chief of Toljang, Personal interview, Churachandpur, 26 November, 2003.

Souvenir of the Kuki Inpi Manipur, 1995-97 Souvenir Committee, Kuki Inpi Manipur, Imphal, 1997, pp. 19-21.

Solution, a press release issued by the Publicity Wing, Naga Lim Guards, 8 November 1993.

The Anniversary Souvenir of the KIM, 1994, The Souvenir Committee, KIM, 1994, pp. 21-23.

The Freedom, a local English daily, 19 April 1993, p. 1.

——— 24 April 1993, p. 1.

——— 11 June 1993, p.

The Imphal Free Press, a local English daily, 22 January 2007, p. 1.

Thongkhulen, Personal interview, T. Gojang, Senapati, 10 February 2004.

Traditional Policy and Standpoint of Kuki Inpi Manipur, signed by Holkhomang Haokip, President KIM, 1 September 1995.

Yamthing, Personal interview, 18 March, 2004.

9

LAND AND ECONOMIC DEVELOPMENT IN THE HILLS OF MANIPUR

—E. Bijoykumar Singh

Introduction

The hills of Manipur cover 20,089 sq.km hosting a population of 8,82,130 with a density of 44 persons per sq.km. against the population density of 631 per sq.km. in the valley. The people in the hills, mostly tribals, have remained poor even after more than half a century of state intervention for their upliftment. The hill areas have always been the biggest challenge for policy makers. As per the 2001 census, 1,74,330 out of 2,56,658 main workers in the hill districts are cultivators and 10998 are agricultural labourers. Agriculture is the most dominant means of livelihood in the hills. Manufacturing, processing, servicing and repairing in household industry with 7,498 persons and other services with 63,532 are the next most important livelihoods, yet there is no disagreement on the fact that there exists large scale poverty in the hills in-spite of the natural wealth in terms of abundant land and known forests. The stagnancy has aroused resentment in the hills, threatening the integrity of the state. Scarcity of resources cannot explain the extent of poverty. The per capita land in the hills works out at 2.27 ha and in the valley it was 0.16 ha. It indicates that the factors of production available in the hills have not been optimally used.

Land is an important factor of production. It is also a preferred store of wealth. There is a legitimate interest in ensuring optimal utilization of land both in the static and dynamic sense. The paper seeks to identify the interface between sustainable use of land and existing production relations in the hills. The current setup involves substantial opportunity cost. The important questions are:

- Is the land system in the hills compatible with productive efficiency?
- Can it be improved by land rental and land sale market?
- If the land market is not sufficient, what type of land reform can we have?

Problems of Development Among Tribals

The problems of development among tribals have been identified as follows:

i). Absence of infrastructure and communication system like good roads, transport and postal service and mass media

ii). Uncertain tribal land ownership system

iii). Low productivity of tribal agriculture

iv). Lack of good educational facilities

v). Lack of power supply

vi). Lack of marketing facilities

vii). Absence of adequate social services like medical and health, water supply and housing and

viii). The absence of well organized bodies for people's direct participation in the developmental works.

In this scheme uncertain tribal land ownership system and low agricultural productivity have been mentioned among the list of factors behind the persistent poverty in tribal or hilly areas. To this, list the author would like to add governance of hill areas as another debilitating factor accentuating poverty among the tribals.

Table 1
Comparative productivity of land in Manipur*

District	*Area in sq.km.*	*Productivity of primary sector per ha in Rs.*		
		1990-91	*2001*	*Percentage change*
Senapati	3271	1822.7	2359	29.4
Tamenglong	4391	641.3	703.7	9.7
Churachandpur	4570	853	1092	28
Chandel	3313	670.4	988.5	47.4
Ukhrul	4544	841.8	1044.2	24
Hills	**20089**	**932**	**1185.6**	**27.2**
Imphal	1228	8026	12198.7	52
Bishnupur	496	9889	14391.1	45.5
Thoubal	514	15015.6	17710.1	17.9
Valley	**2238**	**10046**	**13950.4**	**38.9**
Manipur	22,327	1845.4	2465	33.6

Note: *GSDP per ha at 1993-94 prices. The district level GSDP was calculated by the Directorate of Economics and Statistics, Govt. of Manipur.

The productivity of primary sector can be used as an index of proper use of land because the activities in this sector i.e. agriculture including livestock, forestry and logging, mining and quarrying and fishing are directly associated with land. It shows that productivity of land in the valley is several times higher than that of the hill districts. Not only the productivity of hill districts is low, their growth rates are also low except for Chandel .This divide can be bridged only by proper use of land in the hills.

Improvement in the asset base of the poor has been viewed as a central strategy to relieve endemic poverty. In a poor agrarian economy it means improving the terms in which the poor have access to land. In India, land reforms which are mostly efforts at land redistribution through legislated ceilings on land holding have not changed significantly the tribal land relations. Besley and Burgess (1998) survey of major events in land reform in 14 major states in India since 1950 has only one entry – Lushai Hill District (Acquisition of Chiefs Rights) Act, 1954 enacted in Assam directly related with land tenure system among tribals. The Report of the Working Group on land relations also does not discuss the issue of converting communal ownership to individual ownership. The issue of alienation of tribal land is considered in detail. The conversion of community land into individual ownership will not lead to any significant alienation of tribal land. The large segments/plots owned traditionally by the Kuki chiefs will be broken down in smaller units. The usual policy of as little interference as possible has continued in this area. Land ownership is treated as a fundamental issue in the 1st Five Year Plan.

Besley & Burgess (1998) state that Indian state level data shows that there is robust evidence of a link between poverty reduction and two kinds of land reform measures i.e. tenancy reform and abolition of intermediaries. The pattern of land ownership which determines whether the land is cultivated by the owner or rented out is an important determinant of agricultural productivity. The empirical evidence on tenancy contracts suggests that asymmetric information can reduce agricultural productivity. Because of private information, enforcement problems etc., market contracts in general are inefficient in agriculture where many tasks cannot be monitored. Empirical analysis of Nicaraguan farmers shows that the distribution of property rights in land influences the choice of crop mix. Farmers are more likely to grow tree crops on the plots they own rather than on the land they rent. Growing of tree crops along with annual crops is more profitable however it is much more labor intensive than growing annual crops alone. Bandiera (2002) states

The empirical analysis of crop choice in rural Nicaragua shows that owner cultivators choose a riskier, more effort intensive and more profitable crop mix. The analysis also shows that the inability to commit, rather than limited liability, seems to be the main source of inefficiency.

Another interesting inference is that since inability to commit is the main source of inefficiency, any kind of land reform that makes tenancy more secure or promotes the use of long term contracts would be similar to land distribution in terms of its effect on choice of effort and production techniques. The traditional approach is to place the onus for innovations on tenants. Bhaduri (1972) places the onus on the land lord A landlord decides whether to adopt any innovation in techniques or not. In a semi feudal economy a landlord's income has two components i.e. property income which he earns as rent and usurious income which he earns by lending to the tenants. The tenant's income rises with innovation thereby reducing his credit requirement. It reduces the owner's net income. This serves to reduce the incentive for introducing any innovation.

The Issue of Proper Use of Land

When population was sparse and land abundant the issue

was the appropriate use of labor. When population grew land became a critical factor of production even constraining the production frontier, only to be crossed through technological breakthrough enhancing the productivity of factors of production. This led to the emergence of notion of property rights in land, beginning with notions of community rights to tracts of land which gradually metamorphosed to ownership right by a single individual or family. In the case of the hills in Manipur this metamorphosis is yet to take place.

The Manipur Land Reforms and Land Revenue Act 1960 has not been implemented throughout the state. It is being implemented in the entire valley and only in a few villages in the hills. In the hills there is community ownership of land as in Africa. In Africa most of the land is held under forms of group or communal tenure and individual claims are weak. A small proportion of land is under owner cultivation because property rights are not well defined. There are two systems of land ownership among the tribals in Manipur. Among the Nagas there is a three tier land ownership system: the village community land, the clan land and the individual land. Among the Kukis, the entire village land is owned by the village chief and the villagers are his tenants. The villagers have right to cultivate but no ownership right which would enable them to sell the land like any commodity in the market. Land belonging to the tribals cannot be sold to non tribals.

The land ownership system evolved when there was plenty of land and population density was also low. The dominant mode of agricultural operation in the hills is shifting cultivation. This practice also evolved to economize on a scarce factor i.e. labor in the hills. The thinly populated villages, given the difficult topography, were always short of labour. Terraced cultivation is practiced in some districts at a lower scale. In 1983, annual area under shifting cultivation in Manipur was 900 sq. km, the highest in north eastern India with a fallow period ranging from 4 to 7 years. The minimum area in Manipur under shifting cultivation one time or other is 3600 sq. km.

This arrangement either in a Naga village or a Kuki village can be examined as a tenurial arrangement where the village chief is the landlord and the villagers the tenants. Just as the tenants are bound to the landlords in a semi feudal setup through an intricate credit market, the villagers are also bound to the village chiefs through an intricate system of reciprocity. However the incentive system is similar. The villagers who are the tenants are not likely to invest in land because their right to cultivation is only for a short jhum cycle and there is no guarantee that they will be back to the same plot in the future. The village chiefs are not keen because any innovation is likely to reduce their usurious income component. There is the possibility of a decline in net income. The desire for innovation of the land owner and the tenant is also circumscribed by the absence of well developed markets for the produce, credit and insurance.

Markets and institutions in the hills deeply influence the lives of people in the hills. Land, labour, credit and insurance market should function properly. Since these markets are inter linked, failure in one market leads to problems in other markets as well. The economics is simple: lack of information, the need to provide appropriate incentives and limits to contractual enforcement create efficiency failures. Unequal distribution of income or wealth may worsen this failure. The land market can open up with plots rented out or sold from landowners to those with relative abundance of labor or other inputs of production. The existence of input markets ensures to bring the ratios of various factors in line for efficient production

Pooling of land can take advantage of technological returns to scale. If the increasing return is due to large scale marketing, land can be farmed separately. Cost of setting up the marketing network can be pooled. However if the increasing returns emanate from production level there is an incentive problem. As long as the production is joint, individual owners will have a tendency to slack off.

The Proposal

At low population densities there is no incentive to invest in soil fertility and fertility can be restored by keeping the land fallow. Ownership security is not required to induce investment. When population densities rise, the fallow periods have to be shortened. Thus restoration of fertility and enhancement of productivity of land already under cultivation require higher investment. In this case ownership of land becomes an important incentive for making the right investment. As the demand for credit grows to finance the more expensive inputs associated with modern technology, the issue of land as collateral against bank loans becomes important. Legal ownership guarantees that the returns to the investment accrue to the investor. Tenants have less incentive because they have to share the produce with the land owner either through share cropping or fixed rent arrangements. In the case of share cropping the tenant will consider any investment worthwhile only when his share is increased more than his investment.

Land should be put to the best use. It need not be agricultural use. If it is required for an educational institute or for industrial purposes, land in hilly areas can be taken over by the authority after adequately compensating all whose livelihood has been adversely affected by the alternative use of land. It includes the cultivators whose livelihood depends on the land. The displaced persons need to be resettled and rehabilitated before the project starts. The current practice of resettlement /rehabilitation activities being undertaken even after the project has been completed is undesirable. Even in agriculture there is a strong logic to grow the crop in which the hills have a comparative advantage, not over the valley, but over the rest of India. The development of markets as part of globalization will ensure that the cultivators get the best price for the crop in which they have specialized. Shifting cultivation used to be justified when the farmers had to be self sufficient and needed to be protected against the vagaries of market, when labor scarcity was the constraint. In shifting cultivation a typical farmer grows a number of crops at any time. There is no market either for inputs or output. The technology was also obsolete. However the productivity was low enough to keep the farmer always poor.

The topography of hills is such that one cannot have properly irrigated tracts of land at affordable prices. Horticultural crops have comparative advantage over food grains. However horticultural plants take much longer than food grains in maturing. There is also the need to ensure that they are not damaged before maturity. The investment of money, labour and time become meaningless if one is not certain to whom the income would accrue once the product becomes marketable. The land ownership pattern needs radical change. Among the Kukis, the villagers should no longer be treated as tenants cultivating a piece of land at the mercy of the village chief. The entire village should be under individual ownership of the villagers. The Kuki chiefs may be compensated at a reasonable price and the tenants on whom ownership rights have been conferred should be required to pay a fraction of the price for the land over a period of time. The reasonable price of land should be based on present value of the future flow of income from the land. Similarly in the case of the Nagas, communal and clan land should give way to individual land. Communal and clan land should never constitute a large portion of the land.

Markets for inputs and outputs have to be developed. A farmer can buy all his inputs and requirements from the market and can sell his output also. He will be insured against the risk of crop failure by the insurance market. His labor requirements can be obtained from the labour market. He can sell his surplus or unutilized factors of production. The technology has improved significantly both in terms of production techniques and HYV seeds. The farmer no longer needs to be in low level equilibrium trap. He can specialize and produce a higher amount. His surplus can be easily exchanged for his requirements because there is a market. In this changed situation if he continues to do shifting cultivation, his opportunity cost of pursuing shifting cultivation has increased. He is producing much less than what he could have produced. However his interface with the market is inhibited by the inadequate development or absence of a land market. He simply does not have an ownership right over land. Because a land market is interliked with labor, credit and insurance markets, the failure in land market affects all other markets. For example higher investment will require credit from banks which will be forthcoming when the farmer's land serves as collateral, something which the bank can dispose of legally in the event of default of loan. Because he does not own the land he cultivates, his land cannot be pledged as collateral for his loan. With the development of a proper land market, when he is conferred ownership right over the land he cultivates; land can be put to its best use. This can be assured when land can be sold and bought in the land market just like any commodity. This is based on individual ownership of land.

To account for special provisions for the tribals the only restriction on the market may be that tribal land cannot be bought by non tribals. However the introduction of land market should be accompanied by development of labor, credit and insurance markets. The low level equilibrium of shifting cultivation used to ensure that enough labor and credit were available and also that the farmers were insured against any crop failure and subsequent food shortage. This will reduce efficiency failure substantially and will ensure the best use of land. The development of the land market is of top priority in eradication of rural poverty.

The conferring of ownership right to people in hill areas in place of communal ownership will have the desirable effect when labour, credit and insurance markets are also developed simultaneously. Infrastructure to enhance the mobility and skill of labourers, banks to provide adequate credit needed for investment and insurance companies covering their activities should be developed. Otherwise the change will lead to serious dislocations in the hill areas. The land market may lead to impoverishment of the villagers who sell off their land. It may also lead to transfer of de facto ownership to non tribals who may buy up the land. It is at this juncture that governance plays an important role. The development of these markets simultaneously has to be ensured by the state. Contracts have to be enforced. Negative market externalities have to be accounted for. This is consistent with the view that in backward areas the role of the government is as crucial as before. It is an area where there has been too little of government, not too much of it.

Conclusion

Any move for the extension of the MLR and LR Act 1960 in the hills has met the standard response that any such regulation should adequately reflect the tribal ethos etc. The village chiefs and the elite in the hills have succeeded in stalling the move. This has continued for more than 40 years. Any amendment of the said act to meet these requirements or extension of the act over the entire state should be taken up on a priority basis. The conferment of ownership rights to the villagers and subsequent development of the land market should go hand in hand with the development of the credit, labour and product market. These markets are known for their imperfections. It is where the government should play the leading role to make them functional. At stake is the integrity of the state due to the persistent failure of the state to deliver. It should be noted that the policy framework is based on individual ownership of land. This inconsistency between the framework and the ownership pattern has led to serious implementation failures.

REFERENCES

Bandiera,Oriana (2002), 'Land distribution, incentives and the choice of production techniques in Nicaragua', *DEDPS* 34, April, Suntory centre, London School of Economics.

Besley,T . and R.Burgess (1998), "Land reforms, poverty reduction and growth: Evidence from India", *The Development Economics,* Discussion Paper Series no. 13, STICERD, London school of Economics.

Bhaduri, A. (1973), 'A Study in agricultural backwardness under semi feudalism' *Economic Journal* 83.

Binswanger,H.P.,K.Deininger and G.Feder (1993), 'Power, distortions, revolt and reform in Agricultural land relations', *Policy Research Working Paper* no. 1164 The World Bank.

Govt, of India (2006), *Report of the working group on land relations for formulation of 11th Five Year Plan,* Planning Commission.

Horam, M. (2000) (ed.), *The Rising Manipur including other North Eastern States,* Manas Publications, New Delhi.

Kamei,G. (2000), 'Problems of development in the Tribal areas of Manipur', Horam (ed.) *The Rising Manipur including other North Eastern States,* Manas Publications, New Delhi.

Ray, D. (2003), *Development Economics,* Oxford University Press.

The World Bank (2007), 'India: Land policies for growth and poverty reduction', Oxford University Press, New Delhi.

10

USE OF LAND FOR ECONOMIC DEVELOPMENT: Role of Democratic Institutions in Senapati and Ukhrul Districts

—*N. Vijaylakshmi Brara*

Let me start with the quote from C J.Thomas's background paper, "Land is used in the hill areas as a mere piece of community property not as a source of enterprise and income." This fact was also a worrying and as well as a starting point for our project intervention.

The issue of Land in the Northeast has been more emotive. It has been an integral part of traditions and cultures of various societies. By more emotive, I mean that it is not that the emotional attachment with the land is not there elsewhere. After all various wars all over have been won or lost to extend one's territory, kingdoms and empires. The whole issue of patriotism is grounded in the concept of *matrabhoomi*. But, at the same time, land, in other societies is also seen in terms of its commercial value, as a source of income. In the

Northeast this issue of commercialization has started to make its slow movement. In fact this is the reason why the issues of ownership, inheritance, legal records, and boundaries have started raising their heads. People have started thinking in terms of marketing their agricultural produce, and therefore are thinking in terms of growing what ever is in demand and are also discussing the commercial volume. The rise in business entrepreneurship is also giving rise to change in the land ownership patterns. Today people want to have individual land holding but collective marketing. They want to have land-holding rights but at the same time want to collectively decide the issues, which will enhance the productivity and at the same time maintain their natural equilibrium. Now everybody in the villages know the value of land and therefore are also aware that while using it for farming it also has to be maintained and continuously renewed. They also know that to be able to get access to the market they need good roads. The infrastructures such as the roads have to be made on somebody's land. The agreement to that effect is being sought. All these interventions have started to take place in the hill districts of Senapati and Ukhrul. Some of the modest interventions have been made by the NERCORMP project.

I am interested to showcase the interventions made by this project because, today when we are thinking of strategizing the development initiatives in the Northeast through the Vision 2020 and also envisioning a "Look East Policy", we have to understand the NERCORMP/IFAD model. Nearly all the agencies, which have to either evaluate this project or come for just studying it, have called it a successful and implementable programme.

Before we enter into the realm of NERCORMP interventions, lets us first understand the land use pattern in Manipur. It will then give us the context and therefore the felt need for some small measures of reforms.

The Land Holding System in Manipur

There are broadly three land systems, based on the customary norms of broadly three ethnic communities that govern land rights in Manipur. In the hill areas, the community, not the state, owns most of the land; though private plots of terraces and forests as well as private encroachment of common property (not sanctioned by customary law) is prevalent in some places. The Kukis and the Nagas both have a system of community ownership governed by unwritten custom and tradition. There are, however, two fundamental differences between the Nagas and the Kukis: in the case of the former, the tiller or direct producer has inalienable occupancy and inheritance rights, which cannot be superseded by the Chief, while in the case of the Kukis the chief has far greater overriding power over land use and access. The Nagas enjoy the rights of inheritance and occupancy and every village has more than one clan. They have a three-tier system of land ownership – clan, village and private land. The Kuki-Chin-Mizos have a more semi- feudal system of landownership with built in disincentives against private or farm investment. There is a well-developed system of grain rent collection called *tangsen, bushan, changsen* or *fathang*. Furthermore, the Chief exacts labour from the cultivator families, often at the rate of four days per person per annum.The Kuki families are therfore far more at the mercy of their Chief, who often tends to be autocratic and arbitrary. The third system of property rights is prevalent in the valley, where complete private individual ownership exists and is protected by the state through its laws and institutions.

In the Naga areas the land holdings are under the control of the village administration, which exercises executive, judicial and administrative autonomy. The Naga Chief is bound by the advice of the village elders and council. This is not necessarily true of the Kuki areas where the Chief is seen to be more arbitrary in exercising his authority. However, in doing so even he is bound to take the village elders into confidence. Again, though both tribes own village lands, in Naga villages, individual households have land tenures and can sell land to anyone from their own village although transactions with people outside the village are prohibited. In Kuki villages on the other hand, no individual household can lay claim to any land. The Chief distributes this land to village people for paddy cultivation, and in return the latter have to give a portion of their paddy to the Chief. Apart from these systems there are also several other systems of smaller tribes like the Hmars where the entire village community owns the land, but in practice has to give the Chief a portion of their paddy or hunted animal as the case may be.

The attachment to land is not entirely due to its economic importance. Territory plays an important role in shaping cultural and ethnic identity.

The elite in tribal societies owes its emergence in part to the 'modern' administrative system's preference for individual land ownership. Privatization of land has led to its commodification, resulting in mortgaging and sale of land within the community. This has created class distinctions and land alienation. It is also reinforcing patriarchy since the *pattas* are made only in a male's name and thus excludes women from land ownership.

The emergence of an impoverished and even landless class of tenants is recorded in several places in the hills, most notably in Kuki areas but even amongst the Rongmei, the Thangkuls and other Nagas. Immigration and encroachment on land are especially important. The struggle to acquire resources (most notably land) amidst changing land relations has translated into ethnic conflicts.

Land and forests are the two basic resources for subsistence in the hills. An essential requirement of this region is an healthy and adaptive system of land rights that can tackle the incipient problems of differentiation, jhum, inequality, and the emergence of a local elite.

It is in this background that the NERCORMP Project took certain interventions whereby promoting the spirit of collectivity, inclusivity and in some measures, a certain kind of redistribution of land.

A Brief Background of the Project

NERCORMP is a joint developmental initiative in North East India of the North Eastern Council (NEC), Ministry of DONER and International Fund for Agricultural Development (IFAD). Its broad objective can be summarized as follows:

To improve the livelihoods of vulnerable groups in a sustainable manner through improved management of their resource base in a way that contributes to preservation and restoration of the environment

The Project was launched against a backdrop of not many successful Rural Development interventions in North East. Equally glaring was the weak and often, absence of right Social and Developmental Institutes at the grass root level.

Therefore one main objective was to perform a SUCCESSFUL DEVELOPMENTAL PROJECT and at the same time come up with a TRUE DEVELOPMENTAL MODEL evolved from the grass root. It also aimed to establish a sense of stakeholdership/ownership by the Communities.

This project can proudly claim and even proclaim the establishment of two growth engines in each of our project village; The SHGs and the NaRMGs (Natural Resource Management Groups)

NaRMGs are the Community Developmental Planning and implementing Bodies. Membership is drawn from both men and women of 50% each. Eventually, both husband and wife of a household, become members. NaRMGs along with SHGs have become the key pillars on which the Project rests and builds on. As of today there are 1012 NaRMGs in the Project. NaRMGs are vibrant and are shouldering the given responsibilities. It has managed to set up and co-exist with other Traditional/Legal Institutions of the village.

Concept and approach of the NaRMG is towards collective deliberation, decision and action. Many issues not addressed regularly or never addressed in the past are now being regularly dealt with in NaRMG Meetings. This has opened up the eyes and consciousness of the Communities to many areas in ways never seen in the past. NaRMGs indeed are becoming a Force and engine towards growth. They have also got themselves federated and call themselves the cluster associations. This is normally a group of 10-15 villages in adjoining areas. They Select one or two items as focus/thrust items depending on suitability, soil, topology, temperature adaptability etc. They pay strong emphasis on the selected crops/activities by way of trainings, Extension services etc. They also organize market linkages.

Some of the Cluster Focus activities in different Districts are given below:

- West Garo Hills – Ginger, Areca nut, Patchouli, Livestock, Orange
- West Khasi Hills – Ginger, Pineapple, Patchouli, Livestock, Litchi, Orange, Broom stick etc.
- NC Hills – Banana, Pineapple, Ginger, Livestock, etc.
- Senapati – Passion fruit, Green Pea, King Chilly, Livestock, Tree Tomato, Tree Beans etc.
- Ukhrul – King Chilly, Banana, Passion fruit, Pineapple, Terrace field cultivation, Geranium, Livestock etc.

One of the key areas of Project interventions and achievements have been in development of Community based Biodiversity, Conservation and Community Forestry Management Systems which is becoming a movement among many Project villages.

This has resulted into a creation of a wide SPECTRUM and NETWORK of Community based Biodiversity Conservation areas such as Catchment Forest resources, Sacred grovess, Stream Banks Forest reserves, grazing land reserves, wildlife reserve, Bird sanctuary, Pitcher plant sanctuary, Fish pool reserves, Thatch grass and Bamboo reserves and so on.

Many of the pristine forest patches and also degraded forest areas in critical locations such as water catchments / resources areas have been declared as Community Forests with strict Management Rules and Regulations.

The network of Forest / Biodiversity Resources in all the Districts is now about 1835.89 sq. kms. It is likely to further scale up in the near future.

Land Use, Development and NaRGM

The traditional systems of resource management have long existed among the Tangkhul Naga. Like any other tribe in the North East, the Tangkhuls have intrinsic link to forest and land and it is a systems approach. In short, land for the Tangkhuls is everything and they have experienced many struggles for survival and self determination over their natural rights and the territories in the form of ethno-cultural clashes since the time when the British ruled this state. They can give up their lives even for an inch of land. In the whole territories of the Tangkhul community, there is not an inch of land called waste land. Land is being utilized for some or the other purpose.

Land use system of the Tangkhuls:

- Wet terrace cultivation
- Jhum/shifting cultivation
- Home garden
- Settlement area
- Village reserve forest
- Fuel wood Reserve
- Grass land
- Green Belt

The Tangkhuls have three land holding system.

- Private land
- Clan Land and
- Community land

Out of these three land holding system, private and community land ownership are predominant.

Private Land: Private lands are generally found at the vicinity of the settlement areas in non-jhum belt of the district. Private land is well marked with boundary stones and maintained strict vigilance of any intruders is maintained. Cutting even a single tree or extraction of NTFPs, needs permission from the land owner. In the jhum belt area, individuals owns the jhum blocks but it is managed/utilized by the community as common resource property so that everybody gets a share of the land.

Community land: Utilization of land in the community land needs permission from the village authority (VA). The community land is reserved for the purpose of village development and whenever need arises, the village authority or council opens the land to the community. For example every village maintains a village reserved forest and it is opened only when they feel the needs to harvest the resources from this reserved forest and only partial extraction is allowed for a short duration. In this way the whole community land is regulated under the village authority. However, one shortcoming about community land is, not measuring and recording the vastness of the areas. It is often decided by imaginary calculation of the ridges, brook, hill range etc. This practice often leads to land disputes between the neighbouring villages.

Transfer of Land

In the Tangkhul society land is inherited only by the male folk. There is also a slight variation among different zones. For example in the jhum cultivation area, only the eldest son of the family inherit land where as in the wet terrace cultivation area, all the male members get land though varying in proportions. If there is no male member in a family then it is inherited by a cousin who is called as *shimluikat*.

When an individual landowner wants to sell his land, he has to first inform to his brothers, then within immediate family called the *meiphung*, next to the clan members and finally open to the community. If there are no buyers within the village it is open to the neighboring village. As per the customary norm this procedure has to be followed.

Transferring or selling of land to non Tangkhul Naga is strictly prohibited by the village authority as well as by the apex organization, the Tangkhul Naga Long.

The land holding system did not change with the emergence of the NaRM-G in the village set up. Whenever the NaRM-Gs, SHGs or any organization or individual within the village requisitions land from village authority for the development/welfare of the villagers, the Village authority discusses the matter at the council level and allots accordingly.

With the introduction of focus item in the project villages, the community land or even individual land have been donated to the NaRM-Gs or SHGs. Prior to donation of land, an understanding has to reached between the two parties, the general agreement reached between the village council and NaRM-Gs/ SHGs/lead farmers is that they will use the allotted land so long as the NaRM-Gs/SHGs exist .

With the result today they have vast stretches of banana cultivation and king chilly cultivation and have been able to raise their commercial volume to such an extent that they have managed to take over the major city markets.

The Impact of the Project on Land Tenure System with Special REference to Kuki Areas in Senapati District

The Kuki chiefs are till today the Feudal Landlords. They own all the land in their village. Hence any long-term intervention in the sustainability of land in terms of attempting to increase the volume and its productivity was turning out to be a difficult proposition. The NaRMG collectives were not encouraged to till the land, which is ultimately not theirs. Therefore, this feudal tenure system was the stumbling block to any land based development activity. The NaRMG members were afraid that in the long run the benefit of any land based activity will profit only the Chief of the Village as he is the sole owner of the land.

After some unsuccessful interventions, the NaRMGs along with their NGOs were able to negotiate with the Village chief to donate land to the Villagers free of cost! An agreement of land donation was signed between NaRMGs members and village Chiefs, which was counter-signed by Government Officials granting it a legal validity. The lands are used for passion fruit, medicinal, horticulture and forestry plantations. The strength of the collectives in these villages, through the various capacity building trainings, brought a certain level of confidence in the villagers. This intervention is a landmark

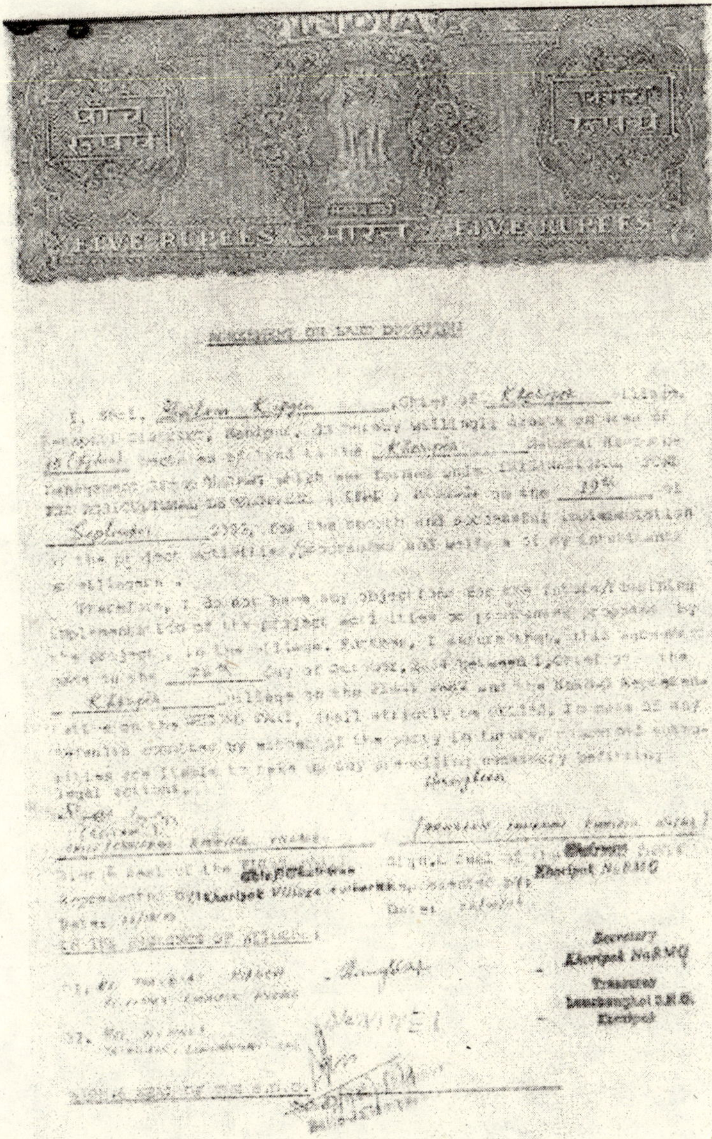

Fig: Shows the land donation agreement between village chief and Khoripok NaRM-G

in the history of the Kuki tribes of the Northeast. This example will be cited as a historical landmark in the history of land reforms of the tribal belt of the Northeast India. The village chiefs have been able to understand that sharing of Natural Resources, particularly land, is a very important developmental tool. Below is an example of the land donation agreement between the villagers and their chief and further below is the list of the chiefs who gave away the land as well as the size of the area. This can be equated to the *bhudaan* movement started by Vinoba Bhave.

Table 1
Lands donated by the Village Chief

Sl. No.	*NaRMG*	*Date of Agreement*	*Size of land donated*
1	Lhangkichoi	23/9/04	45 hac
2	A. Songpijang	23/9/04	25 hac
3	Leikot	20/9/04	20 hac
4	Phaijang	23/9/04	35 hac
5	Haiken	21/9/04	15 hac
6	Phailenkot	23/9/04	23 hac
7	N. Khonom	26/9/04	20 hac
8	Thomjang	26/9/04	20 hac
9	Gampum	5/4/03	35 hac
10	Zalenphai	5/9/03	20 hac
11	S. Khonomphai	16/6/03	10 hac
12	T. Gamnom	5/5/03	7 hac
13	Waichei	26/9/04	30 hac
14	Naphai	26/9/04	30 hac
15	Moljol	14/9/04	10 hac

(Contd...)

Sl. No.	*NaRMG*	*Date of Agreement*	*Size of land donated*
16	Tengkonphai	7/6/04	30 hac
17	Ng. Phainom	15/6/03	35 hac
18	C. Aisan	9/6/03	5 hac
19	Khoripok	19/9/04	15 hac
20	Haibung	4/10/03	15 hac
21	Manamjang	19/9/03	7 hac
22	T.Mongbung	26/10/03	5 hac
23	A.Geljang	3/12/04	15 hac
24	S.Mongbung	24/10/04	15 hac
25	Twichamphai	25/10/04	10 hac
26	Thingsat	3/11/04	10 hac
27	Bolsang	5/11/04	10 hac
28	N.Chaljang	20/10/04	10 hac
29	T.Thangkan	22/10/04	8 hac
30	Thangalsurung	28/9/04	20 hac
		Total	**593 hectares**

The Kukis today in our project areas are no more insecure and are also no more under the threat of being ousted by the chief. They have collective ownership of land and have become commercial farmers. This remarkable intervention through their collectivity is something they could not even dream of. Today, it is their reality.

11

Agrarian Structure and Agricultural Production in Manipur

—*N. Bhupendra Singh*

Introduction

There is a constant change in the agrarian structure of Manipur mainly due to mounting population pressure. But, whether the change is consistent with the socio-economic objectives adopted by the state, has become a major issue. A clear understanding of the existing agrarian structure and the emerging patterns of agrarian reconstruction becomes highly pertinent both from the stand point of policy formulation and also of understanding the growth imperatives.

The present study attempts to analyse the emerging pattern of agrarian structure in the state during 1990 to 2006 using factual data available in different sources. Concurrently, an attempt has also been made to examine the trend of agricultural production. In doing so, due to certain limitation of the NSSO data on land holdings, the discussion on the size distribution of ownership and operational land holdings has been confined to the rural areas of state only, while other remaining indicators used in the study are for the entire state.

The present study has been divided into five sections including introduction. In section II various aspects of agrarian structure including the distribution pattern of agricultural household assets are discussed. The structure of land ownership is the main determinant of agrarian relations. Section III discusses the agrarian relationships which reflect the occupational distribution of labour force. The production trend and emerging demand-supply gap of agriculture products are analysed in section IV. Lastly, the conclusion drawn from the analysis is given in section V.

Agrarian Structure

The distribution of operational holdings is getting increasingly marginalised at least in the rural areas of Manipur. During 1992 to 2002 the total numbers of operational holdings have increased by 630 hundred which amounts to 37.21 percent while the area operated have increased merely by 109 hundred hectare which is about 8.34 percent. The inproportionate increases in the number of household operational holdings have lead to the reduction in the average size of operational holding from 0.77 hectare in 1992 to 0.61 hectare in 2002. The distribution of operational holdings into different size classes in the rural areas of Manipur is given in Table 1.

In 1992 marginal holdings constituted about 71 percent of the total operational holdings and 37 percent of the total area operated. However, in 2002 it constituted 83 percent and 60 percent respectively. In other words, the numbers of marginal households have increased by about 59 percent while the areas operated have increased by about 73 percent. As the proportion of increase in the number of households is slightly less than that of operated areas, there is a marginal improvement in the average size of marginal holding from 0.41 hectare in 1992 to 0.44 hectare in 2002. In the case of small holdings, while the number of households is increased by 4 percent the areas operated has declined by 4 percent which has lead to a decline in the average size small holding from 1.35 hectare to 1.24 hectare. Similarly, the average size of semi medium holding has also declined from 2.40 hectare to 2.31 hectare as the decline in the proportion of areas operated is more than the number of households. Though the number and areas operated by medium holding is very small its average size is growing as the increase in the former is less than the latter. The number of households with large size operational holdings is likely to be very few in numbers.

Table 1
Distribution of Operational Holdings in Rural Areas of Manipur (NSS)

Size Class	*1991-92*			*2002-03*		
	No. of hhs (00)	*Area (00 hect)*	*Average area*	*No. of hhs (00)*	*Area (00 hect)*	*Average Area*
Marginal (Less than 1 hectare)	1204 (71.12)	489 (37.44)	0.41	1918 (82.57)	844 (59.65)	0.44
Small (1 to 2 hecters)	340 (20.08)	459 (35.15)	1.35	355 (15.28)	441 (31.16)	1.24
Semi Medium (2 to 4 hectares)	148 (8.74)	355 (27.18)	2.40	45 (1.94)	104 (7.35)	2.31
Medium (4 to 10 hectares)	1 (0.06)	3 (0.23)	3.00*	5 (0.21)	26 (1.84)	5.2
Large (10 hectares &above)	-	-	-	-	-	-
All Holdings	1693 (100)	1306 (100)	0.77	2323 (100)	1415 (100)	0.61
Gini Coefficient		0.361			0.238	

Note: *All figures are drawn from the sample data and in most of the cases the estimated figures are rounded up to nearest whole number. Hence in some cases the value of the calculated average size may not fall within the specified range of the particular class. Figures in the parenthesis indicate the percentage distribution.

Sources: 1. NSSO. 1997. Operational land Holdings in India 1991-92: Salient Features, 48th Round, Report No. 407.

2. NSSO. 2006. Some Aspects of Operational Land Holdings in India 2002-03, 59th Round, Report No. 491.

The increase in the number of marginal and small holdings and shrinking in other size classes implies that the division and sub-division of holdings is widely practiced in the rural areas of Manipur. At the same time there is an increase in the number of landless households from 33 hundred to 72 hundred.

During the period from 1992 to 2002 there is a decline in inequality in the distribution of operational holdings as it revealed by the value of estimated Gini coefficient. It may be attributed mainly to the distribution of holdings in favour of marginal and small holdings without any significant change in the average size of holding. The decline in the estimated value of Gini coefficient is likely to be concurrent with the socio-economic objective of the state. But, the question of economic viability of marginal and small holdings can be confirmed when we discuss the productivity trends of agricultural output in section IV.

The data on the distribution of operational holdings is also available in Agricultural Census Report. Though the census data are not always dependable as they are mostly based on the revenue records they have generally been used in many studies. The size distribution of operational holdings based on census data is being reproduced in Table 2.

Table 2

Distribution of Operational Holdings in Manipur

	1990-91			*1995-96*		
Size Class	*No.*	*Area*	*Average*	*No.*	*Area*	*Average*
Marginal	68598 (48.29)	37820 (21.61)	0.55	69320 (48.56)	38940 (22.39)	0.56
Small	49062 (34.53)	67135 (38.37)	1.37	49300 (34.53)	66505 (38.23)	1.35

(Contd...)

	1990-91			1995-96		
Size Class	*No.*	*Area*	*Average*	*No.*	*Area*	*Average*
Semi Medium	21452 (15.10)	54892 (31.37)	2.56	21225 (14.87)	53550 (30.78)	2.52
Medium	2916 (2.05)	14611 (8.35)	5.01	2870 (2.01)	14445 (8.30)	5.03
Large	43 (0.03)	523 (0.30)	12.16	40 (0.03)	525 (0.30)	13.13
All Size	1,42,071 (100)	1,74,981 (100)	1.23	1,42,755 (100)	1,73,965 (100)	1.22
Gini coefficient		0.3456		0.3396		

Note: Figures in the parentheses indicate the percentage distribution.
Source: GOM, Agricultural Census of Manipur 1990-91& 1995-96, Department of Agriculture.

From the above table it can be observed that the marginal holdings dominated the distribution of operational holdings both in 1990-91 and 1995-96 censuses. However, the proportion of households and area operated for marginal holdings is much smaller than what is observed in NSSO series. In the case of other size classes' i.e. small, semi-medium, medium and large holdings, the same is much larger. Nevertheless these proportions (number of households and area operated) for marginal holdings have increased but declined for other size classes. Similarly, the inequality in the distribution of operational holdings has also decreased over time. This corroborates our earlier findings of frequent division and sub-division of operational holdings in Manipur.

The distribution pattern of land holdings is very much related with the distribution of assets of the cultivating households as the agriculture productivity is likely to be dependent upon the types of assets used. It is, therefore, pertinent to examine the structure of assets owned by the cultivating households. The information on inventory assets owned by the cultivating households is available in the various rounds of Debt and Investment Survey, NSSO. The distribution of assets per reported cultivating household in 48th and 59th round of NSSO is shown in Table 3.

Table 3
Distribution of Assets per Reported Cultivating Household in Rupees (48th and 59th Round NSS)

Assets	*As on 30.06.1991*			*As on 30.06.2006*		
	Average Value (Rs)	*Percentage*	*Gini Coefficients*	*Average Value (Rs)*	*Percentage*	*Gini Coefficients*
Land	52776	55.87	0.5082	121153	60.58	0.5919
Building	25680	27.18	0.4011	43442	21.72	0.3675
Livestock & Poultry	3000	3.18	0.1303	5523	2.76	0.09225
Machinery & Equipment	4094	4.33	0.7309	6543	3.27	0.6858
Household durables	7516	7.96	0.3439	13628	6.81	0.3593
Financial assets	1377	1.46	0.5928	9671	4.84	*
Loan receivable	20	0.02	0.4566	38	0.02	0.4730
Total	94463	100		199998	100	

Note: *Due to the presence of negative values in some of the size classes the value of the Gini Coefficient can not be calculated for Financial assets.

Source: 1. NSSO. 1998. 48th Round, Report No. 419.

2. NSSO. 2006. 59th Round, Report No. 500.

The average value of assets owned by the cultivating household have increased from about Rs. 94 thousand in 1991 to Rs. 2 lakh in 2002. Out of all the assets owned by cultivating household, land is the most important asset. Its share in the average value of the assets owned per reporting household have increased from 56 percent in 1991 to 61 percent in 2002. At the same time the accumulation of asset in the form of land has become more skewed. Similarly the share of financial assets also has increased from about 1 percent to 5 percent. But the shares of building, livestock and poultry, machinery and equipment and household durable assets has decreased to 22%, 3%, 3% and 7% respectively. The low rate of assets owned in the form of machinery and equipment means low rate of private fixed capital formation. Actually, the private fixed capital formation per rural household has also declined from Rs. 348 in 1991-92 to Rs. 336 in 2002-03. Further, high rate of inequality in machinery and equipment owned implies that they are mostly owned by more affluent farmers while rest of the farmers, mainly farmers with marginal and small holdings, continue to depend on bovine sources to carry out the farm activities. Since private fixed capital formation plays an important role in the development of agriculture sector the decline in the share of livestock and poultry and machinery and equipment is a source of concern.[1]

Agrarian Relations

The economic development is generally known to be associated with a decline in the share of agriculture both in terms of net domestic product and labour force. While the share of agriculture in net domestic product of the state declined from 31.19 percent in 1993-94 to 23.14 percent in 2004-05 their share in the work force continue to hover over 50 percent. The major cause for this divergent trend in agriculture's share in net domestic product and work force is the rapid growth of population in conjunction with the inability of industrial development to increase its share in labour force absorption.

Table 4

Distribution of Main and Marginal Workers in Manipur

Census Year	*Culti-vator*	*Main Agri. Labourer*	*Others*	*Total Main Workers*	*Culti-vator*	*Marginal Agri. Labourer*	*Other*	*Total Marginal Workers*
2001	2,85,809 (43.35)	41,819 (6.34)	3,31,736 (50.31)	6,59,364 (100)	93,896 (32.85)	71,811 (25.12)	1,20,142 (42.03)	2,85,849 (100)
1991	4,37,499 (61.77)	47,350 (6.68)	2,23,434 (31.55)	7,08,283 (100)	-	-	-	66,621

Note: 1. Figures in the parenthesis indicate the percentage distribution.
2. The classifications for marginal workers in different sector are not available in 1991 census.

Source: GOM, Statistical Abstract of Manipur 2005, Directorate of Economics & Statistics, Imphal.

During 1991 to 2001[2] the population of the state has increased by 4.6 lakh and work force (main plus marginal) by 1.7 lakh. The pressure of population and work force on land is also reflected in the size distribution of land holdings. The manner in which the additional work force is distributed among different occupations provides an overview of the dynamics of change in rural economy of the state. The occupational distribution of work force in the state available in population census is shown in Table 4.

There is evidence to suggest that crop cultivation has exhausted its capacity to accommodate the increasing labour force. In 1991 out of the total work force of 7.75 lakh, 7.08 lakh were main workers and only 67 thousand were marginal workers. Of these 7.08 lakh main workers about 68 percent were employed in agriculture sector. In 2001, the numbers of main workers were reduced to 6.59 lakh but the number of marginal workers increased to 2.9 lakh, from mere 67 thousand in 1991. The percentage of main workers employed in agriculture sector has reduced to 50 percent and the rest 50 percent is mostly absorbed in the service sector. In the case of marginal workers about 58 percent were engaged in agricultural activities. The increase in marginal workers attached with agricultural activities is concurrent with the increase in the number of landless households.

The occupational distribution of work force is also available in various rounds of National Sample Survey Results and is shown in Table 5.

The percentage of work force engaged in agricultural activities hover around 26 to 29 percent (both in usual principal status and principal plus subsidiary status) in urban areas but in the case of rural areas it continues to remain high though fluctuates between 64 to 75 percent. In rural areas the percentage of work force (usual principal plus subsidiary status) involved in agricultural activities which increased to 75 percent in 1999-00 from 64 percent in 1993-94, has declined to 69 percent in 2004-05.

Table 5
Percentage of Population Working in Agriculture Sector

Round/Year		*Rural Person*		*Urban Person*
	PS	*PS+SS*	*PS*	*PS+SS*
2004-05	67.8	69.3	25.9	28.3
1999-00	74.4	75.3	25.5	28.3
1993-94	64.2	63.8	27.1	29.3

Sources: 1. NSSO. 1997. 50th Round, Report No. 409.
2. NSSO. 2001. 55th Round, Report No. 458.
3. NSSO. 2006. 61st Round, Report No. 515.

Persistence of high rate of work force engaged in the agriculture sector has led to widespread speculation of the existence of disguised unemployment. Looking into the population scenario the pressure of swelling labour force on land is not likely to ease in the near future. It is, therefore, time to think of diversifying the rural economy other than those based on crop land that can generate gainful employment.

Agriculture Production Trend

Agriculture in Manipur is mainly confined in the production of rice. It accounts for about 98 percent of the area under cereal cultivation in 2006-07 while the rest is maize. Similarly, the production of rice constitutes about 98 percent of the total cereal production in the state. Therefore, an examination on the performance of rice cultivation in the state can summarize the extent of development of the agriculture sector. The time series on area, yield and production of rice in the state is given in appendix 1.

The per hectare yield of rice have increased from 1742 kg in 1990-91 to 2505 kg in 1995-96 thereafter it hovered around 2329 kg. The yield rate recorded in the state is comparable to many states of the Indian union. The relatively high rate of yield per hectare on predominantly marginal and small holdings implies that there seems to be inverse relationship between productivity and farm size. However, its production fluctuates widely due to the fluctuation in the area cultivated. During 1990 to 2006, the area under rice cultivation grows at an annual compound growth rate[3] of 0.4 percent while its production and yield grows at the rate of 1.78 percent and 1.38 percent respectively. It shows that the increase in rice output in the state is mainly due to increase in yield per hectare. In other words, the growth of rice output in the state is mainly induced by yield effect while area effect is negligible. It implies that the marginalisation of holdings and dependence on bovine sources hardly affects the productivity/per hectare yield of rice.

The increase in the production of rice at an annual compound growth rate 1.78 percent is not sufficient to meet the requirement in the state. The production of rice is far short of the demand in the state. It can be confirmed if we look at the gap between the production and required quantity estimated by the Directorate of Economics and Statistics, Government of Manipur. The gap between the two is widening. The estimated annual requirements[4] have increased from 431 thousand tonnes in 1999-00 to 497 tonnes in 2006-07 and is likely touch 546 thousand tonnes by 2011 at the present population growth rate of 2.25 percent.[5] It means the production is short by 66 thousand tonnes in 1999-00 and 108 thousand tonnes in 2006-07. Assuming the present growth rate of rice output in the state to continue, the gap is likely to touch 121 thousand tonnes by 2011. The problem is more serious if we consider the net production[6] instead of gross production. The state is at the throes of severe food crisis.

Considering the pressure of swelling population, urbanisation and development process, there is hardly any scope for further extension of arable land, at least in the valley area. However, at least for the time being, the problem of shortage in rice production seems not because of the limited scope for extension of arable land but because of the pattern of arable land being utilized in the state. The major portions of the cultivated land are under mono cropping implying thereby underutilization of these arable lands. In simple words, if we can step up the cropping intensity to double or triple cropping with the help of excess labour force, the problem of shortage in rice production can be easily solved. It, however, would require to step-up the rate of capital formation, more particularly public capital formation in irrigation, as most of the farmers are dependent upon the vagaries of monsoon. The irrigation system is in pathetic condition in spite of allocating massive public investment in agriculture.[7] Similarly, other infrastructures like road, electricity, storage, proper marketing system, agricultural research etc. also need to be improved. Such exercise would induce the farmers to invest in farm sector.

With fossil fuels increasingly being substituted by bio fuels extracted from agricultural products, commercialisation and diversification of this sector to generate extra income without sufficient food stock would to lead to severe food crisis in the state. In the coming years, hill areas of the state which constitute about 90 percent of the total geographical areas, need to play a significant role in tackling the problem of food shortage. An alternate farming practice should be introduced, like the one initiated by NEPED in Nagaland, which are economically viable, socially acceptable and ecologically sustainable.

Conclusion

There is a frequent division and sub-division of holdings due to excessive population pressure. As a result, land holdings – both ownership and operational – in the state is increasingly marginalised. But its productivity has not been affected much till now. However, further continuation of the process would have a deleterious effect on the productivity even under the new technology.

The increase in the number of landless households and marginal workers suggest that crop cultivation has exhausted its capacity to accommodate the increasing labour force at the given level of cropping intensity. There is a widespread speculation about the existence of disguised unemployment. On the other hand the available crop land has not been utilised to the optimum level because of the widespread practice of subsistence mode of farming. The majority of the holdings are under mono cropping and a very few holdings are under double cropping. If we can increase the cropping intensity to double or triple crops, utilizing the existing excess labour force, the problem of shortage in the production of rice can be easily solved. It, however, would require a massive public capital formation in irrigation and other related infrastructure. Such exercise would induce the farmers to invest more in farm sector. With the realisation of self-sufficiency in food production the sense of participation in the commercialisation and diversification process would grow.

NOTES

1. For more details on capital formation in agriculture sector of Manipur see N B Singh. 2007. *Capital Formation in Agriculture Sector of Manipur*, Akansha Publishing House, New Delhi.
2. 2001 census exclude Mao Maram, Paomata and Purul sub-division of Senapati District. Therefore, the total population and number of workers (main plus marginal) of the state may be more than the recorded figures. But the present discussion is mainly base on the available records.
3. The annual compound growth rate is calculated with the help of log linear regression model.
4. The annual requirement of rice per person is assumed to be 193.38 kg.

5. Mid-year projected population for the state in 2011 is 28,23,387. For more information see *Economic Survey of Manipur 2006-07*, Directorate of Economics & Statistics, GOM, p. 7.

6. Gross production less seed requirements, feed and wastage equals Net production. Usually net production has been taken as 92.4 percent of the gross production for rice.

7. During 1990 to 2003-04 about 90 percent of the total public investment in agriculture sector is in the development irrigation facility in the state.

Appendix 1
Area, Production and Yield of Rice in the State (1990-91 to 2006-07)

Year	*Area (000 hect)*	*Yield (kg/hect)*	*Production (000 tones)*
1990-91	157.41	1741.76	274.17
1991-92	160.30	2123.83	340.45
1992-93	151.19	1806.47	273.12
1993-94	161.87	2154.94	348.82
1994-95	163.93	2186.97	358.51
1995-96	134.93	2505.37	338.05
1996-97	166.10	2211.20	367.28
1997-98	157.90	2227.17	351.67
1998-99	166.89	2290.07	382.19
1999-00	157.05	2323.97	364.98
2000-01	156.96	2431.77	381.69
2001-02	162.57	2382.11	387.26
2002-03	153.11	2192.35	335.67
2003-04	157.83	2415.51	381.24
2004-05	176.31	2472.52	435.93
2005-06	166.26	2322.09	386.07
2006-07	165.37	2353.22	389.17

Source: GOM. Crop Estimation Survey Various Issues, Directorate of Economics and Statistics

REFERENCES

Ahuja, Kanta (1986), 'Agricultural Labour and Rural Employment', M. L. Dantwala et.al (eds.). *Indian Agricultural Development Since Independence: A Collection of Essays*, Oxford & IBH Publishing Co. Pvt. Ltd., New Delhi, pp. 400-431.

Dantwala, M. L. (1986), 'Agrarian Structure and Agrarian Relations in India', M. L. Dantwala et. al (eds.). *Indian Agricultural Development Since Independence: A Collection of Essays*, Oxford & IBH Publishing Co. Pvt. Ltd., New Delhi, pp. 59-88.

Deshpande, R. S. (1998), 'Land Reforms and Agrarian Structure in Maharashtra', *Journal of Indian School of Political Economy*, vol. x, no. 1. January-March, pp. 1-23.

Gadgil, Sulochana and Siddhartha Gadgil. (2006), 'The Indian Monsoon, GDP and Agriculture', *Economic and Political Weekly*, vol. 41, no. 47, November 25, pp.4887-4894.

Ghosh, Nilabja. *Organic Farming in North-East Hill Region in India*, http://iegindia.org/dis_nila_86.pdf.

Government of Manipur. *Agricultural Census of Manipur 1990-91& 1995-96*, Department of Agriculture, Imphal.

Government of Manipur. *Crop Estimation Survey of Manipur*, various issues.

Government of Manipur. (2006), *Statistical Abstract of Manipur 2005*, Directorate of Economics and Statistics, Imphal.

Government of Manipur (2007), *Economic Survey of Manipur 2006-07*, Directorate of Economics & Statistics, Imphal.

Laxminarayan, H. and S. S. Tyagi. (1982), *Changes in Agrarian Structure in India*, Agricole Publishing Academy, New Delhi.

NSSO (1997), *Operational land Holdings in India 1991-92: Salient Features*, 48th Round, Report No. 407.

NSSO (1997), *Employment and Unemployment in India, 1993-94*, 50th Round, Report No. 409.

NSSO (1998), *Household Assets and Liabilities as on 30.06.1991*, 48th Round, Report No. 419.

NSSO (2001), *Employment and Unemployment Situation in India 1999-2000*, 55th Round, Report No. 458.

NSSO (2006) *Household Ownership Holdings in India, 2003*, 59th Round, Report No. 491.

NSSO (2006), *Some Aspects of Operational Land Holdings in India 2002-03*, 59th Round, Report No. 492.

NSSO (2006), *Employment and Unemployment Situation in India, 2004-05*, 61st Round, Report No. 515.

Rudra, Ashok, (1992), *Political Economy of Indian Agriculture*, K. P. Bagch & Company, Calcutta.

Sharma, H. R. (1997), 'Land Reforms: Status and Opportunities', Bhupat M. Desai (ed.). *Agricultural Development Paradigm for the Ninth Plan under New Economic Environment*, CMA Monograph No. 179, Oxford & IBH Publishing Co. Pvt. Ltd., New Delhi, pp. 712-739.

Singh, N Bhupendro (2007), *Capital Formation in Agriculture Sector of Manipur*, Akansha Publishing House, New Delhi.

Thorat, Sukhadeo (1997), 'Trends in Land Ownership, Tenancy and Land Reform', Bhupat M. Desai (ed.), *Agricultural Development Paradigm for the Ninth Plan under New Economic Environment*, CMA Monograph No. 179, Oxford & IBH Publishing Co. Pvt. Ltd., New Delhi, pp. 684-711.

12

ROLE OF AGRICULTURE IN THE ECONOMIC DEVELOPMENT OF MANIPUR

—*K. Gyanendra Singh*

> *General economic development requires agricultural development either to precede or to go hand in hand. Rate of saving and investment cannot be high unless it is high in agriculture. Per capita income as a whole cannot increase unless there is development in agriculture and increase in income in the agricultural sector* (Datt and Sundharam 1996).

Manipur, a tiny Northeastern state of 22,327 sq. km., is known as 'Jewel of India' as coined by our late Prime Minister Jawaharlal Nehru. A charming place encircled by nine hill ranges on all sides with a small and oval valley at the centre, the state is inhabited by four major ethnic groups, viz., the Meiteis, the Nagas, the Kukis and the Meitei Pangals (Muslims). The valley area which account for 10.02 percent of the total geographical area is the most populous area registering a density of 631 persons per sq. km. according to 2001 census, whereas the hill area with 89.98 percent of the total geographical area has a density of 44 persons per sq. km. This indicates that the major economic activities are concentrated in the valley.

Historical Background

The Manipur economy is predominantly agricultural in nature. Right from historical days, agriculture has been a major activity in the economy. It was known for its rice economy. Rice formed the staple food of the people. They cultivated their fields and grew rice. Peasantry had become a solid aspect of life. They had enough cheap wholesome food to eat (Singh 1992). While jhum cultivation was practiced in the hills, in the plains it was wet rice cultivation. The crop raised in the valley (at Thoubal and its vicinity) was the mainstay of the state (McCulloh 1980). About nineteen varieties of rice were grown and the produce of one year was enough to feed the population for two years. Average yield per pari (2.5 acres) was about one hundred and fifty baskets annually, each basket contain about sixty pounds (1 P = 0.45 kg.) (Brown: 2001). So the average yield was 1620 kg. per acre.

Though Manipur excelled in agriculture, its manufacturing base was very weak. Weaving was the most important industry. The cloths produced were of excellent quality and extraordinarily cheap (Allen 2002). Other manufactures were subsistence in nature and comprised of leather, cooking pots, pottery, jewellery, iron and steel, carpentry, turning, dyeing and silk. Salt was another important produce of the state. It was of very good quality and free from smell. It was manufactured from the well blessed salt wells in the state (Brown: 2001).

The state was not very open to trade. Trade was of scanty nature. Major trade was carried on with Cachar and the principal items of exports were cloths, yarns, buffaloes, ponies and Burma ditto. In return betel nut and pan, cloth, yarns, brass and other metals and *hukas* were taken. But it enjoyed a positive trade balance with Cachar. In 1868-69 the total exports from Manipur to Cachar was Rs. 3533 and total imports from Cachar was Rs. 1975, a positive balance of Rs. 1558 (Brown 2001).

Native Rule

The establishment of native rule after the Anglo-Manipuri War of 1891 brought drastic changes in the socio-economic and political structure of the state. The Raja became only a nominal head and the central pivot of the overall administration of the state was vested in the hands of the Political Agent (Singh 1989). The worst affected by the new rule was the traditional economy. The old system of *lallup* which exacted great public works was abolished and in place, a house tax of Rs. 2 per house in the valley and Rs. 3 in the hills was introduced. A new system of *Patta* was also introduced, according to which, any person having a claim on any land after 1892 was to obtain a patta from the government and the patta holder was given an inheritable and transferable rights of the land he held. In lieu of the kind tax, a land tax of Rs. 5 per pari was imposed on the patta holders. This deprived the traditional rights of the King over the land (Singh: 1998). But the landed properties exclusively belonging to His Highness and his near relatives had never been affected by any sort of levy, etc. (Singh 1989). Taking advantage of the new land system, the nobles and tenants of the King began to apply for independent lands on a mass scale.

The new government issued pattas for as many as 14,000 paris in 1892-93 only and in the next year 24,887 paris were issued. This process led to the concentration of land in the hands of a few like the rural rich, members of the Durbar, salaried bureaucrats and other employees of the government. Though the Durbar passed a resolution in 1924 prohibiting any person from acquiring more than 10 paris of land, there is little doubt that it had any effect. On the other hand, the condition of the farmers began to deteriorate. They found it more and more difficult to pay their land tax. Besides, in 1913 the local authorities increased the land tax to Rs. 5.15 per pari in lieu of the abolition of *Pothang* and in1914 many of the customary feudal services were replaced by cash payment. The farmers, thus, began to borrow money from local money lenders at a very high interest rate. If they were unable to pay land revenue, they resorted to surrendering their lands or otherwise the defaulted lands were forcibly put to auction by the revenue officials (Singh 1998).

Another significant change after 1891 was that Manipur was opened to free trade policy of the British. There was not only change in export basket but the period also witnessed the emergence of a new dominant business class, the Marwaris, who entered under the protection of the colonial authority. They controlled both the external as well as the internal trade. The opening of cart route to Dimapur via Mao Thana in 1896 further added impulse to the ongoing trade (Allen 2002).

Table1
Exports from Manipur to the Surma and Assam Valley

Name of Articles	*Average value of Exports during the three years ending 1903-04, via*	
	Jirighat (Rs.)	*Mao thana(Rs.)*
Cattle	27022	2610
Timber	85577	-
Rice husked	731	93998
Total Export	154947	113949

Source: Allen: 2002

The above table shows the exports from Manipur to the Surma and Assam Valley during the three years ending 1903-

04. As it is seen from the table, during this period of British control the state was used as a source of rice, cattle and timber. Rice was the main item of export, its value averaging at Rs. 94729 in three years, i.e., 35.23 percent of the total exports. Timber and cattle were the other two main items, with their values averaging at Rs. 85577 (31.83 percent) and Rs. 29632 (11.02 percent) respectively in three years. Gradually rice became an important item of export from Manipur during the 1930s.

Table 2
Rice Exports during 1900-1939

Year	*Quantities of Rice Exported*
1900-01	Rs. 69866 worth of rice
1905-06	Rs. 127330 worth of rice
1911-12	108086 mds.
1922-23	80000 mds.
1926-27	40000 mds.
1930-31	151725 mds.
1934-36	254619 mds.
1938-39	372174 mds.

Source: Singh: 1998

It can be observed from the above table that rice formed the main item of export since 1930 onwards. Its quantity increased from 151725 mds. in 1930-31 to 25,4,619 mds. and 37,2,174 mds. in 1934-36 and 1938-39 respectively.

Table 3
Imports to Manipur from the Surma and Assam Valley

Name of Articles	*Average value of Imports during the three years ending 1903-04, via*	
	Jirighat (Rs.)	*Mao thana(Rs.)*
Cotton twist, yarn and piece goods	9687	54161
Dry fish	19636	211
Salt	1418	19353
Betel nuts	57532	2850
Total Import	103901	138737

Source: Allen: 2002

While the state was used as a source for rice, it served as a market for the manufactured goods produced outside. Among the main items of import, cotton twist, yarn and piece goods contributed the highest share, its value averaging at Rs. 63,848 for three years, i.e., 26.31 percent of the total imports. Betel nuts and salt are the two other major items of export with their value averaging at Rs. 60,382 (24.89 percent) and Rs. 20,771 (8.56 percent) respectively.

The policy of exploiting the natural resources and flooding the market with cheap machine made goods is one of the economic policies of colonialism. The same has happened in case of Manipur. The above table clearly shows that rice, which was the mainstay of the economy of the state, was exported heavily. Initially the impact of such exploitation was not very serious. But the outburst came in 1939 (*Nupi Lan*) when the price shot up above average due to failure of crops because of flood. Other worst affected sectors during the British control were the salt industry and the traditional handloom industries which could not compete with cheap machine products imported from outside the state.

Independence was in no way a better solution to the deteriorating economic conditions of the state. While trying to recover from the shocks of the colonial exploitation and the Second World War, the merger of the state with the Indian Union in 1949 further worsened the scenario. This period of the time was marked by high growth rate of population and the undue importance given to infrastructure in the subsequent five year plans instead of agriculture and industry has left the state far behind her counterparts.

Table 4
Growth Rate of Population in Manipur

Year	*Total population growth rate (%)*	*% of urban population to total population*	*% of rural population to total population*
1951*	12.80	0.50	99.50
1961	35.04	8.68	91.32
1971	37.53	13.19	86.81
1981	32.46	26.42	73.58
1991	29.29	27.52	72.48
2001	30.02	23.88	76.12

Source: Statistical Abstract Manipur 2004
* *Note*: In 1951 Census, an area of only 2 sq. miles, covering Imphal bazar, the office and residential positions looked after by the then Imphal Town Fund was considered as Imphal Town but in other census years the area of Imphal Municipality was taken as Imphal Town.

There was a continuous growth of population in Manipur. Its growth rate increased from 12.80 percent in 1951 to 35.04 percent and 37.53 percent in 1961 and 1971 respectively. It however declined to 32. 46 percent and 29.29 percent in 1981 and 1991 respectively but in 2001 it slightly increased to 30.02 percent. Another feature of the population in the state is marked by a high percentage of rural population. Though it declined from 91.32 percent in1961 to 86.81 percent and 73.58 percent in 1971 and 1981 respectively, it increased to 76.12 percent in 2001 from 72.48 percent in1991. The concentration of our population in rural areas is also reflected in the occupational pattern.

Table 5

Occupational Distribution of Main Workers in Manipur (% share)

Classification of workers	*1961*	*1971*	*1981*	*1991*	*2001*
Cultivator	65.43	67.00	63.60	61.77	43.35
Agricultural labour	0.61	3.65	4.99	6.69	6.34
Secondary	23.05	12.23	13.35	9.66	6.55
Tertiary	10.69	16.47	17.05	20.33	43.76

Source: Statistical Abstract Manipur, 2004

The occupational distribution of main workers in Manipur shows that more than 60 percent of our working population is engaged in primary activities. But the share is declining over the years. The percentage share of cultivator which was 65.43 percent in1961 increased to 67 percent in 1971 but declined to 63.60 percent and 61.77 percent in 1981 and 1991 respectively and further to 43.35 percent in 2001. But in case of agricultural labour, the share has increased from 0.61 percent in 1961 to 3.65 percent and 4.99 percent in 1971 and 1981 respectively. It further increased to 6.69 percent in 1991 but slightly declined to 6.34 percent in 2001. The increase in the share of agricultural labour is an indication of increasing landless labour. But there is a shift of the working population from primary activities to other sectors.

This may be because of the non-sustainability and subsistence nature of the agricultural sector in the present scenario.

The similar trend is also found in case of secondary sector. The share of main workers declined from 23.05 percent in 1961 to 12.23 percent in 1971. It slightly increased to 13.35 percent in 1981 but declined to 9.66 percent and 6.55 percent in 1991 and 2001 respectively.

There a shift of the working population from the two sectors to tertiary sector. The share of main workers has increased from 10.69 percent in 1961 to 16.47 percent and 17.05 percent in 1971 and 1981 respectively. It further increased to 20.33 percent and 43.76 percent in 1991 and 2001 respectively. The occupational distributions of the main workers show that the economy is moving towards tertiarisation. This phenomenon can be observed from sectoral shares of the state domestic product.

Table 6
Share of Agriculture and other Sectors in NSDP in Manipur (% share)

Year	*Agriculture*	*Secondary*	*Tertiary*
1961	52.82	10.28	34.04
1970	55.68	8.86	33.76
1980	46.24	18.16	32.80
1990	32.01	9.48	52.25
2000	25.90	20.12	48.75
2005	23.14	24.64	47.42

Source: EPW and CSO

The share of agriculture is declining over the years. Its share has been declining from 55.68 percent in 1970 to 46.24 percent and 32.01 percent in 1980 and 1990 respectively and further to 25.90 percent and 23.14 percent in 2000 and 2005 respectively.

The share of secondary sector kept on fluctuating up to 1990s. Its share declined from 10.28 percent in 1961 to 8.86 percent in 1970. It increased to 18.16 percent in 1980 but declined very sharply to 9.48 percent in 1990. From 1990 onwards it has increased to 20.12 percent and 23.14 percent in 2000 and 2005 respectively.

In case of tertiary sector, its share has increased over the years with slight fluctuations. Initially its share declined from 34.04 percent in1961 to 33.76 percent and 32.80 percent in 1970 and 1980 respectively. Since then its share has increased to 52.25 percent in 1990. Again the share fell to 48.75 percent and 47.42 percent in 2000 and 2005 respectively.

The declining share of agriculture and increasing share of secondary and tertiary sectors in the net state domestic product (NSDP) is a sign of economic development especially when tertiary sector growth is fueled by manufacture. But in case of Manipur, the economy is moving towards the tertiary sector and the secondary sectors, but the vital sector of manufacturing has stagnated around 8 percent through time.

Table 7

Secondary Sector and its components in NSDP in Manipur (% share)

Year	*Manufacturing*				
	Regd	*Unregd*	*Total*	*Construction*	*Electricity, gas & water supply*
1961	-	-	8.34	1.68	0.25
1970	-	-	6.57	1.89	0.40
1980	0.48	6.24	6.72	11.67	-0.23
1990	0.08	5.68	5.76	7.91	-4.18
2000	0.06	8.20	8.26	11.54	0.31
2005	0.21	8.67	8.88	15.71	0.05

Source: Calculated from EPW and CSO

The above table showing the secondary sector and its components gives a very grim picture. The rise in the share of secondary sector in the total NSDP is the result of construction. The share of construction has increased from a mere 1.89 percent in 1970 to 11.67 percent in 1980. The share, however, declined to 7.91 percent in 1990 but showed a healthy picture in subsequent years sharing 11.54 percent and 15.71 percent in 2000 and 2005 respectively. The share of manufacturing is very low, with its share revolving around 8 percent throughout the years. Major share of manufacturing comes from unregistered manufacturing units, whereas the share of registered units is almost negligible. The share of registered manufacturing units is less than 1 percent over the years. Similar trend is also observed in case of electricity, gas and water supply contributing less than 1 percent over the years. Thus we can see that growth in secondary sector is brought about by construction rather than manufacture. This shows the backwardness of industrial sector in the state.

Table 8
Tertiary Sector and its components in NSDP in Manipur (% share)

Year	*Transport, storage & communication*	*Trade, hotels & restaurants*	*Banking & insurance*	*Public administration*
1961	1.60	14.57	0.93	3.37
1970	1.64	12.05	0.95	5.53
1980	3.02	5.81	1.33	7.65
1990	4.73	4.01	2.31	12.40
2000	3.46	11.22	1.72	15.77
2005	4.97	9.23	2.58	14.21

Source: Calculated from EPW and CSO

Coming to the tertiary sector, major contribution is coming from public administration. Its share has increased from 3.37 percent in 1961 to 5.53 percent and 7.65 percent in 1970 and 1980 respectively. It further increased from 12.40 percent in 1990 to 15.77 percent and 14.21 percent in 2000 and 2005. The share of other components is very low specially banking and insurance contributing only 1.72 percent and 2.58 percent in 2000 and 2005 respectively. The share of transport, storage and communication is only 3.46 percent and 4.97 percent in 2000 and 2005 respectively. The share of hotels and restaurants is 11.22 percent and 9.23 percent in 2000 and 2005 respectively. The analysis of the tertiary sector shows that growth in this sector is brought about by public administration. In short we can say that it is the government job generated growth rather than through infrastructure and banking services.

The economy of Manipur, as seen from the above analysis gives a very grim picture. The decline in the share of agriculture in total NSDP, though a healthy sign of development is not accompanied by a corresponding decline in the share of workforce in this sector. A major share of the population is still engaged in primary activities.

Moreover, growth in secondary and tertiary sectors is the result of construction and government jobs. This is in one way the result of how grants-in-aid from the centre have been utilized in the state.

Table 9

Grants-in-aid from the Centre as % of total revenue of Manipur

Year	*Grants-in-aid (% share)*
1981	63.67
1985	87.00
1990	65.41
1995	56.89
2000	56.03
2001	75.66
2002	81.15
2003	76.67
2004	77.19
2005	71.79

Source: Statistical Handbook of Manipur 2002 & Statistical Abstract Manipur 2004

The table shows that more than 70 percent of the total revenue of the state is coming from the centre. The rest is from tax, non-tax and share from central taxes. This shows that only a meager amount is generated within the state and it is wholly dependent on centre for its smooth functioning.

The high levels of dependence on the outside funds virtually retard economic growth if it does not create any spread effects. No doubt outside funding is required for economic growth, but these funds should be utilized in such a way that they act as agents for growth within the state. But in case of Manipur these funds have been used mainly to sustain the economy. Faster growth is not generated within the state and the result is the decline in the rate of growth of NSDP and Per Capita Income.

Table 10
Decennial Compound Growth Rate of NSDP and Per Capita Income in Manipur

Year	*NSDP*	*Per capita*
1961-70	7.37	4.16
1971-80	6.84	3.81
1981-90	4.80	2.14
1991-00	4.68	2.36
2001-05	5.44	3.31

Source: Calculated from EPW and CSO

The decennial compound growth of NSDP is declining over the years. It has declined from 7.37 percent in 1961-70 to 6.84 percent and 4.80 percent in 1971-80 and 1981-90 respectively. It further declined to 4.68 percent in 1991-2000 but slightly improved to 5.44 percent in 2001-05.

Similar trend is also found in case of Per Capita Income. The decennial compound growth rate of per capita income declined from 4.16 percent in 1961-70 to 3.81 percent and 2.14 percent in 1971-80 and 1981-90 respectively. But it has improved to 2.36 percent and 3.31 percent in 1991-2000 and 2001-05 respectively.

Conclusion

The economy of Manipur is in fact stagnant. There is virtually little growth in the productive sectors of agriculture and manufacture. The decline in the share of agriculture is not covered by other sectors. The increasing share of secondary and tertiary sectors to total NSDP is not contributing to the real growth of the productive base of the economy. As seen from above, major share of growth is coming from construction and government jobs. These are actually not directly productive and in many ways retard economic growth through the negative effects of a distorted rent seeking political economy. The national phenomenon is that major share of domestic product is coming from manufacture, trade, hotels, restaurants, banking and insurance, etc., even if there is a decline in the share of agriculture. Moreover, the lopsided importance given to transport and communication and social services in the Five Year Plans of Manipur, contrary to the importance given to agriculture and industry in national plans, had also resulted in moving agriculture towards the path of stagnation (Singh 2005).

Manipur, being a land-locked state, has a very narrow scope for industrialization. Coupled with poor infrastructure is the non-availability of core natural resources which acts as a hindrance towards industrialization. The topography and geographical isolation resulting in high transport cost is also another constraint to development. Moreover, services like trade, hotels and restaurants and banking services are not fully developed so that it can create the spread effects. So land is the only resource at our disposal for development. We need to pay more attention towards this sector. There is a need to strengthen the weak resource-industry linkage. Agro-based industries should be set up. Any future planning should give high priority to these areas. The development of agricultural sector and setting up of agro-based industries along with the development of infrastructure and other social services will lead the state towards the path of development.

REFERENCES

Allen, B C (2002) (first published: 1905), *Gazetteer of Naga Hills and Manipur*, Mittal Publications, New Delhi.

Brown, R, (2001) (first published: 1874), *Statistical Account of Manipur*, Mittal Publications, New Delhi.

Central Statistical Organisation, http://mospi.nic.in

Datt, Ruddar and K.P.M. Sundharam, (1996), *Indian Economy*, S. Chand & Company Ltd., New Delhi.

Domestic Product of States of India 1960-61 to 2000-01, EPW Research Foundation, Mumbai, 2003.

Government of Manipur (2005), *Statistical Abstract of Manipur 2004*, Directorate of Economics and Statistics,

Government of Manipur (2005), *Statistical Handbook of Manipur 2002*, Directorate of Economics and Statistics,

McCulloh, M (1980), *Valley of Manipur*, Gian Publications, New Delhi

Singh, Ch Priyoranjan (2005), 'Manipur Economy: Historical Roots and Structural Evolution', *Eastern Quarterly*, Volume 3, Issue III, October-December.

Singh, K Manimohan (1989), *Hijam Irabot and Political Movements in Manipur*, B R Publishing Corporation, New Delhi.

Singh, N Lokendra (1998), *The Unquiet Valley*, Mittal Publications, New Delhi.

Singh, R K Jhalajit (1992), *A Short History of Manipur*, R K Jhalajit Singh, Imphal.

SECTION III

TRIBAL LAND SYSTEMS, IDENTITY AND CHANGE

13

LAND OWNERSHIP SYSTEM OF THE NAGA COMMUNITY: Uniqueness in Tradition

—U A Shimray

Land has been the inherent economic guardian of the traditional society like the Nagas and is the main source of their livelihood systems. Naga social and cultural system and identity are closely linked with the land. Every Naga village is self sufficient with their respective village land and territories. Traditionally, the village chief is the nominal owner of village land and forest. Village land and its natural resources are accessible to the whole village community and are regulated by traditional customary laws where no individual has exclusive property right over the community land. In other words, land is community owned and includes land owned by the clans and land owned by individuals/ households. Transferring of landed properties is based on the customary law. Therefore, any threat to land and forest is not merely an economic issue but also an attack on their identity.

The focus of this paper is to understand the land ownership system with respect to the customary practices of the Naga community with reference to the *Tangkhul Nagas*. The paper also, examines the changes in ownership system, process of land alienation and state's policy towards land. The Manipur Land Revenue and Land Reforms Act, 1960 (MLR&LR Act) covers the state of Manipur except the hill areas. Hitherto, the MLR&LR Act has been amended several times and the recent Amendment Bill intends to remove the word 'except hill areas thereof'. This means that the extension of the Act, shall also apply in the hill areas of Manipur where land ownership system is based on the respective tradition of the hill communities.

Manipur Peopling

Manipur, also known as the *land of jewel*, is a tiny state situated in the eastern most part of the North-eastern region of India. The state is bounded on the north by Nagaland, on the east by the *Somrah* ranges and Upper Chindwin river of Myanmar, on the south by Chin Hill (Myanmar) and Mizoram state and on the west by the Cachar Hills district of Assam. Manipur state shares the longest frontier with Myanmar (Burma). Geographically, Manipur state is landlocked, having two distinct topographic entities; the central plain or Imphal valley and the hill ranges that surrounds the valley. The almost bottle-shaped state has an area of 22,327 sq.km.

Manipur state is a home for several ethnic groups. Each and every ethnic community possesses diverse social and cultural systems and linguistics. Interestingly, ethnic division coincides with the topographical divides, that is, hills and valley (Chattopadhyay 2006: 108). The valley is traditionally inhabited by the *Meetei* community and the migrant *Pangan* (Muslim) and they are recognised as non-tribal. Hill communities (tribals) belong to the *Naga* group and the *Kuki-Chin-Zomi* group. Government of India (1991) recognised 29 (twenty nine) ethnic groups as "Scheduled Tribes."

The hill areas constitute the major part of the state's geographical area with 90 per cent of land surrounding the narrow central plains known as the *Imphal* valley. Population density in the valley area is considerably high with 630 persons per square kilo meter, whereas,in the hill area it is only 37 persons per square kilometre. Administratively, there are nine districts. The hill-based districts are (1) Senapati, (2) Churachandpur, (3) Chandel, (4) Ukhrul, and (5) Tamenglong. While the valley areas consist of four districts- (1) Thoubal, (2) Bishnupur, (3) Imphal East and (4) Imphal West. The division of the state into Hills and Valley has geographical, ethnic and political significance.

Manipur state presents a remarkable social, cultural and linguistic diversity. Out of the state's total population (2001 Census), the non-tribal communities constitute the largest share of population accounting for 65.8 per cent. Among the tribal communities, the highest proportion is recorded among the Nagas with 18.7 per cent, followed by Kuki-Thadou (6.64 per cent) and Zomis (5.08 per cent). Demographically, the non-tribal Meetei community is the largest ethnic group in the state (based on 1991 population census).

According to 2001 population census, the state recorded a total population of 21, 66,788 persons with a decadal growth rate of 17.94 per cent during 1991-2001. The decadal growth rate has been declined in the last population census. Among the districts, Tamenglong, Senapati and Ukhrul, found considerable decline in decadal growth rate but in other districts, the rate of decline is marginal. Overall, the decadal growth rate is found considerably higher in the hill districts than the valley districts (see Table 1). The negative decadal growth rate (-24.89 percent) in Senapati and the unusual positive rate (66.62 percent) in Chandel is mainly explained by the Kuki-Naga ethnic clashes and the consequent demographic displacements.

Highest tribal population is recorded in Ukhrul district with 95.53 per cent followed by Tamenglong (95.38 per cent), Churachandpur (93.23 per cent), Chandel (91.93 per cent) and Senapati (78.45). In the valley areas, very low tribal population is recorded with only 3.98 per cent.

Table 1
Manipur Total Population and Growth Rate

State/District	*Total Population*			*Decadal Growth Rate*		*Proportion of Tribal to Total Population*	
	1981	1991	2001	1981-1991	1991-2001	1991	2001
Manipur	**14,20,953**	**18,37,149**	**21,66,788@**	**29.29**	**17.94**	**34.41**	**34.2@**
Hill Districts	***4,91,876***	***6,51,157***	***7,55,022***	***32.38***	***15.95***	***89.97***	***90.71***
Senapati	1,55,421	2,08,406	1,56,513@	34.09	-24.89@	84.07	78.45@
Tamenglong	62,289	86,278	1,11,499	38.51	29.23	96.59	95.38
Churachandpur	1,34,776	1,76,184	2,27,905	30.72	29.25	93.49	93.23
Ukhrul	82,946	1,09,275	1,40,778	31.74	28.82	93.23	95.53
Chandel	56,444	71,014	1,18,327	25.81	66.62	85.52	91.93
Valley Districts	***9,29,077***	***11,85,992***	***14,11,766***	***27.65***	***19.03***	***3.90***	***3.98***
Thoubal	2,31,781	2,93,958	3,64,140	26.83	23.87	-	-

(Contd...)

State/District	Total Population			Decadal Rate	Growth	Proportion of Tribal to Total Population	
	1981	1991	2001	1981-1991	1991-2001	1991	2001
Bishnupur	1,41,150	1,80,773	2,08,368	28.07	15.26	-	-
Imphal	5,56,146	7,11,261	839258*	27.89	17.99	-	-
Imphal West#	-	-	4,44,382	-	-	-	-
Imphal East#	-	-	3,94,876	-	-	-	-

Notes: *Including the district of Imphal West and Imphal East
#District created in 2001 Census.

@ Excluding **Mao-Maram, Paomata** and **Purul** sub-divisions [The data of this Sub-division was cancelled by the Registrar General and Census Commissioner reasoning as technical problem].

Source: Office of the Registrar General and Census Commissioner. 1981 & 1991. *Series-14 Manipur, Final Population Total.* New Delhi.

Office of the Registrar General and Census Commissioner. 2001. *Final Population Totals*, Series 1 India, Paper-1 of 2001. New Delhi.

Population Density

Population density is one important parameter in understanding land-man ratio of any region. The spatial distribution of population is not uniform and there is wide regional variation in population concentration. In Manipur the distribution of population is rather based on ethnicity (tribal and non-tribal) or hills and valley. According to the 2001 population census, the population density in Manipur is 97 persons per square kilometer. The data indicates that there are drastic differences in land-population ratio in hill based districts and valley based districts. The hill districts have very low population density recording 37 persons per square kilometers in 2001. On other hand, valley based districts indicates high population density of 630 persons per square kilometer. The decade 1991-2001 shows, increases in population density in both the regions however, the increase is more prominent in valley areas (see table 2). The table shows that the valley region is experiencing immense population pressure on land.

Table 2
Population Density

State/ District	*Area [in Sq. km]*	*Percentage share of State's total area*	*Density of Population perSq. Km*		*Change in Population Density*
			1991	*2001*	*1991-2001*
1	*2*	*3*	*4*	*5*	*6*
Manipur	**22,327**	**100.00**	**82**	**97**	**[+]15**
Hill Districts	*20,089*	*89.97*	*32*	*37*	*[+]5*
Senapati	3,271	14.65	63	47	[-]16
Tamenglong	4,391	19.66	18	34	[+]16
Churachanpur	4,570	20.46	38	49	[+]11

(Contd...)

1	*2*	*3*	*4*	*5*	*6*
Chandel	3,313	14.83	21	35	[+]14
Ukhrul	4,544	20.35	24	30	[+]6
Valley Districts	*2,238*	*10.02*	***523***	***630***	[+]***107***
Thoubal	514	2.30	**572**	**708**	[+]**136**
Bishnupur	496	2.22	**219**	**420**	[+]**201**
Imphal	1,228	5.50	**579**	**683**	[+]**104**

Source: Office of the Registrar General and Census Commissioner. *General Population Tables, 1991, Series-15, Part II A, Manipur*. New Delhi: Office of the Registrar General.

The Nagas: Village and Land

The Naga community is one of the largest ethnic groups in the North Eastern region. Nagas consists of several sub-ethnic groups. Each community possesses distinct language and well-demarcated ethnic territory. Within this broad rubric of Nagas ethnicity, they share a common historical root, socio-cultural and economic systems and political aspirations. In Manipur there are fifteen Naga groups and they traditionally inhabit the four hill districts: Senapati, Ukhrul, Tamenglong and Chandel. According to the 1991 population census, the recognised Naga ethnic groups ("Scheduled Tribes") in Manipur are: *Anal, Chiru. Chothe, Kabui, Kacha Nagas, Koireng, Koirao, Lamkang, Mao, Maram, Maring, Monsang, Moyon, Sema,* and *Tangkhul* (The Naga groups like *Thangal, Poumei, Liangmei, Tharao* are yet to be listed as Scheduled Tribes separately).

Village is the smallest unit of settlement having a definite territory by tangible social, cultural, political and economic bonds. Sachchidanand (1968: vii) opines: "In most parts of India, the village is not merely an administrative or revenue unit, but the basic unit of our social polity. It is enshrined in the tradition from time immemorial. The village community is a historical as well as a social fact. The inhabitants of the village have intimate social, economic, ritual and political relationship which is regulated by age old traditions and institutions." The importance of village as a subject matter of human study was realised very late and of the tribal village still much later (Vidyarthi and Binay 1976). Tribal villages differ from the non-tribal villages both in composition and characteristics. Major factors for the differences are ecological settings, culture, society, economy and institutions.

Traditionally, Nagas live in villages often situated on hill tops. Once they settle in a place, it becomes a permanent settlement and they rarely move out to a new place. Naga village is a well-defined demarcated unit having their own village land and territory. The unit structural village system is comprised of households of different clans. Villages are complementary components and interdependent in relationships, socially, economically and culturally. Moreover, the village system and its functions are a source of their tradition and culture. Naga villages function as compact and well-knit societies where the customs and discipline were observed. Shimray (1985: 43) wrote: "A Naga village state has (i) population (ii) territory and (iii) sovereignty as its components. Naga village is an independent unit and accordingly enjoys the right of sovereignty. Every village state pursues an independent foreign policy and implements its own customary laws on all walks of life of its citizens. Each village state had its own defence system. Administration was indigenous and independent. Its economy was local and self-sufficient. In the village, customary laws were to be feared and respected. Naga customary laws were strictly enforced. Every Naga obeyed these laws for he himself was the maker of the laws." The village administration is taken care of by the village council. The village council is headed by the village chief or headman. The functions of the village authority are broadly executive, administrative and judiciary. Das (1985: 16) points out that: "The Naga village is something like a protective shell, where they can lead a life based on their own cultural values. A village to them is a breathing space that has to be nurtured at any cost."

The village is often irregular in settlement patterns and is well-defended. All the villages have their own demarcated boundaries viz., streams, rivers, ridges or stone. However, there are inevitable inter-village boundary disputes, which is common phenomenon even now.

Naga concept of land includes village land, territory, forest, economy and culture. At the same time, they are the objects which they possess and control that is inherited and immutable. Nagas have their own way of understanding land and its implications. Such implications manifest through their daily activities and livelihood. Moreover, land is the basic foundation of the Naga social, cultural and economic systems. Within the given village territory and its ecosystem the values, belief and cultural practices are regulated by the traditional social institutions. Morris and Marsh (1988: 27) state that: "Territoriality is such a deeply ingrained aspect of human life that we tend to assume that it is something we have acquired during our evolution."

Land and forest provides not only an important element in their livelihood systems but also security and a sense of belongingness. Naga historical root is also strongly linked with the land they live. The land is more than just a habitat or a political boundary; it is the basis of their identity. In functional aspects, Naga socio-cultural organisation play significant role in the ecological complex. For instance, Nagas' social and cultural practice manifests their close relationship with the local ecology. Worshipping nature is well presented in their traditional folk songs and folk dances.

The Naga villages are nearly independent system having self-sufficiency and pursue their economic activities within the given village land and territory. One villager cannot pursue economic activities in another village's territory except hunting and fishing. Land is intrinsically interfaced with the political, cultural and economic parameters. And these parameters sustain the Nagas' livelihood systems. As Gadgil and Guha (1995) called it, "ecosystem people" depend on the natural environments of their locality to meet most of their material needs.

Land and Ownership System: A Case of the Tangkhul Nagas

The *Tangkhul Nagas* is one of the Naga ethnic groups largely inhabiting in Ukhrul district of Manipur. Population Census of India, 1991 recorded total Tangkhul Naga population as 1,07,244 persons. Ukhrul district shares a greater frontier with Myanmar (Burma) and has a total area of 4,544 sq. km. The international boundary (Indo-Myanmar) cut the Tangkhul Nagas into two citizenship-Indian and Myanmarese. The larger number of Tangkhul Naga population dwells on the Indian side of the frontier. The Tangkhul Nagas who lives in Myanmar is known as *Somra* Tangkhul Nagas.

In Tangkhul Naga society, community land is one important economic asset. The community land consists of undivided land which belongs to the village community. Any bonafide household or member is free to use such land for any agricultural purposes temporarily. Ruivah (1987) pointed out that this might be owned by an individual household or by the lineage members in the name of the head of the lineage, temporarily. However, once the household stops operations, the plot automatically reverts back as community land. In community land every household has the right of use and occupation without paying any land revenue to the village council.

The village chief and council lay down certain provisions in using community land particularly size of the areas or plot which one can occupy. Hitherto, tradition sanctions certain rights to acquire ownership in community land, if the household or person has made permanent improvement on it by way of construction of permanent cultivation of crops or plants or converting into sedentary terraced paddy fields. As said, if a person makes permanent improvement for agricultural purposes then it is eventually recognised as individual/household property. Hodson (1911: 50) emphasis that: "By means of long and ardous labour, a terraced field may be built up and provided with water so that the large terrace represents the expenditure of a vast amount of energy and farming ability as well as much practical engineering skill."

Land and ownership system is followed according to the customary practices and is transmitted from generation to generation. In Tangkhul Naga society, only males can inherit the landed ancestral properties that are, homestead, terraced paddy fields and jhum areas and household owned woodland (or *Thingkham*). This is accentuated by the patriarchal system of the Tangkhul Nagas. If a man leaves no sons, the properties will go to the nearest relatives called *Shimlui-kat*. Customarily the immovable property especially agricultural land and homestead cannot be passed down to the daughter(s).

Such tradition of transferring properties has been sustaining since they first settled in the village site. At the same time, individual ownership is a kind of practice that would mean possession of land with rights to use it or dispose it in any manner according to the customary practices. "The term 'ownership' encompasses such questions as to who has the rights to use a particular plot of land, who exercises control and who has legal claims to certain portions of village land and forests" (Shimray 2007: 45). Broadly, we can categorise individual household owned land as *'ancestral land'* and *'acquired land.'* Ancestral land, as the name suggests, is passed down to the male line from generation to generation. Acquired land on the other hand, is land obtained by purchasing by an individual. In the process land can be re-classified as ancestral land when it is passed down to the children of the one who has acquired it

Land transfers or sale of land is possible only within the prescribed limits and also requires certain social and customary sanctions. No land is to be sold, mortgaged, leased, bartered and gifted or otherwise transferred to an outsider. Land selling or transfer follows the following procedure. At the first stage, selling or mortgage or barter of land is to be conducted among the nearest family members (nearest clan members). In case the immediate family members cannot purchase the land, a seller scouts among the members of other clans for prospective buyers. Selling of land to outsiders (non-members of the village) is not a simple task. An important stipulation of selling of land to outsiders is that the buyers have to become bonafide members of the village and must permanently settle down and absorb to one of the village clans.

In Tangkhul Naga society, patrilineal family system is dominated by virilocal marriage and patrilocal residence after marriage. When the eldest son of a family marries, the parents are obliged to leave their house along with the unmarried children. The same process is repeated on the marriage of another son and may be again and again if the couple has many sons.

Changes in Land Use System

Today, there has been an inevitable change in land ownership system, such changes largely affecting community land and village forest. The main factors responsible for the changes are the socio-economic transition, population pressure on land and also internal transformation in the village system. On the other hand, emergence of "elite households" and money economy in the village has played a vital role in the "change dynamics". Dutta (1986: 94) understood that: "The tribal society that is supposed to be traditionally egalitarian where community ownership is the rule, there is a large scale encroachment in the community land by a powerful section of the society."

In olden days, land was considered as the most important asset connoting "power" and "status." However, it has changed altogether with the coming of money economy. Such emergence eventually transforms land as commodity, which can be bought and sold. This newly wealth based on money economy, put pressure on land which eventually modifies the ownership system. Money economy had multiple roles as an agent of change. Land is available as commodity in which sale and purchase is possible that results in the best portion of the land being under the ownership of the rich households. As Luithui (1987: 58) understood that: "The introduction of currency value by the British had led to the alteration of the local standard of wealth, power and influence to some extent. The British introduced Western system of education which is assisted by the Christian missionaries to bring the Nagas in touch with modern civilization and use educated class as a link between the rulers and ruled".

Generally, land use system and tenure are not codified on a written basis but it is based on oral custom. The fact is, because of such a system it is made easy for house holds to target and extend land and claim as individual/household ownership, particularly in community land. Such a process eventually shrinks the community land in the long run. Even though there is a clear-cut demarcation between privately owned land and community land, in reality the village community lands are often usurped and turned into individual land. Nongbri (1987) also pointed out that if a particular plot of land is operated by one individual household in the village community land and it makes permanent improvement on it and continues to occupy it, that land in course of time is recognised as its individual/household property.

Land and Laws

During the colonial period, there was a dual administration system in Manipur state. The Hills were under direct administration of the British Crown, President Manipur State *Darbar* (PMSD) taken care by British's ICS officer. The British administration did not disturb the hill villages whose Headmen (Cheiftainship) were recognised and entrusted with village-level administration. The *Manipuri* (*Meitei*) *Maharaja* was the sole owner and controller of the valley area. "Before, the application of any laws in Manipur, the *Raja* of Manipur claimed absolute ownership of all lands within his territory in the valley from the earliest times and collected land revenue" (Guite 2000: 235). In the colonial period, the Chin Hill Regulation (CHR) was applied to the hill areas and a House Tax of Rs. 3.00 per year per household was imposed. Later it was renamed as Manipur State Hill Peoples Regulation (MSHPR), Act 1947. In the valley, the Assam Land and Revenue Regulation (AL&RR) 1886 was introduced in 1947 and subsequently the AL&RR was replaced by the Manipur Land Revenue and Land Reforms Act, 1960 (MLR&LR Act). The Act extends to the whole of Manipur state "except the hill areas thereof." As stated, MLR&LR Act has been amended several times and the recent Amendment Bill intends to remove the word "except hill areas thereof," which means that the act, will become the statutory authority on land, in the hill areas of Manipur.

In 1956 the Parliament passed the Manipur Village Authorities (MVA) Act, for the village administration (which was implemented in 1957). The Act determines the number of members of a village authority on the basis of the number of tax-paying houses. Prior to upgradation of Manipur into a full-fledged state, the Manipur [Hill Areas] District Councils Act, 1971 was introduced to administer the hill areas.[13] Devi [2000: 182] contends that: "The autonomy granted to the district councils under the Act is only in name."

Here, the way in which the state attempts to expand its control and influence in the tribal areas of Manipur is apparent in the attempt to include hill areas under MLR&LR Act. In the latest amendment, the Bill has proposed that the sub-section (2) of section 1 where the words "except the hill areas thereof" and the provision thereto shall be omitted. Section 2 states that- "It extends to the whole of the State of Manipur 'except the hill areas thereof', provided that the State Government may by notification in the Official Gazette, extend the whole or any part of any section of this act to any of the hill areas of Manipur also as may be specified in such notification."

The MLR&LR (Amendment) Bill, 2005 as introduced in the Manipur Legislative Assembly on 15-7-2005 and the statement made by two honorable MLAs Shri. I. Hemochandra Singh and Dr. Nimaichand Luwang on behalf of the House Committee wrote:

> This Act is not a uniform land law for the entire state and excludes the hill areas from its area of operation. Section 1(2) of the Principal Act while defining the extent of this Act excludes the hill area from its ambit. A provision has been added below Section 1[2] whereby a separate notification is required for extension of the MLR&LR Act in the hill districts of the State.

The statement further mentioned that:

> Manipur with a total area of 22,327 sq. km., comprises of 9 (nine) revenue districts out of which 5 (five) districts fall

in the hill areas. There is immense pressure on land in the valley areas comprising of the remaining 4 (four) districts causing tremendous pressure on land. The lack of a uniform land law has created and fermented social tension amongst the multi ethnic society of our state. It is also the popular desire of many sections of the people of the population in the state that there must be one uniform land law which is equitable. One must be allowed to settle everywhere in the state and there should not be any restriction for settlement in the hill areas for every citizen of Manipur.

Jusho (2004) emphasises that the tribal movements operating in Manipur further vitiated the atmosphere of peaceful co-existence among the people, particularly between the non-tribal and the tribals. The demand of the hill tribes for creation of a separate state sounds harmful as it would hurt the territorial boundary of Manipur. They are more apprehensive of the demand raised by some sections of tribal for introduction of Sixth Schedule of the Constitution in the hill districts of Manipur.

On the other hand, tribal communities are demanding for the extension of "Sixth Schedule" in all hill districts. However, the demand is not popularly supported by a non-tribal community, who favour extending of MLR&LR Act in the hill areas.

Concluding Remarks

Land is the basic foundation of the Nagas' livelihood systems. The uniqueness of the land ownership system is its communitarian holding system which is immutable in tradition.[14] In other words, Land is communally owned with collective responsiblility. This community property is intrinsically guaranteed by traditions and customs. Transfer of landed property has to follow according to the tradition. Such given traditions and customs guaranteed that land *per se* is not only manifestation of identity but also unique culture of the Nagas. Yumnam (2002: 215) understood that in hill areas, every community has their own respective traditional and customary land usage and management system. Chieftainship and traditional village authorities still continue to exist with all its rights and privileges in the hill areas. Traditional self-governing institutions are those institutions which have served and have been serving the cause of the communities by ensuring continuation of life and property through a system of guiding principles, organizational structures and governing procedures.

The recent Sixth Amendment Bill of MLR&LR Act intending to extend the Act to the hill areas is seen as the state taking over ownership of resources from the community.[15] Ngaihte (2000: 253) rightly points out that: "The act seeks to end communal holding and replace it with individual holding or ownership." In fact such extension would rather threaten traditional land use, ownership, livelihood and identity of the tribals. In the process, the subsistence economies and livelihood would be destroyed. Politically the Bill is controversial in nature because it encroaches upon the traditional rights of the hill communities including traditional institution and management. Here, it needs to be understood that land is the fundamental organ of the tribal community in determining the political, economic, cultural systems and their identity itself. Therefore, introduction of any kind of Acts that related to land need to redress the social and cultural entities. Otherwise, social conflict, political uneasiness and turmoil would not cease in the future.

NOTES

I would like to thank SRTT [Sri Ratan Tata Trust] through Institute for Social and Economic Change [ISEC], Bangalore, for the financial support to participate and present the paper at the National Seminar on "Land, Identity and Development: Manipur Experience," November 16-17, 2007, Imphal, Manipur.

REFERENCES

Chambers, R. and G. Conway (1991), 'Sustainable Rural Livelihoods: Practical Concepts for the 21st Century,' *Institute of Development, Paper 296*, Brighton, UK.

Chattapadhyay, S. (2006) 'An Analytical Study of Fiscal Reforms in Manipur,' *Manpower*, Vol. XXXXI No. April-June.

Daimai, Kaikhamang (2000), 'Tribal Land Use System in Manipur (With reference to Liangmais),' Horam, M.,(ed.), *The Rising Manipur*,: Manas Publications, New Delhi.

Das, R. K. (1985), *Manipur Tribal Scene Studies in Society and Change*, Inter-India Publications, New Delhi.

Devi, Ksh. Bimola (2000), 'Administrative changes in the Hill Areas of Manipur,' Horam, M. (ed.), *The Rising Manipur*, Manas Publications, New Delhi.

Dutta, B.B. (1986), 'Tradition vs. Modernity: Problems of Forestry Planning in the Khasi Hills of Meghalaya,' D. Gupta, Malabika, A.K. Gangopadhyay, T. Bhattacharya and M. Chakraborty (eds.), *Forestry Development in North-East India*, Omsons Publications, New Delhi.

Gadgil, M. and R. Guha.(1995), *Ecology and Equity: The Use and Abuse of Nature in Contemporary India*, Routledge, London

Guite, K.C. (2000), 'MLR & LR Act, 1960 and Sixth Schedule in Relation to Hill Area,' M. Horam, (ed.). *The Rising Manipur*, Manas Publications, New Delhi.

Horam, M.(2000), *The Rising Manipur*, Manas Publications, New Delhi.

Hodson, T. C. (1911), *The Nagas Tribes of Manipur*, Low Price Publications, New Delhi.

Hutton, J. H. (1921), *The Angami Nagas: With Some Notes on Neighbouring Tribes*.: Macmillan, London.

Jusho, Hitson (2004), '*Politics of Ethnicity in North East India*', Regency Publications, New Delhi.

Luithui, S. (1987), *Land and Power Structure Among the Nagas*, Unpublished Dissertation, CPS, JNU, Delhi.

Morris, D. and P. Marsh. (1988), *Tribes*, Pyramid, London.

Ngajokpa, F. (2000), 'Land Use System of the Marams,' M. Horam (ed.), *The Rising Manipur*, Manas Publications, New Delhi.

Ngaihte, L. Chinzakham. (2000), 'Land Use and Ownership System: Churachandpur District,' Horam, M., *The Rising Manipur*, Manas Publications, New Delhi.

Nongbri, T. (1987), 'The Khasi Land Tenure System: Need for Conceptual Refinement,' B.B. Dutta and M.N. Karna (eds.), *Land Relations in North-East India,*: People's Publishing House, New Delhi, pp. 71-81.

Ruivah, K. (1987), 'Land ownership and its problems among the *Tangkhul Nagas*,' B.B. Dutta and M.N. Karna (eds.), *Land Relations in North-East India.* People's Publishing House, New Delhi, pp. 54-64.

Sachchidanand (1968), *The tribal Village in Bihar*, Munshiram Manoharlal, Delhi.

Shimray, R.R. (1985), '*Origin and Culture of the Nagas*, Pamleiphy Shimray, Delhi.

Shimray, U. A. (2007), *Naga population and Integration Movement: Documentation*, Mittal Publications New Delhi

Vidyarthi, L., P. and K.R. Binay. (1976), *The Tribal Culture of India*, Concept Publishing Company, Delhi.

Yumnam, Amar (2002), 'Traditional Self-Governing Institutions of the Hill Tribes of Manipur: An Economist's View', Goswami. (ed.), *Traditional Self-Governing Institutions Among the Hill Tribes of North- East India,* Akansha Publishing House. New Delhi.

14

Land Use and Ownership Pattern Among the Khoibus

—H. Phomrong & Donyaishei Hongsha

The Khoibus are an indigenous group of tribal people inhabiting mostly at Machi Block, 42, Tengnoupal constituency, Chandel district, Manipur state, North eastern corner of India bordering Myanmar. Our forefathers called themselves as '*Uibo*'. We are also called '*Uipowaa*' by the Marings, with whom the tribe lives together in close proximity. The neighboring Tangkhul villagers call us as '*Apo*'. We were also called '*Upong*' by the people of Chindwin basin civilization. The term 'Khoipu' derived from 'Khoi' which means bee and 'Pu' owner. Therefore, Khoipu means the people who own bees. Historically the Khoibu people had good relationship with the Meitei Kings and the neighbouring communities and often exchanged honey as gift with them. It is in this connection that the term Khoibu is believed to have been coined by the Meitei Kings.

The principal village of the Khoibu community is called Khoibu Khullen which is the oldest and the first Khoibu settlement in this particular region. It is located in the Heirok

Hill range in the eastern hills of Manipur with a latitude of 23.68° N, and the longitude of 93.03° E – 94.78°E. Sangsak road, an all season road running in the hills between Ukhrul and Tengnoupal subdivision of Chandel district in the south, links the village. There is also an approach road leading to the principal Khoibu Khullen village which is about 2 km from the link road. It is a distance of 116 km from Imphal via Tengnoupal on the NH – 39, leading to the international border town, Moreh. The distance between Tengnoupal and Khoibu Khullen is about 41 km from NH – 39.

The area of indigenous land possessed by the Khoibu Khullen is about 300 sq.kms out of the total state geographical area which is 22,327 sq.kms. The State of Manipur comprises of two parts: the first part is the central oval valley measuring 8% of the total area. The second part is the hilly region which covers 92% of the total land of the state. This land stands at an altitude varying between 762 metres (1500ft) to nearly 3048 metres (10,000ft) above the sea level. This land is a part of Assam - Burma tertiary ranges, which sweeps in a long curve from the north-eastern corner of Assam to cape Negrais in Myanmar. The central plain of Manipur lies in the latitude of about 792.4 metres (2600ft) high (Ansari, 1973.13).

The Khoibus originally had hereditary type of Chiefship. The original royal clan of the Khoibu is *Charang*. The oldest known living village is Khoibu Khullen, meaning principal Khoibu village, referred to above as Khoibu Yon. The village is still in existence now. The original hereditary chiefship is still continuing in this village and is still held by the *Charang* clan. Other villages established and hived off from the parent Khoibu Khullen village do not necessarily reserve the office of the Chiefship to *Charang* clan. A person belonging to any clan heading the party in establishing such a new village became the chief of the village. Chiefship of a village among the Khoibu is assumed to be hereditary, but the hereditary nature of village chiefship is not rigid except the chiefship of Khoibu Khullen held by the original *Charang* clan. The chiefship in the new villages can be hereditary and the office of the chiefship may continue and then pass on to his eldest son if the chief is good and if he has a suitable son to inherit it. But the office of this type of chiefship can be terminated by the village people if he is detrimental to the village. However, the chiefship in the parental Khoibu Khullen village cannot be terminated by the villagers and it is the original chiefship inherited from father to son. It is purely hereditary. Respect is shown to *Charang* as the royal clan of Khoibu.

Khoibu Land and Land System

The indigenous land of the Khoibu community lies in the transborders of Myanmar and Manipur state, particularly between Ukhrul and Chandel district of Manipur.

Mr. Duncan, the then Commissioner of Ukhrul had clearly demarcated the Khoibu Khullen territory in the state of Manipur in 1936-37. According to Duncan's sketch map (plates: Khoibu territory) *Yawn ei uiyok*(name of Forest), the village land boundary consist of *Meibungching* (a hill range) in the north east, *Hanggoilok*(name of a stream) and *Teret Lok*(river flowing towards Myanmar in the east) in the northwest, *Emdiching* (name of a hill range) *Molgat*(name of another stream) in the southwest and southeast form the border of the vast area of Khoibu territory.

Since time immemorial the Khoibus have their own systems of land holding in consonance with the other Naga Communities. The village land holding system among the Naga communities can be classified into three categories:

i) Individual holding of land

ii) Clan land

iii) Community land.

The above system of holding of land is like rings circling one after another. The innermost represents the individuals holding, the second or the middle ring, its area represents the clan's land and the outermost represents the community land.

i) **Individual Holding**: Each and every family in the village has its own plot sufficient enough for the construction of house and gardening etc. An individual also owns a terrace cultivation field; this may be in any place. This kind of holding entitles the individual to have full rights over it either to sell or to hold.

ii) **Clan Land:** The second or the middle ring of the circle is owned by the clan. Here an individual cannot exercise full rights over land. One needs to take permission from the concerned clan if any person wants to use it for any purpose. This portion of land is mainly utilized for gardening and fire wood collection.

iii) **Community Land:** The third circle, representing the outer most portion of the land is commonly owned by the community. This land is mainly used for Jhum/ shifting cultivation; the community decides when and where to cultivate. Here all the community has equal shares and equal rights to it.

The land holding system of the Mizo-Chin-Kuki group is slightly different from the land holding system of the Naga groups. The Mizo-Chin-Kuki groups practice chieftainship. In this kind of practice, the chief purchases the land by himself and manages this under his authority, and the revenue thus collected annually also goes into his exchequer.

In the case of the Khoibus, there are three divisions of land patterns in concentric circles having common ownership.

(1) The central part is a reserved land under the control of the village headman(*Charang Amaa*) and the heads of each seven clan such as *Charang, Hongsha, Dangsha, Tongtang, Khaling, Saka* and *Ronglo*, since time immemorial. However, with the coming of modern village administrative system, the village authority has replaced the ancient practice with a new system. In the new system, the village's reserved forest is kept for the community, to protect the residential area from wild jungle fire. Nobody is allowed to cut any tree from this forest without the prior permission from the village authority. However, in the case of domestic needs the village authority can give restricted permit to cut the tree for the purpose of house construction and firewood.

(2) The second outer layer is a cultivable land called *Tuishakram* or *Kasoiram*, which is surrounded by rivers from three different sides. In the western side lie the rivers *Ranmong Khraa* and *Thamakoo Khraa* which flow towards the northern side and join the river *Minpui Khraa* which forms the boundaries on the north. In the eastern side flow the river *Yongdang Chathai Khraa*.

There are three parallel mountains in Khoibu ancestral land such as Bongchoupui, Mangthelbung and Kharambung. The mountain Mangthelbung lies in the centre of the second layer (Tuishakram) and both the mountains Bongchoupui and Kharambung lie in the third Layer (Wangkheiram). Bongchouppui lies in the western side and Kharambung lies in the eastern side of the Khoibu village. In this area many of the Khoibu families have their own Louning (Individual land holding of 2.5 hectares). Land was distributed to the households of the parental village in the ancient times. In the process of distribution, only the lineage heads (*pipas*) are entitled to own this share, thereby excluding other younger brothers in the family from that share. However, these younger brothers, although they are not entitled to land, may own the same if they are able to purchase land or get a grant from a willing brother. This practice is called *Louning* system. In this area they carry out jhum or Shifting cultivation. Some families can cultivate 1-2 *Lounings* in a year. The remaining *Lounings* are given to other families who do not have *Lounings*. In return, they pay some tins of Paddy as annual tax. There is enough land to cultivate for about 70-80 families with a rotation of 10-15 years of Jhum cycles. (In case, any one wishes to establish a new village within the jurisdiction or the purview of the so called Tuisakhram, 2nd Layer).

(3) If the forest is not fully grown, they shift to Wangkheiram (3rd layer) which is another stretch of land beyond Tuisakram. This Wangkheiram has two sides. One side is called Tlongtlaiwang and the other is known as Yonyerwang. This area which consists though of two sides and having a large area, is, the third layer which belongs to common villagers and it is a land opened for all individuals of the Khoibus. In the event of any village which wants to cultivate or use this type of land (Wangkheiram) taxes have to be paid to the parental Khoibu Khullen village in kinds (about 3 tins of Paddy). However, if this type of land is to be cultivated by the villagers of the old parental village, then, no tax is to be levied.

In this Wangkheiram (3rd Layer), if any clan or group wishes to establish a new village, they can do so with the permission of the *Amaa* and *Pipas*. For instance, the present existing villages like Yamloching, Biyang, Thalem and Khoibu Centre are in existence through this traditional system. The traditional system of the Khoibu allows any new village to be established and the area is opened for all. Due to the largeness in area of Wangkheiram, the households of the Khoibu are not able to use the area completely and therefore, people from other communities are also allowed to cultivate this land by paying the required taxes to the parental Khoibu village.

The headman and his members in the council, authorize the people of Yongerwang (North Block of the village) to collect the revenue of the northern side and Tlongtlaiwang (southern block of the village) to collect the revenue of the southern side. The total revenues thus collected annually are used in the form of festivals and their rituals which come off annually and triennially.

This outer layer covering almost 70-75 percent of the total land area is kept as community land. All the revenues in this community land are equally accessible by all the villagers on ritual payment and on proper information to the authority.

The territorial land of the Khoibu is a virgin land, rich in flora and fauna. There are a number of varieties of plants. Some of the plants commonly found in this forest are bamboos, bay leaf, amla, banana, cotton, papaya, maize, potato, rice(different varieties), soyabean, parkia, gourd, turbot (Benincasa hispida), cucumber, pumkin, arum, brinjal, bitter brinjal(solanacae family), cabbage, groundnut, chilli, yendem (calocasia giganta), sougri (hibiscusncannabinus), lady's finger, karol akhabi (momordica charantia), bottle gourd (luffa cylindrical), squash, banon (vigina sinensis), sweet potato, tomato, pea, troitree, (atisdesma diandrum) coriander, mireipak (cryngium foetitdium), singe (zanthoxylum alatum), theripok (citrus hystrix), keireem (houtluynia), onion , garlic, ginger, mint, mayangpaa (ocimum canum) etc.

Besides these vegetables, spices and fruit yielding plants, there are many species of wild and domesticated plants like lemon masherhie (citrus variety), mango, Jack fruit, pear, teitohei(spondias pinnata), Khongmahei(rhus semita), heikhaa(prunus domestica), kahei (juglans regia), chongnaihei (gareinia cowa), guava, sugarcane, pomegranate, waahei(squerers seneiserrata), grap, plum, theilangkoi (amoora rohituka) and various species of beans etc.

Above all, there are also many plants of economic, mashou (schima wallichii), tera (samalia malabarica) etc.

Medicinal Plants and Traditional Medicine

The story of evolution of medicine is a long story stretching from prehistoric times to modern times encompassing man through different ages and phases of evolution. Every community and culture has a developed system of medicinal cure since ancient times. The act of healing found among the Khoibu of Manipur began thousands of years ago.

The Khoibus try to provide relief to different kind of sicknesses and sufferings through the practices of various indigenous methods along with prayers, rituals, sacrifices etc. and driving out the evil spirits from the human body by using chants. The elements of primitive medicine are still prevailing among the Khoibus using herbs and medicines from animals as different remedies. Some of the traditional system of treating different diseases and ailments by the Khoibu tribe of Manipur are given as follows:

HERBAL PLANTS

Sl.No.	*Herbal plants (local Name)*	*Methods*	*Treatment*
1	Ansapui	To eat raw	Cold, fever, body ache
2	Aikhoo	To eat raw/burnt	Dairrhoea, dysentery, Vomit
3	Andong	To apply by grinding	Burn and bruises
4	Awaamachanghei	To cook/boil	Dog bite
5	Ankum	To boil the bark and drink	Digestive system problem
6	Benacha	To boil and drink	Women menstrual problems, Dysentery
7	Chalung	To apply by grinding	Burns
8	Chalung	To grind and apply	Cold cough, fever, hair soap
9	Changalnam	Eat or apply raw	Food poison, high temperature etc.
10.	Chongnaihei	To boil and eat	Stonecase, bone fracture
11	Hithlaknaa(tobacco)	Chew and apply	Dog bite, snake bite
12	Hatle	Boil the leave and drink	Pile, stomach ulcer,

(Contd...)

Sl.No.	*Herbal plants (local Name)*	*Methods*	*Treatment*
			etc.
'13	Ikaithibi	Boil and eat	Pile
14	Khamna	To burn the leaver	Measles
15	Kanbor	Half burn the leave and apply	Body ache
16	Laichangkhraa	To burn	Use for evil spell
17	Loulurpui	To eat raw/boil and eat	Fever, body ache
18	Louhei mathuk	Boil the stem and leaves and drink	Body ache, Joint pain, weak health
19	Marou	Eat raw/burn and eat	Dry cough
20	Onamrui	Boil with rice and apply	Fracture, sprain
21	Pangkilou	Boil the stem & leaves and drink	Cold, cough, scabies
22	Pongheitol-na	Grind the budding leaves and eat	Digestive system, dysentery
23	Puklu-hei	Eat raw/mixed with honey	Throat problem
24	Phalup	Boil the leaves and apply	Cold, cough, fever
25	Pakasay	Grind and apply	Swelling/boils
26	Parbomkuk	Grind the root and apply	Swelling/boils
27	Partawai	Grind the root and apply	Swelling/Boils
28	Ramhoi	Eat the root raw	Cold, cough, indigestion problem
29	Khongmahei	Soak the fruit and drink	Diarrhea, constipation

Jhum Rituals

Jhum cultivation is practiced in the area of Tuishakram (2nd Layer) and Wangkheiram (3rd Layer). At the very beginning, the village high priest (*Amung*) performs the rituals by invoking the fate of the entire villagers for the coming year at *Aitlangthoi* (name of a festival probably in the month for January/February). He, then, chooses the area for cultivation of that year. This shifting cultivation is done with a cycle of 10-15 years. Longer period produces better yield. The *Among* (High Priest), *Chamon Khulpu* (Asstt. Priest) and *Charaaroi* perform various rites and rituals in different seasons of the year.

The Khoibu ancestors commonly practice the following rites and rituals for good yield of the crops and for the protection of the lives of the people. Some of the practices are given below:

Sl. No.	*Name of the Rituals*	*Time Period*	*Activities involved*
1.	Yawn Meirui	Kashan	Seeing luck for the whole year
2.	Chaa-Kabu thoi	February	Seed sowing festivals/ asking the goddess of paddy for good yield
3.	Chaasang Kada	April	Ritual for good yield
4.	Kharu Kashoi	May	Ritual done for preservation of the sown seeds to the goddess along with the observation of genna the next day
5.	Khalampui-Kathoi	October	Ritual carried out to Khoibu Langmaiching for the problem of paddy from natural calamity, insect & wild animals

6.	Lungshel Kalaad	October	Ritual to the same God for good yield and to protect the villagers from sicknesses

Festivals

There are a number of festivals of the Khoibus related to harvest. When the harvest is plentiful, and the yield of the crops is abundant, the following practices are carried out.

(1) ***Sharou Kayer*** **(Distribution of special meat):** This festival is associated with the grandest feast of the community by the distribution of customary meat to all the participants. In this occasion of harvest even the pregnant ladies are given two shares of customary meat along with the hoisting of a tri-colored flag (Red, white, yellow).

(2) ***Yaamana Katan*****(eldest brother as host of the threshers):** In this festival the eldest son of the family hosts the occasion. In the festival, a *Mithun* has to be butchered and offering of a sumptuous feast is offered to all the fellow villagers. The festival is medium importance with flags.

(3) ***Ningshon-Cha-Kada*****(a daughter as the host):** Usually the eldest daughter who is still an unmarried woman is the host in this festival. The harvest starts in the morning, and even if the harvest is completed within the same day, the act of putting of the paddy into the granaries has to be done in the morning of the next day. Both the male and female folks compete with one another to have a bigger share of the paddy. Whatever share the male collected has to be put into the common granary but the share collected by the female is earmarked for the daughter as her individual possession.

Traditional Occupations

YAA Kachan (Hunting)

The practice of hunting has been a part of the culture of the Khoibus since ancient times. It is one of the main occupations that prevail among the tribal people. Hunting is mostly carried out during leisure. It is divided into two types; 1.Group hunting and 2.Individual hunting. Group hunting is done mostly during free time but individual hunting is done at will. It is carried out any time and in any season of the year. Any hunter going for such adventure must not have any physical contact with his wife to avoid accident and bad luck.

Kharu Kashu (Fishing)

Fishing is another activity carried out usually during spring time during March and May, when the volume of water in the river is at its lowest ebb. Two types of fishing is practiced by the Khoibu community. One is group fishing and another is an individual fishing. The group fishing is carried by using poisonous herbs and nets.

Sinrai Kashin (Handicrafts)

There are many activities taken up by the ancestors of the Khoibu as a part of enhancing economy or means of livelihood. Common among such activities are:

Pharaa Kasha (Winnowing Plate): Every family member of the household of the Khoibu village engages himself in the making of *pharaa*. It is made with cane and bamboo. The Khoibus supply *pharaas* to different parts of Manipur state. Besides the above activity, there are various works of cane and bamboos such as *Leikho-Kasha* (spreading paddy mat) *Phak-Kash* (Mat), *shangphai-Kash* (Baskets) etc.

Yuma-Kayok (Animal Doestication)

The rich and vast forest of the Khoibus favour

domestication of animals. Most of the areas of land are suitable for the living of many types of animal. Some of the animals found in this forest are mithuns, pigs, goats, cows, horses and chickens. Among the mentioned animals, mithuns are taken to be most important because they are used in any customary festivals and occasions related to marriage, harvest and construction of new houses.

Land Reforms

Since time immemorial the Khoibus have their own pattern of ownership of land. Shifting and jhum cultivation are discouraged as a general policy. But this cannot be applied to the Khoibus as the villagers' main source of livelihood is jhuming. Jhuming, as a matter of fact, renews the cycle of plants. This practice allows almost every arable land to have a cycle of new plants every 10-15 years and thereby bringing fresh forest and better conditions of crop yield. If an area is not cultivated for 40-50 years, then, it becomes difficult for the villagers to clear land for the next cultivation.

Therefore, until and unless a proper scientific alternative is arranged, banning of jhum cultivation in this community would be exposing them to starvation and banning of jhum would be impracticable.

The Manipur Land Revenue Act, 1960 and other Land Reforms Acts cover mostly the valley areas. These Acts are not applied in the far hill areas of the Khoibu. Moreover, the Forest conservation Act, 1980 deprive the inherent ownership right to land of the tribals. And any move for the development of land and forest should be done with the consent of the people possessing this land.For instance the Khoibu tribe was once a recognized tribe with reference to the letter No.2/AG.49/0659-96 Dated, Imphal, the 6th June, 1947 issued by the *Dewan* of Manipur State showing the list of 24 recognized Scheduled tribes and two (2) scheduled castes where the Khoibu tribe was placed in Sl.No.18. Unfortunately, the Govt.

of India in its Amendment of the constitution scheduled caste and scheduled Tribes List (modification) order, 1956, part-X, Manipur, Notification No.SR) 2477A Ministry of Home Affairs, Govt. of India issued 29 scheduled tribes by including some fresh tribes. In the recent tribe Recognition of Manipur, issued by the Govt. of India Tarao Kharam, Poumai and any Kuki were recognized in 2003 dropping the Khoibu tribe inspite of repeated appeals to the concerned authority.

It is therefore, the responsibility of the government of India and ICSSR in particular to muse and ponder deeply and bring development at the faster pace through the adoption of suitable technologies which would be appropriate to this region without undermining the old traditional practices and without disturbing the ecological balance.

Some of the remedies and measures for land development of the Khoibus may be suggested as follow:

- Encourage cattle rearing through SHG
- Encourage bamboo planting and bamboo works through the provision of proper infrastructure (tools and Implement of modern designs).
- Encourage researchers in medicinal plants, roots and insects through project system from the concerned departments.
- Encourage passion fruit farms, parkia farms, banana farms etc.
- Encourage tribal co-operatives, labour co-operatives & Govt. corporations.
- Lastly, revival of the lost identities of the existing tribes in the North- Eastern Region of India.

REFERENCES

Binodini Devi, P. (2002), 'The Maring Tribe of Manipur', *Monograph*, Department of Anthropology, M.U.

Hill Area Committee-Manipur (2002), *A Report on Expert Committees on Khoibus.*

Horam, Ringkahao (1994), *A Country Report*, NPMHR, North East India.

Jha L.K (n.d), *India's Forest Policies: Analysis and Appraisal.*

Khoibu Union, (2003), *Historical Background of Khoibu Tribe.*

Singh, J.S., S.P. Singh, and C. Shastri (1981), *Science and Rural Development in Mountains.*

Singh, S. (n.d), *Forest, Tribals and Forest Policy*, Principal Chief Conservator of Forest Govt. of Manipur.

Singh, L.A (1998), *The Manipur Land Revenue and Land Reforms Act, 1960.*

Sukumar Singh, S. (2006), *The Economic Plants of Manipur and their Uses.*

Tribe Union, (2006), *Ethnography on Khoibus.*

Tongtang, Angshem and Deben Sharma (2004), *A Development Perspective of Khoibu* DHP.

Uipo Marou Assembly (2003) , *Khoibu (Uipo) Tribe a Profile.*

15

LAND RELATIONS: Chiru Community Perspective

—Samson Chiru

A son's wrong selection of field site makes for eight years of starvation (famine)

—Chiru Proverb

Introduction

In human history, it is land and its resources that are the main source of livelihood of man. As man's society becomes more complex and developed, the need for land also increases correspondingly for various other purposes. All battles amounting to full-fledged wars have been fought for land and its resources. Manipur state is no different.

The Treaty of Yandaboo (1826) is the piece of document that heralded the recognition of Manipur being an independent state.

As to tribal areas, the territory of the Naga nation, it is a well-defined territory and successive kings and rulers had recognized our boundaries. The Ahoms put pillars to mark the boundary and they stand even now as silent witnesses to the truth of our claims. Our national boundaries cover an area of approximately 12,000 sq. km with a population of four million. Our lands are rich in minerals and other natural resources, and we have guarded them from wasteful exploitation. We are not in a position to use much of our resources but we claim the right to exercise permanent sovereignty over our natural and cultural resources so that we use these resources for the development of our people.

The British recognised the fact that our territory on the Eastern side extended up to Sagiang Division and Kachin State, which is under the occupation of the Myanmar State, and on the Western side it extended to the Arunachal Pradesh, Nagaland State, four districts within Manipur State and parts of the Assam State. At no point of our history did we give up or concede to give up an inch of our land.

The Naga resistance to the division of their territory is also documented. "From 1832 to 1880, the Naga people fought against the might of the British army with courage and tenacity that the British had to arrive at a settlement in accordance with the Naga customary law on 27 March 1880." The British tried their best to conquer certain territory of the tribes after the fall of Ahom kingdom no doubt, but as cited above, the Ahoms remained silent witnesses to the truth of the claims made by Nagas of their land. In the 1880s, somehow after forty eight years of war with the tribesmen, the British succeeded. However, the tribesmen rejected any sort of imposition of tax upon land. Save for house tax imposed by the British as part of allegiance to the crown, taxes were not imposed in terms of economic contribution. Tribal pattern of administration was undisturbed and so was traditional system of land tenure. The Chirus' traditional land tenure system as such remains virgin to this day.

System of Hill Administration in Manipur

In Manipur Hill Areas, the Hill Areas Committee (Article 371C) and Department of Tribal Development look after the welfare of the tribals, their land and resources. Hill Area Committee was constituted while Manipur was still a Union Territory status by the constitution (Twenty-seventh Amendment) Act, 1971, sec. 5 (w.e.f. 15-2-1972). Manipur Autonomous District Council system existed for sometime but became defunct. (out of the eight sisters of the North-Eastern region, Assam, Meghalaya, Mizoram and Tripura subscribed to Autonomous District Council).

Panchayat Extension to Scheduled Areas Act (PESA) 1996 is not being subscribed by the tribes either, in Hill Areas of Manipur. Therefore, all the different tribes numbering twenty-nine have their own system of land ownership. And land reforms, if at all carried out, will affect the tribes and their land system, which varies from one tribe to another and also from one village to another. The Kukis practise ownership of land by the Chief (Kulak) whereas, the Nagas practice both the village and clan/lineage or individual ownership of land. The land revenue in Manipur is enforced under the Land Revenue and Land Reforms Act of 1960 and amendment Act 1968. According to these acts, findings of the cadastral survey must be recorded properly so that land revenue maybe collected according to their respective holdings. But the hill people are very much against the acts as they wanted to retain their traditional customs and protect their interest according to their own traditional way of life.

Some of the Chiru villages, inhabiting the buffer zones i.e., sandwiched between the Hill Areas and the Plain/Valleys where majority of the state's population occupy also do not undertake the proper cadastral survey. In an isolated case, they succumbed to the (sale) transfer of certain wet cultivation areas to the non-tribals so as to meet their expedient needs of the family. In such cases, measures may be initiated to prevent further transfer of land ownership of the various categories of land prevalent in the Chiru tribe.

The Bohteh System and the Village Ownership of Land

Land relations system existing in the Chiru community has been inscribed in the minds of elders, transmitting it down in history to the younger generations in its purest form and not written records (Sketch records in recent Chiru Christian villages had been maintained by the village administration). The Chiru tribe practiced both the system of lineage/clan and village ownership of land tenurial system. Bohteh System (Pattadar System) is based upon lineage/clan. However, one clan family may dominate the others in the area of land owned somehow by mere hard work and with that he is able to own more land than the other clan families.(Mind you, I fall in the category of not owning much as I look I should be). Still there was always sharing and distribution of land in settlements of the Chiru tribes.

Usually, major chunk of the lineage land goes to the eldest son of the family. Eldest daughter does not own land as a matter of right.

The Chiru tribe has a participial system of society. On the issue of equity of land distribution, all clans as listed later, own land, howsoever small and different in size and fertility. By this is meant, even in terms of land that can be utilised either for shifting cultivation or for permanent wet cultivation. This ownership of land, in due course of time, gets transferred by way of establishment of new families by the respective families from one generation to the other. Thus, fragmentation takes place.

Fragmentation of Ceilling on Land Holding

The Bohteh System is a land owning system in which ownership gets transferred from one generation to the next by way of land being fragmented and transferred to the children, usually son/s, as Chiru community practice patrilenial system of society. Save in case of no son in the family, the daughter is given the ownership right. However, if she is divorced then the land given to her should be reverted back to the original family clan lineage. Adoption of son may also take place and in such cases land is given to such adopted sons. Certain land ownership right takes place by being given from one clan to another. Usually such transfer takes place between close family matrimonial allegiances from the forefathers to the present time. The Chiru tribe is quite small in number or rather almost all the villagers are connected somehow in matrimonial alliance either from patriliniel or matrilineal side. Ownership of land may also take place by mutual exchange transfer of land between two separate family lineages. There are cases where land is being given to daughters for a certain cultivation period in shifting cultivation at least and in most cases such patch of land continues to be utilised by the woman given in marriage, if not permanently, for a fairly good period of time. However, when it comes to land which could be utilised for terrace cultivation such land is retained by her brother for his children (sons). In the case of male side of the distribution of land, even in shifting cultivation or otherwise, once a patch of land is utilised or is given away by the eldest brother to the younger ones, it often continues to be permanently owned by the one to whom it is given. Usually the eldest son distributes as per the needs of his brothers. The latest system of land ownership transfer is usually decided by the head of the family (father during his lifetime). Each son is entitled somehow to some land holding through fragmentation of the terrace (wet cultivation) among the sons by their father. The sons who do not own land, mainly for wet cultivation, may approach the nearest family relation in matrimony, since their forefather's time. Such approach may be initiated in similar manner even in the case of certain shifting cultivable land too.

There are certain reserved areas of land in the village. This land can be distributed in the village through the village chief. Thus villagers approach the chief and the village authority members with a kilogram or more, as the case may be, of sugar and tea leaf (earlier local beer or Zu was served, Christianity has modified this practice) to be served to the village authority court. Thus, the Chirus land tenurial system has two classes of land:

1. Primary or agricultural land, and
2. Subsidiary or building or reserved land. This is further divided into the following categories:
   a) *Village land*: Used for public institutions like dormitory, grave-yard, worshipping place etc. The waste-land without and structure on it belongs to the whole village. The village land is the joint property of the villagers and all the people who belong to that particular village have the right to use it for jhum cultivation. Besides, each village has a small forest land to provide raw materials for construction and repair of houses for village public use. Most importantly, such areas are to prevent forest fires, hostile winds entering the village and also to provide shades to the otherwise heated summer sun.
   b) *Lineage land*: It is owned by a kin group (Bohteh system).
   c) *Individual land*: It is either inherited or acquired land. There is no limit in the size of such holdings. Mostly rich people hold more land and lease out land to those who do not have enough. Land may sometimes be aleinated by way of inability to repay certain borrowings and loans from one family by the other. Sometimes, such repayment may be agreed by way of manual labour service given to the loaner by the loanee.

Land Dispute Settlement Mechanism

There are times when dispute arises between families in the clan. And in this, the chief intervenes. If at all such dispute arises, it is resolved through arbitration, mediation or intervention by the village authority. The decision making authority of the village is discussed later.

Sometimes, when there is dispute over ownership of cultivable land (both wet and shifting cultivation) between/among brothers of the family or between/among one family clan with another family clan, the chief and authority members decide who is supposed to be the legal owner of the disputed land. There are times, if the disputants are not able to negotiate and arrive at a settlement between or among themselves, when the village retains the land. Such disputed land of pending cases is temporarily given to be cultivated by a landless villager till the dispute is resolved. In this way allocation of the land to the landless through judgment pronounced on disputed land by the authority of the village court is a common system practiced in the Chiru community. This is intra clan. There may be inter clan land dispute. The same judgment could be pronounced by the village authority. So far all land disputes are settled by the respective Chiru villages. In cases of inter villages or community disputes, cases may be filed even in the magisterial level.

The Chirus Inhabiting the Buffer Zones of Manipur State

The Chiru villages in the buffer zones i.e., between the Hill Areas and the Plains/valley may tend to have the right to dispose their terrace fields to other community outside the village (this is illegal in customary law or at most legal if the land adjoining the plain areas of Manipur was earlier bought by the tribes and was just a resale case) but not the land adjoining the Hill Areas of Manipur. For it is found that most of the wet cultivation in the Chiru villages is adjoining to

Manipur plain areas. And it is difficult for them not to allow the other communities like Meeteis to indulge in buying tribal land when the tribal family or individual has emergency needs to sell land. This could be construed as exceptional land relationship between the Chirus inhabiting the Buffer zones (adjoining the plains of Manipur state). But over all, in no way the Chiru tribe sells land to outsiders, particularly, the Meeteis.

Origin of Chiru Tribe

Chiru community traces their origin to the Chin Hills. The nomenclature of the tribe—Chiru— is derived from the double /dou syllables— Chi— meaning salt and bu/buk/beei meaning—spot or land i.e., land of salt. It could be that the Chiru community thought this 'ru' i.e., seed grows into 'chi' salt. Chi means salt and ru means seed. And thus, the word Chiru. It could also mean to them as pieces of crystal bones. For 'ru' has similar meaning with 'ruu' i.e., seed and bone. Probably, on leaving the land of salt, they said adieu to the land and thus, Chibeei or Chubai meaning goodbye. There are various other versions of the nomenclature of the Chiru community.

According to Meijinlung Kamson, former Member of Parliament from Manipur while addressing the Chiru youth in Delhi 1997, "The Chirus are the original inhabitants of the Manipur state. They fall in the old Kuki group. They originated from the place called Chibu —Land of Salt, in Manmar/Mizoram (Chin Hills)". In a similar vein, Rishang Keishing, the present M.P. (Raja Sabha) in his speech at Nungsai Chiru village said," The Chirus are the oldest inhabitants of the Manipur State. Their smallness in number is mainly because of the absorption into the Meetei community." According to Alar Thoitak, President, Kom-Rem, North East India, "The term 'Chiru' is said to have been derived without a specific meaning. It is just said that it denotes 'Rem' which means simple 'hill people'. Rem means simple. Accordingly, the Rem tribes consisting of the Kom tribe and other Rem tribes have similar custom, culture, traditions, folktales, folklore, folk songs, indegenious games and sports etc. It is also said that Aimols, Chirus, Koms, Koren, Purum etc. (Kom-Rem)are the indigenous Mongoloid and simple hill people."

He further reveals, which is in consonance with the other scholars, through the traditional folk tales, folk songs, legendary stories etc. the Chirus are the settlers of a place called Chibu which is believed to be a place in the Chin Hills of Myanmar. Thereafter, the Chirus migrated to different places like Tripura, Mizoram, Assam and Manipur as early as 13th century A.D. whereas their exodus from Chin Hills is dated back around 10th or 11th century A.D.

The most reliable sources of their migration from various places in due course of time is mentioned in their folklore and folk tales composed by the local Chiru tribe of the places like Parphawng, Parbung (Myanmar/Mizoram/Churanchanpur).

The Chiru tribe is said to have migrated under pressure of the advance of the tribes from the South Tripura, to their present homes from sites in the south-east of the valley beyond Moirang. It was said that Chirus were instructed by the local king to collect 8(eight) containers of crab's flesh at least 250-500 grams each totaling 2000-4000 grams of flesh of crabs per head which is quite unreasonable and irrational, an indirect pressure to vacate the land in which Chirus have been inhabiting for generations.

There is also a legend that connects with the Three Brother's theory which according to it, the three brothers became the progenitors of Kukis, the eldest son, Nagas, the middle son and the Meeteis, the youngest son. But as to which camp do the Chirus belong, there is no history. Thus, Chirus are Chirus. Except in the recent 20th century (1911) British administrator and writer T.C. Hudson mentioned in his book, 'Naga Tribes of Manipur' that Marings who are from the Naga camp borrowed the curious fillet from Chiru tribe. This somehow may indicate that Chirus are culturally akin to Naga camp but linguistically again they are akin to Kuki-Chin camp. Most of the British and Indian/or native scholars have convergence and divergence as to which camp the Chirus belong. Some wrote that they belong to the Kuki group and others wrote that they belong to the Naga group.

Traditional Chiru Village Administration and Decision Making Authority

Like any tribal societal and polity set up, the traditional Chiru village has a village chief who is aided by Village Council Members. (Normally a village chief is traditionally supposed to be chosen from Danlah clan or sub-clan; however, with the introduction of Chairmanship in village administration, other clans have also been inducted as Chief-cum-Chairman). They are chosen on the basis of consensus. Basically the Chiru village administration is run by the following designated porfolio holders: 1) *Kulak* (chief). 2) *Theempu / Laisu* (Village rites priest or *Lamsokhar*). 2) *Sangpu* (*Seedsowing* and harvesting priest/). 3) *Theersu* (*Usuall* of Shekho clan that performs rites relating to all agricultural implements both before the beginning and at the end of agricultural cycle) 4) *Besarpu* (Priest of jungle fire or unnatural death). 5) *Meetei Lampu* (social worker or *khosung sunsawraw*) and the last but not least 6) *Kho Tangva* (Village ushers)

The writer of this essay does not intend to write on all the roles of different priests but mostly the role of the priests related closely with land and agri/agro issues. But this does not mean that other priests like Meetei Lampu (Social Worker who play an over all role now in the present Chiru society),

Besarpu(priest of jungle fire and un-natural death) and Kho Tangva (Village Ushers who are instrumental in rendering the services required by the Village Authority) are of less significance. In Dolang Chiru village in the latest system of administration of the village, the eldest male of the family and posted in the said village, if he is a government servant he has to render three years of service to the village authority mandatorily. Other younger brothers may pay a fee to escape this service to the village if they are in government service) The writer is keen to explain the clan system as land ownership is based on the clan/lineage. If at all, clan relations even to matrimonial alliances are to be discussed, it would be too lengthy an essay, which of course, is still practised in the Chiru community. Moreover, marriageable clans system differs from one Chiru village to another. Normally, a girl is taken in marriage from maternal side. Marriage of inter tribes/community takes place and is in vogue. In such cases, a girl taken in marriage by Chiru man is designated a particular clan guardianship and accordingly lineage line continues in the designated clan guardianship of the Chiru tribe.

Role of Chiru Traditional Priests

Seed sowing and harvesting priests are chosen from the Raja clan or any Raja sub-clan. Certain Puja/rites, pertaining to agricultural activities, needed by the village every season in the cycle of production related activities, are performed by this priest. He also performed rites related to pest whenever destruction of crops by pests occurred. He was known as the symbol of village prosperity (*Kholongning*). He has authority in village decision making, being one of the members of the village council. He is appointed on life term basis. On his death the senior most and the man recognised for his abilities replaced his priesthood.

Agricultural implement priests (*Thirsu/Thir Theempu*) usually come from the *Shekho Dingthoi* clan. In every cycle of agricultural season, this priest performed the required rites relating to the implements and tools for the safety of the users of the whole village. The rites are performed usually before the beginning and after the end of the agricultural season.

Theempu/Laisu: Theempu is one who has expertise in performing rituals at the village gate/worship places. This ritual is compulsory in a year. Lamsokhar meaning blocking the route is also performed whenever a stranger enters the village boundary. He also performed rites related to sickness. Theempu is selected from among the members of the Dingthoi clan generally and he holds the membership of the village council.

Besarpu (*Meei le Sarsawng maadai Theempu*/Priest of fire and Un-natural death), as a priest of fire, he performs rite when felling and clearing of jungle for cultivation is to be done so that fire does not spread to the village from the jungle. He performs rites swhenever un-natural death occurred in the village. He is a member of the village authority. He is selected from the *Sampar* clans.

In a nut shell, the functions of the priests are as below:

1) Annual rites;

2) Family worship (*Innroireei/Innsungkhur Rawthawi*);

3) *Laibeeklawn Rawthawi.*

The Major Clans and Sub-clans of Chiru Tribe

The following are the Chiru clan division and sub-division:

Major Clans (*Phunghawi)* and Sub-Clans (*Phungtang/ Phunglawp*)

a) Major Clans and sub-Clans:

1. *Chawngdur* and its seven sub-clans 2. Danlah and its seven sub-clans 3. Dingthoi and its nine sub-clans 4.

Raja and its thirteen sub-clans 5. Sampar and its seven sub-clans. There are, thus, forty one in total in Chiru Phratries division. (See: The Chiru Customary Marriage Law Book translated by Dr. Samson S. Chiru Joint Secretary, Chiru Christian Literature Commitee, North-East India.)

Conclusion

The Chiru tribe nomenclature has much to do with land—land of salt— Chibu. The Bible says, "You are the salt of the earth. If the salt loses its saltiness, then it is useless and thrown". Have the Chirus lost their saltiness? Or have the Meeteis tasted the saltiness of the Chirus that they are being evicted and displaced? Certain territory owned by Chirus for long years have been deprived of by Meeteis. This is a cause of alarm. And what needs to be done is the concern of every good people. Certain sections of the tribe are now being rehabilitated by fellow Nagas in Manipur. This is indeed the generosity of the Nagas. As to their land relations, the Chirus practised Bohteh System in which land ownership, transfer and fragmentation is basically all within the clan (male) so long as wet cultivable land is concerned. Daughters are given land at least for shifting cultivation, howsoever, temporary it may be. But all land utilised for shifting cultivation are not given permanently to the married daughters. Land ownership transfer, even of wet cultivable land, takes place from rich land owner traditional forefather (daughters taken in marriage in the past history) to man/men of the history based on past marriage of their grandparents. Mutual exchange of land of past history of grandparent in matrimonial alliance also takes place in Chiru tribe. Urbanization of the neighbouring areas has brought some changes in the Chiru community in land relations in the Buffer Zones as an exceptional case. However, in no case should the Scheduled Areas and Scheduled Tribes (Fifth Schedule) or Hill Area Committee System in Manipur, allow transfer of land to the non-tribal people. If at all such transfer takes place, displacement by way of developmental project sites, adequate compensation is the pre-requisite of land being acquired by the State. A humane land reforms keeping in mind the sentiments both traditional and religious, is the need of the time.

Analyses, Suggestions and Recommendations

Land reform measures needs to be introduced in the Chiru villages for collateral purposes to avail credit from financial institutions of both the Government and private agencies.

1 Village Authority maybe empowered with the certification power of land for such loan purposes.

2. Reforms in Chiru community is related to cultural and traditional aspects of land ownership (Usually all settlements both within and outside the village were in the form of Beer (Zu) and now is replaced with Sugar and tea leaf for Chai to be served in the village. In the case of settlements outside the village, normally boundary cases, disputes are resolved through mechanism evolved by the respective community leaders).

3. Other forms of exchange such as Cattle and kind also continues as a part of settlement either by way of penalty or otherwise.

4. Land measurement by way of cadastral survey, howsoever random it may be, needs to be introduced so as to know the exact size of the land owned in all the categories of ownership.

5. As regards to uniform system of land ownership in the Chiru villages, the writer feels that what he has been discussing in this essay is applicable to more or

less all the Chiru villages excepting the Buffer Zone Chiru villages with wet cultivation land.

6. More power and authority to the village authority court may be delegated so as to arrive at a more equitable distribution of land ownership in Chiru tribe land.

7. Landless villagers should be given some portion of land so as to ensure inclusive and equitable distribution of land.

8. Shifting of a member of a family from one to another Chiru village may be discouraged.

9. Cultivation by hired labour should be encouraged, particularly of the landless villager with a shares ratio of 1:1 of total yield/produce.

10. Afforestation should be encouraged to protect the eco-system

11. Shifting cultivation should be discouraged by creating awareness programmes of the ill effects and impact on the economy and ecology of the village in the long run.

12. The government through the different levels of administration (Hill Area) should encourage crop rotation/double or triple cropping system in the wet cultivation system.

13. Introduction of Autonomous District Council (ADC) may give more teeth than the existing Hill Area Committee system in the Hill Areas of Manipur.

14. Frequent jungle fire should be discouraged. (Accidents of jungle fire are penalised as the village authority decides in relation to the value of property destroyed by the fire. If the accused refuses to admit his mistake, the village authority orders for test in the water. The

aggrieved person usually cannot remain for long inside the water. Such test in the water is applicable to any other dispute also.)

15. Tree plantation should be carried out on a large scale so as to generate perennial spring water supply both for the purposes of irrigation and drinking water.
16. Animal grazing should be concentrated in certain particular areas so as to prevent over-grazing.
17. Awareness should be given to the villagers over rodents as pesticide and pestilent and manure enhancing insects for more yield.
18. Family planning is optional for the Chiru tribe, keeping in mind its demographic factor of the community, in spite of scarcity of land.

REFERENCES

Second Scheduled Areas and Scheduled Tribes Commission, 2002-2004, Questionnaires.

Dutta, B.B and M.N. Karna (1987) (ed.), *Land Relations in North East India*, New Delhi.

Miri, Mrinal, *Continuity and Change in Tribal Society*, (1993), New Delhi, Concept Publications.

The Chiru Customary Marriage Law Book, (2000), Chiru Christian Literature Committee, Imphal.

Naga Journal of Indigenous Affairs, (2002), Naga People's Forum Publication, New Delhi.

The Legal Status of Naga National Armed Resistence, (2001), Oking Publicity and Information Service, Nagaland.

'Special issue of Khongjom Day', (1992), *Manipur Today*, Imphal.

S.R. Toppo (2000), *Tribes in India*, New Delhi.

16

LAND AND ETHNIC IDENTITY: The Anal Tribe

—*S.R.Tohring*

Today, land and ethnic identity issues have seriously affected India's Northeast. Manipur is one of the most affected states. Ethnic rivalries in Manipur, particularly the last decade of the 20th century, were generally attributed to land, ethnic identity and their related issues like taxes. These complex problems continue to disturb the states of this region, particularly Manipur state. The question is how to heal them. When one looks into the problem, it is very complicated and it has to begin with each tribe or community's ownership of land, ethnic identity and their related issues. The focus of this study will be on Anal tribe which will be dealt under three subheadings viz., the tribe, land and ethnic identity.

The Anal tribe is one of the oldest tribes of Manipur. Today, it is one of the thirty three recognized tribes of Manipur. The Anals are settled both in India and Myanmar but are mostly concentrated in the state of Manipur in India. In Manipur, they are found in three districts viz. Chandel,

Churachandpur and Thoubal, but they are mostly found in Chandel, which has about 64 villages out of a total of 68 Anal villages in the state. The neighboring district of Churachanpur has three Anal villages and the Thoubal district has one Anal village. According to 2001 census, the total Anal population in the state is 13,853. Myanmar has three Anal villages namely, Nagakala, Napaleen and Haika.

Originally, the Anals were animists but with the advent of Christianity a few Anals were converted to Christianity. Soon, Christianity became the religion of the Anals. Today, 99 percent of the Anals are Christians. One of the most important impacts of Christianity on the Anal is that the early Anal Christians were introduced to modern education and they began to take up the responsibility of converting and educating their tribesmen despite stiff resistance and persecution from their own brethrens. The current educational status of the Anals is low in comparison with other tribes. Yet, their level of awareness about the importance of education is high. In late 20th century they established their own literature society in Chandel District. Economically, the Anals are still in a primitive stage as they continue to practice jhumming or shifting cultivation. As a result of economic backwardness, pace of social development for this tribe is negligible. Nevertheless, political consciousness of the Anals is high, thus, any question on their identity is strongly reacted.

Land

In this study, the concept of land refers to territory whether inhabited or claimed or both. If, we look at ethnic issues or tribal relations, land assumes a very important position. Since olden times, for possession or ownership of land, wars occurred. Today, politics over land has assumed inproportionate dimensions. This could be seen from proliferation of ethnic movements. Most of the major ethnic groups in North-East India have launched armed movements. The goals of these ethnic groups are mostly to get freedom for their home land or ancestral home land. In this situation, ethnic relations over land are very fragile, any alteration or cross of a boundary is interpreted with cynicism. Owing to this, in recent years, series of inter-ethnic conflicts were witnessed in North East. In the state of Manipur, a sequence of ethnic conflicts occurred in the last decade of 20th century namely, Meetei-Pangal, Naga-Kuki, Kuki-Paite, Meetei-Kuki etc. The analysts concluded that land was one of the major causes of these conflicts.

The history of the Anals mentioned the land they occupied and traversed through but the concept of Anal's land became more concrete after they inhabited the land they are presently occupying. The earliest written historical source of Manipur, *The Royal Chronicles of Manipur*, mentioned the Anal villages as 'Anan village' from 16th century A.D. This shows that there was a concept of Anal's land. Prior to British rule, Anal's land was a sort of independent and autonomous land. The tribe enjoyed a freedom to rule themselves. Maharajas of Manipur who ruled the low land of present Manipur state raided and conquered some Anal villages. From these they demanded tributes and compelled them to accept their supremacy. Nevertheless, Maharajas never changed nor interfered in the customary practices of the Anals. There were also Anal villages untouched by the rulers of Manipur. Besides the rulers of low land Manipur, it was the Kukis with whom the Anals fought tribalistic warfare over land et'al. Since 1840s Kukis began to settle in and around Anal territory. If one goes by Anal's oral history, the mentioned of wars between the Kukis and Anals are there. It seems that the Anals were defeated by the Kukis (Kamhos) and the consequence was that Anals left part of their territory to the Kukis. During the British rule, there were cases between the Anals and the Kukis over land which had been adjudicated by the colonial administrators and political agents. Today, Anals and some of the Kukis are staying adjacent to each other in Chandel district of Manipur.

The Anals have been known for giving importance to their land, and preserving their land. A noticeable fact is that they continue to settle permanently in the area they first inhabited. The ownership pattern of land in Anal community continues from the time a concept of land ownership emerged. The ownership of land amongst the Anals is the same as most of the Naga tribes. There are three kinds of ownership, namely, village ownership, clan ownership and individual ownership.

In village ownership, all the residents of the village have the right to usethe village land. In *Anal No* (Anal Customary Law) it is stated that "within the village territory, all the things and their products like rivers, streams, wild-beasts, fish, birds, trees, woods, thatches, grasses, rocks, sands, grippers etc., belong to the said village and are to be utilized by the villagers in common". But this right is subjected to the customary law and the consensus of the villagers headed by village chief and elders. At the beginning of Anals settlement in the area they are currently occupying, they had three Anal villages namely, Khumbung, Anal Khullen and Rangsom. From these villages, particularly Khumbung and Anal Khullen, originated the present villages of the tribe. The current Anal villages could be clustered into two types: offspring villages and purchased villages. In the former type of village, it is established with the consent of the parent village in a part of latter's land whereas in the latter type of village a person or persons bought a portion of land and set up a village. Today, both types usually obtained government recognitions. The ownership pattern of these two types differed. In the first type, all the residents have equal right over village land but in the second type the individual (or individuals) who bought the land has more power over the land. The boundary between villages "is generally demarcated by tracking mountains, streams, rivers or marked on rocks or anything that cannot be easily erased out" (Anal No, p.6). The vastness of village territory varies, usually the older villages possessed larger land than the newly formed villages.

In clan ownership, villagers other than the clan as well as village authority have no say or right. It is owned by the clan and depends wholly on the clan decision to exploit or preserve. According to *Anal No*, "every clan of a village possesses a private land within the territory of the village for jhuming/gardening purposes. The land owned by each clan is demarcated by a small or big tracks of brooks, hill etc". In individual ownership, all the right stays with the owner alone. Yet, this right could not be misused to disturb other villagers' rights. Today, individual ownership is gaining momentums over village and clan ownerships. The reasons are: clan ownership is breaking up amongst clansmen and the village land is depleting as it is bought or notified as reserved land or divided among the villagers. Nevertheless, village and clan ownerships are continuing along with individual ownership.

The inheritance right of village land is very complex. If the village ceased to exist and the old residents reside in a nearby area, the right to look after or use, continues to stay with them but if the inhabitants move to other far off areas or get extinct, then the land is either sold away or handed over to a nearby Anal village or villages. In the case of clan's land, if a clan gets extinct or leaves the village, the nearest clan inherits the land. In the case of individual ownership, the ownership of land is passed on to the sons. Generally, equal distribution of land amongst the sons is practiced but parental home and other important heirlooms are inherited by the youngest son.

Since olden times, land disputes emerged from encroachment on the land by others. Among Naga tribes, it resulted into war, head-hunting and raid. With the dawn of modernity among them such practice dwindled. However, many types of land disputes persist even today. In Anal Naga community, land dispute within the tribe is on the rise. There are many types of land disputes. Here, only three types are noted, namely, inter-village land dispute, inter-clan land dispute and individual level land dispute. Inter-village land dispute is usually a dispute resulting from alteration or crossing of demarcated boundary. A case like this is settled in accordance with the customary law of the tribe or by the consensus among the contending parties. In the inter-clan land dispute, a clan is involved in land dispute with one or more clans of the village or vice versa, the matter is settled by the village authorities or elders of the clan. In individual land dispute, an individual is involved with one or more individuals or vice versa. This is usually settled by elders and village authority.

There are also disputes like intra- clan land dispute and family dispute over land. Such disputes are adjudicated within the village by the authorities and elders of the village. After India's independence, Chief Associations were formed viz., Chakpi Area Chief Association, Maha Area Chief Association, Western Valley Chief Association, Sulam Area Chief Association and the Anallon Chief Association which is an apex of all these Chief Associations. These associations endeavor to look after their subjects and also to arbitrate cases which a village or villages could not pass judgments or when a petitioner (petitioners) wants to be tried by higher authorities. Thus, the Anal tribe has it own system to resolve intra-tribe land conflicts. Till now all the land cases, except those who wanted to be adjudicated in a government court, have been resolved by their own means.

The Anals are very conscious of their land. Most Anal elders know about their land and whether it belongs to a clan or the village. They constantly watch and inspect their areas. Thus, if there is a question about the land or the thing on it, they have an answer. Political aspiration is also molding their land consciousness. Since recent years, many reforms related to land have been initiated by them. Some of the important restructurings are: firstly, selling of land to non-tribal and other tribal communities has been strictly regulated. Secondly, they are systematizing inheritance right. Thirdly, parting a piece of land for their female child is also gradually taking place.

Ethnic Identity

There is no minority tribe like the Anal tribe whose ethnic identity has been questioned for academic or political purpose despite the assertion of the Nagas and the concerned tribe that their ethnic identity is Naga. A surprising thing is that the Anals received greater attention on their ethnic identity as a Naga rather than their economic, political and social backwardness. This study shows how often it has been highlighted not only amongst the academic circle but also in the media by the academicians, journalists and politicians. It also traces how the ethnic identity issue of the Anal tribe emerged and continues to be questioned even today. In the light of these controversies, the discourses on the Anal's identity, social, political, cultural, linguistic and historical aspects of the Anal tribe are analyzed in this paper.

Media highlights on the Anal's ethnic identity came up during the Naga-Kuki ethnic clash of 1992-1999. Prior to this clash, Anal ethnic identity was a matter of an academic debate rarely or never reported in the newspapers. During the Naga-Kuki conflict of 1992-1999, a subject of Anal ethnic identity emerged as a sort of newspaper war from an academic debate. The excerpt of two newspapers clippings will show this. They are given below.

Anals may live as Anals only: KNF (Kuki National Front)

Among others the KNF ask the ZYF to clarify whether the Anals are Nagas on the basis of linguistic classification, customs, dialects and historical aspects of their origin. The Anals are more akin to the Kukis, who were entitled as Kukis in 1821 much earlier to that of the Nagas as the 'Nagas' in 1948 in Manipur. Are the Nagas campaigning by adding Naga as suffix to the Anal?..... The KNF says that there is not a single Naga in Chandel district but the Anals were killed only as the Nagas since they used the word Naga as suffix under the instigation of seven or eight tribes. The Anals will be forgiven only when they stand as the Anals even if they do not wish to be the Kukis.

(*The Freedom*, Imphal, Manipur, 18th May 1996)

The above statement of the Kuki National Front (KNF) shows their claim on the Anals as Kuki and their action of killings the Anals was a result of the Anals maintaining their ethnic identity as Nagas. KNF statement also shows that their claim is based on the writings of British administrators and ethnographers like G.A Grierson and J Shakespeare.

The Anals represented by the president of the Anal Naga Student Union (ANSU), Mr. David Hulang, issued a press release:

Anals cannot be assimilated as Kuki: (ANSU)

I. Custom: The Anals have no customary affinity or similarity with the Kukis proved by marriage, land law, village administration, dress, family inheritance and ancestor property. The KNF without authentic knowledge of the customary laws of the Anal claims that the Anals are akin to the nomadic Kukis.

II. Dialect: All the Mongoloid tribes living in the Indo-Burma belt from South East, Tibet in the North and Chindwin in the East, Brahmaputra in the West down to the Chittagong Hill tracks have common food habits, similar physical feature/structure, way of living, similar names, a few common words, example: - mit, na, sam, dui, tui, thing and mei etc.

III. Historical Aspect: a) The Identity of Anals (Pakan tribe) cannot be determined by Gazetteers/records of the British aliens of the 18th century.

b. The Anals are the indigenous people of Manipur, History of Moirang (a Meitei kingdom) and the Anal traditional songs /tales prove our existence in the present inhabited areas since the beginning of the 1st century AD or much earlier.

c. The Anal cultural and traditional relationship with the Meitei brethren dates backs to 33 AD. the marriage alliance of the Meitei King Wangbarel (Pakhangba) with an Anal lady belonging to the Wanglum clan of Anal Khullen proves it.

d. The barbaric nomads/gypsy Kukis invaded the Pakan areas during the mid 1840s. As per Anal record the present villages occupied by the Kukis-HAIKA, RALVAL, AIBUL, LAMPHAI, KHANGBAROL, AISI, etc, were rested by the Makhengs Khongais or the so called Kukis. All the Pakan Naga group have many similarities/affinities with the other Naga tribes in culture and traditions-rituals/customs, ancient ornaments, marriage, inheritance, landownership etc. Therefore, the Anals can never be a kin to the so called Makheng (Kuki) who are the recent invaders of our motherland. The above points prove our identity as Nagas and no force or argument can confuse the Anals in regards to our identity.

(*The Freedom*, Imphal, Manipur, 21st May 1996)

The reactions of the Anals represented by ANSU could be seen from the above press release. The language and the tone of the statement show their anger not only against the Kukis who question their ethnic identity but also the British colonialists. The British administrators and ethnographers, since their penetration into this remote area, were divided on the Anal ethnic identity. Some of them, particularly G.A Grierson and J. Shakespeare, grouped or made references to the Anal as 'Old Kuki' while others like Pemberton and Carry identified them as Nagas. The writings and references of the British colonialists have a great impact on the post-independent scholars, researchers, administrators and politicians. The tribe ethnic identity developed into not merely a debate within academic circle but has also become a tool for political purpose. During the recent peace talks between the NSCN (IM) and the Government of India, Samrat Choudhury in *The Hindustan Time* reported that:

> Padmanabhaiah describes the question of blurred identities, especially of smaller tribes like the Anals, as 'social dynamism', groups shifting allegiances, he says.
>
> (*The Hindustan Time*, 19th January 2003)

As we all know Padmanabhaiah was an interlocutor between the NSCN and the Government of India. If the ethnic identity of the minority tribes particularly the Anal tribe is a political gimmick between the NSCN and the Government of India, then, one has no knowledge about their politics in dealing with each other. But as a concerned researcher, a fair study on the ethnic identity of the tribe in question is a need of the hour.

The origin of this debate could be traced back to British colonialists. During the British rule, ethnographers, administrators and linguists were divided on the Anals' ethnic identity: one group which includes Capt. R.B. Pemberton and Carrey advocated that Anal is Naga while the other group constituted by R. G.A Grierson and J.Shakespeare classified Anal as an Old Kuki. After India's independence, most of the references done on the Anal ethnic identity follow one or the other group. They quote and re-quote the earlier writings of the British colonialists to suit their own views. If one looks into the oral history of Anal and the *Royal Chronicles of Manipur*, Anal ethnic identity is established as Naga. Further, if one compares Anal history and the writings of colonialists on Anals' identity, there are many fallacies and loopholes in the colonialists' writings.

The Royal Chronicles of Manipur is the oldest written account of Manipur. In it, it mentioned Anal as "Anan Naga". The word Naga is suffixed to Anal in almost all the mentions of the Anals. The history of the Anals says that they are Nagas. During the Kuki rebellion of 1917, the Anal Chief of Duthang wrote to the Commissioner, in which he requested him to consider them as not partaking in the rebellion and also that the Anals be treated as non-Kuki.

Thirdly, most of the British colonialists who classified Anal as Kuki or Old Kuki ,focus on their origin, house construction, etc. However, most of these are false. The theory of cave as a point of origin is common among the tribes of Manipur which encompasses the Nagas and the Kukis. Anal is no exception to this, it advocates that they originated from *Khul* or cave. The location of this *Khul* is a point to south western China. According to the colonialists, the Anals in constructing their houses, raise the piles, therefore, the Anals are Old Kukis. However, if we look at the Naga tribe like the Aos, they also practice this type of house construction. Thus, raising posts in house construction is prevalent among the Nagas also. Therefore, these traits could not prove Anal as Kuki. According to R.Brown (1974),

> The people in large track in the south east are called by the name Anal Namfow. In personal appearances they are much like khonjais, with whom, they are at deadly feud, and they appear to have an affinity: the practice of hereditary

chief which is no longer practiced. Interior villages, however retain this old customs of hereditary heads. The houses of the Anals are made like the khonjais. Social customs like marriage also have an affinity to the Kukis.

The truth is Anals never had hereditary chieftainship. Prior to political organization of village, the heroes like Thumkhel, Bera etc ruled and protect their village or land. These heroes could not be regarded as chiefs but they were the strongest or the best of their territory. In other words they were appointed to protect and rule the village due to their might and superiority in warfare. Once modern sense of political systems emerged, chiefship was always democratic in nature. A village chief and others were elected for a specific period. Even today, Anal villages continue this practice. In regard to appearance, both the Nagas and the Kukis are mongoloids belonging to the Tibeto-Burman family. Therefore, it is difficult to determine a difference between them on the basis of appearances and it is inappropriate to use appearance as a criterion to distinguish them.

In conclusion, Anal tribe is one of the sixty six Naga Tribes. It has all the aspects of a tribe. The land they are occupying is compact and undisputed. The land ownership system in this society is systematic but land consciousness has led to many disputes amongst them. Yet, till today the tribe customary law is still able to deal with them. In regard to their ethnic identity, even today, questions have been raised frequently against them. This needs appropriate study and discussion.

REFERENCES

Anal Naga Taangpi, (1999), *The Brief History of the Anals*, Unpublished, N.p.

Anal Naga Union, (1998), *Souvenir of the Second Anal Bungna*, Unpublished, N.p.

B.D. Thumdal, (2000), *A Profile of Anal Land and the Identity*, Unpublished, N.p.

Brown, R., (1893), *Statistical Account of the Native States of Manipur and Hill Territory Under its Rule*, Sanskaran Prakashah, Delhi.

Carry (1893), *Military Report on the Chin Lushia Country*, Shimla.

Chakravarti, Rana (1987), *People of Manipur*, B. R. Publishing House Corporation, Delhi.

Culloch, M. Maj(n.d), *Account of the Valley of Munnipore and the Hill Tribes.*

Customary Law Committee, (2000), *Anal no* (Anal Customary Law), Unplubished, N.p.

Datta, R.B. (1989), *Tribal Identity and Tension in North East India*, Omsons Publications, New Delhi,.

Gangte, T. S. (1993), *The Kukis of Manipur: A Historical Analysis*, Gian Publishing House, New Delhi.

Grierson, G. S. (n.d.), *Linguistic Survey of India*, vol. III, Part III.

Horam, M., (1975), *Naga Polity*, B.R Publishing House Corporation, Delhi.

Kabui, Gangmumei (1985), *Anal: A Transborder Tribe of Manipur*, Mittal Publication, Delhi.

Kanthung Ruwndar,(n.d.)*The Social and Political Life of the Anal Tribe in Manipur*, Unplubished Dissertation, Manipur University.

Pemberton, R. B. (1966), *Report on the Eastern Frontier of British India*, Calcutta.

Sanajaoba, Naoren, (1995) (ed.), *Manipur: Past and Present*, Vol. 3, Mittal Publication, New Delhi.

Shakespeare, Col. J (1912), *The Lushai Kuki Clans*, MacMillan, London.

Shemmi, Roland, (1988), *Comparative History of the Nagas: From Ancient Period Till 1926*, Inter-India Publications, New Delhi.

Singh, Capt. Rajendra (1981), *The Anals of Manipur*, Published Under the Directorate for Welfare of Tribal and Backward Classes, Manipur.

Singh, L. Joychandra (1995), *The Lost Kingdom: Royal Chronicle of Manipur*, Prajatantra Publishing House, Imphal.

Smith, W.C., (1925), *The Ao Naga Tribes of Assam*, MacMillan & Co. Ltd., London.

Soppit , C.A., *A History of the Kuki Lushai Tribes on the N.E. F. Districts: Cachar, Sylhet, Haga Hills and the North Cachar Hills*, Shillong.

Steward, Lieut., (1955), 'Notes on the Northern Cachar', *Journal of the Asiatic Society of Bengal,* Vol. XXIV.

Zehol, Lucy (1998), *Ethnicity of Manipur*, Regency Publication, New Delhi.

17

CRITICALLY ASSESSING KUKI LAND SYSTEM IN MANIPUR

—*T.T. Haokip*

Introduction

The paper attempts to make a critical look at the Kuki land system of Manipur from the point of view of traditional setting, its interface with democratic governance, continuity and change and the options and challenges for reforming the system. Many questions the validity of Kuki land system in a democratic polity mainly because the land within the jurisdiction of a Kuki chief belongs to him and his legal heirs and not to the villagers who live in it. Interestingly, the Kuki chiefship and its control over land have come to stay in spite of the onslaught of modernism and advancement in all works of life. In addition, the control and ownership over land by the Kuki chiefs is linked to identity and territoriality as the chiefship is considered the perennial source of Kuki customary laws. Further, the existence of specific and distinct land systems in both the hills and the valley has brought out the clash of interests and bitter rivalries among different ethnic groups, who views social reality from their own perspectives and identity. There have also been conflicts between the traditional chiefs and the state governments on the issue of land reforms. Thus, the issue of land and land systems in Manipur that has the potential to explode into ethnic conflicts requires critical analysis and farsighted actions from the state government and the communities in question.

Land holds a special place in almost all societies of the world. As a key component of any society's wealth, control and ownership over land and territory is linked not only to socio-economic developments but also to identity and territoriality. The issues of 'under development', 'uneven development', 'insurgency', 'homeland movements',' ethnic conflicts', etc in Northeast India in general and Manipur in particular revolve around land question. In the pre-colonial period, the Maharaja had evolved a land system for the valley.[1] The British initiated administrative changes most significantly in land revenue and judicial system in the valley since 1891. Conversely, the colonial state took no initiative to incorporate the hill areas into the judicial and land revenue system of the state but strengthened and consolidated the existing traditional institution of chiefship in the hills. Thus, the colonial state, by adopting different measures and policies had created divisions between Hills and the Valley. Similarly, the Constitution Drafting Committee of Manipur formed on the eve of British departure had two separate constitutions namely the Manipur State Constitution Act, 1947 and the Manipur Hill People's (Administration) Regulation, 1947. The Manipur Village Authorities Act 1956 further enhanced the traditional authority structure and consequently the Manipur Land Revenue &Reforms Act 1960 confined only to the valley areas. The state government's attempt to abolish the institution of chiefship failed, despite having passed the bill in the State Assembly in 1967. Finally, the Autonomous District Councils (ADCs) established under the Fifth Schedule in 1973 for the hill areas. In brief, the retention of the same pattern of existing traditional administration in the hill areas by the colonial state and Manipur governments in the post-independence period not only created 'One state, two systems' of administration but also sustained many fresh divides between the hill and the valley peoples.

The existence of high dependence on land coupled with lack of alternative source of employment in the post-independence period led to a strong assertion of exclusive territorial claims over land by different ethnic groups, creating a potentially explosive situation. At one level, it has brought out the clash of interests and bitter rivalries between the Meiteis, who approximately constitutes 65 percent of the state's population but confined to one-tenth area of the Imphal valley and tribals, who occupied the nine-tenth hill areas of the state. At another level, the Nagas and Kukis have contested over certain areas of Manipur as their ancestral lands.[2] The existence of different systems of land ownership and tenure, both in the hills and the valley reinforced the accentuated ethnic divide between the three major communities of Manipur. Thus, the modern notions of property and territorial rights have replaced the traditional notions of land ownership and habitation. The ethno-geographic and bio-geographic diversity of Manipur however precludes uniform land systems as different communities have different land systems. A critical assessment of land systems in Manipur is therefore imperative for understanding and addressing its various dimensions. The present paper attempts to make a critical assessment of the Kuki land system in the hills of Manipur.

Traditional Kuki Land System

The Kuki land system in reality was and is the land ownership of the Kuki chiefs. It is therefore imperative to discuss briefly how and under what circumstances the institution of Kuki chiefship emerged and had control over land. The institution of Kuki chiefship[3] might have emerged from the context of tribal wars in the past when a single authoritative figure was a necessity. In their grim struggle for existence and constant war with other tribes, they needed a strong leader who could maintain the cohesiveness of the society and protect it from external threats. Thus, the evolution of a strong and authoritarian chiefship of the Kukis was a historical requirement for survival. However, unlike many other tribal societies, the responsibility of consolidating this muscle power devolved upon the clan heads called 'Mi Upa', who in the process became the chief. Thus, the institution of chiefship in Kuki society has been associated with the concept of 'Mi Upa' or man on the direct line of the senior descent. Consequently, the control and ownership of land that became the necessary condition for maintaining the homogeneity of the community in question therefore came upon the chief or 'Haosa', meaning 'a rich person'. The term 'Haosa' however signified his administrative status rather than his personnel wealth, as he was the acknowledged leader within his territory. The institution of 'Haosa' also presupposes the existence of 'Semang-Pachong'[4], (Council of Ministers), generally composed of persons of wisdom, integrity, knowledge of customary law and its interpretations. Another remarkable feature was the special representation given to the minority clans in the council of ministers.[5] The Kuki chief was in theory the guardian of law and the absolute owner of the village and the land within it. It was true that by tradition, the Kuki chiefs exercised considerable rights in the management of land within his jurisdiction. In practice, he could not exercise 'ownership' in a manner to reduce the aggregate share of the members of the community. The village chief did not ordinarily have the rights to deny a resident member of the village his fair share of a plot. In other words, there was no sense of landlordism. Moreover, since the Kuki inheritance goes by the male line through the law of primogeniture, the land within the jurisdiction of a chief belonged to him and his legal heirs and not to the people who live in it. In the like manner, lands for cultivation, terrace lands, residential lands etc of the villagers belong to them and their legal heirs so long as they live in the same village.

The chief had to protect the interests of villagers by providing them security socially, politically and economically. The other important roles of the chiefs were to settle disputes, provide care and protection to his villagers. By virtue of his status as a chief, the *Haosa* enjoyed certain privileges[6] including *Samal,* the hind leg of hunted animals, *Changseo,* a tribute of certain baskets of paddy, *khotha,* a free labour of each villager once in a year and many others. However, the tributary privileges and other services to the chiefs in the past were understood as only material ethics of obedience and not exploitative in nature. Thus, the villagers on the one hand and the 'Haosa' on the other were in duty bound to fulfill their rights and obligations towards each other. Therefore, it would be wrong to draw a similarity between the traditional land ownership system of the Kuki chiefs and the feudal or zamindary systems. The Kuki chiefs were simply the custodians of village lands and not dictators like Zamindars in other parts of India. The Kuki chiefs were mere distributors of village lands just for jhuming cultivation purposes.[7]

There was sufficient room for a Kuki 'Haosa' to become a despot and tyrannical, but such things were rare since the functional power of the Kuki chiefs rested mainly on the proper consideration of the importance of consensus and customs. The Kuki Chiefship emerged primarily for pragmatic and useful purposes. The Kuki chiefs exercised "functional" power in the past. The enjoyment of a large number of power and privileges had made the chiefship the pivot of the society and overall the authority structure had become all-pervasive. Broadly speaking there are two bases of the authority of the chiefs – the subjective basis and the objective basis. The subjective basis consists in the dogma of kingship, law of primogeniture. The objective basis apparently lies in the customary dues and tributes payable to the chief by the members of the village. The most effective basis of the authority of the chiefs is rooted in the ownership of land and land resources. The chieftainship in Kuki society was the perennial source of customary laws, and the mechanism by which customary laws were interpreted and enforced. It would be wrong to view the traditional land system of the Kukis as exploitative consisting of two main social groups – the rulers and the ruled, the lords and the commoners. In the past, the traditional privileges of the Kuki chiefs had not much material implication as is commonly understood today. It only provided the basis of legitimacy of the traditional authority structure of the chiefs. There was no room for dispute over the boundary, as the chief owned the whole village land. Land disputes over the boundary of the jhum field and with other villages were unknown, although land disputes were very much common among the Nagas. In addition, while the Naga chief had to abide by the decisions of the village elders, the Kuki chief was at liberty to reject or modify the decision of the village elders in every matter. The Kuki chief had more responsibility than the Naga chief did in that he had to distribute land for cultivation every year without any discrimination. Lastly, the Kuki chiefs were able to protect the interests of the Kukis more than the Naga chiefs could protect the Nagas. The Kuki chiefs' control and ownership over land did play a unifying role in the society by providing leadership and ensuring tribal solidarity.

Kuki Land System and Democratic Governance

Democracy, in spite of its worldwide appeal is not free from controversies as democratizing countries are increasingly facing a crisis in governance. Indeed, disorder, corruption, fighting for power over control of resources, crisis in governance, political instability, unresponsive government etc often mark the processes of transition from tribal governance into democratic rule. The democratic structures and institutions envisaged to facilitate the democratic processes often fail to fulfill their very purpose. Consequently, democratisation process appears to be sensitive issue and the pride of tribal tradition suddenly flared up and as a result started politicizing their cultural issues and concentrated on the indispensability of the traditional institutions. However, many critiques see the traditional institutions as undemocratic, backward instruments of domination of chiefs over others, exclusion, social oppression and lack of progress, in such areas as political organization, women's rights, social mobility, and economic rights. It is therefore important to examine the interface of Kuki land system with democratic governance. The prevalence of customary land systems in the hills of Manipur has led to confusion and even confrontation between the Kuki chiefs and the Manipur governments since 1960s. The state government, while not directly questioning the validity of the traditional land systems, tried to enact new land laws in order to keep pace with the democratic norms. The important legislations proposed to bring about changes in the traditional land system include the Manipur Village Authorities Act 1956, the Manipur Hill Areas (Acquisition of Chief's Rights) Act, 1967, the Manipur Land Revenue and Land Reforms Act, 1960 (as amended from time to time). A brief discussion of these acts and legislations would be in order in order to know the interface between democratic governance and Kuki land system.

The Manipur Village Authorities in Hill Areas Act, 1956

The Manipur Village Authorities Act, 1956 attempts to consolidate the constitution and function of the village authorities of the hill areas of Manipur.[8] Under the Hill

Peoples' Regulation of 1947, all the members of the village authority including the chief were nominated according to the prevailing custom. However, under the Act 1956, there was no chance of being ipso facto members of the village council until and unless they were elected except the chief by virtue of the tradition of descent. This legally meant the reduction of the powers of the traditional chiefs and the consequent loosening of control of the chiefs over the members of the village authority. The village court could try cases when the value of the suit did not exceed five hundred rupees or in default imprison a person for a term not exceeding one month.[9] All these changes could not substantially legitimize the new legal authority structure in a Kuki village. However, at the operational level, one can find a traditional hangover in the matter of village administration in addition to the prescribed role of the chiefs as the chair of the constituted village authority. Despite the fact that the Kuki chiefs are the recognized ex-officio chairs, they could not give up their traditional function to all intents and purposes. The net result is the preponderance of the traditional role over the statutory role allotted to the chiefs. The chiefs in fact, run the village administration more as per the customary way. They demanded that the proposed amendment should be without any prejudice to the existing rights of the chiefs or those conferred on them by the government. They felt that legislation ought to recognize the existing unwritten powers, privileges and rights of the chiefs in the hill areas. As a result, the Kuki chiefs started to organize protest movements against this Act and the election of the village authority. The Act was declared by the Secretary of Motbung, a Kuki village, a 'very strange and defective' to Kuki custom, tradition and culture.[10] In April 1985, the Sadar Hills Kuki chiefs' organization in a memorandum to the Chief Minister of Manipur unequivocally described the village authority Act as of 'little use to the Kukis in particular'. The Act in their views was "an impediment to the Kuki way of life."[11] The Chiefs' Union Manipur in 1988 proposed that the rights of the chief to the land of the village shall, according to the customary law be applicable to him, continue to vest in him, and that he shall continue to enjoy such customary dues from his villagers whether he is the ex-officio chairman of the village authority.[12]

The Village Authorities Act, 1956, while indirectly recognized the complementary role of traditional village administration and introduced democratic elements has certain inherent defects. The Act is silent as to the financial matters of the Village Authorities and the village courts. Therefore, it follows that it shall not be possible, due to want of finance, for a Village Authority and Village Courts to perform their functions. It is our experience that no work whether developmental, administrative or judicial can be performed well without proper finance. Again all the criminal and civil laws (except some personal civil laws) are applicable to the tribal people. In addition, Section 19 of the Act provides for the constitution of a village court consisting of two or more members to be appointed by the state government. The question is can there be a village court without the chief or chairperson of the concerned village. Further, a provision in the Act, which states that all the proceedings before a village court should be recorded in Manipuri, made the Act unpopular among the tribal. Therefore, the first task before the government of Manipur is to convince the village chiefs about the value of democratic principles by protecting the customary laws wherever necessary. The tribal people are not likely to accept any Act, which fails to protect their customs and traditions. In Nagaland, the law allows the use of customs of the tribal people for various purposes and as a result, development could reach at the grass root level. In the same way, the Government of Manipur should understand the need, aspirations and sentiments of the tribal people before passing any Act. Sharing this view about the Act of 1956, Pu Rev. D. Singson states, "the Village Authority Act should be modified in accordance with Kuki culture."[13] In the opinion of Pu C. Haujakam, "the Kukis have been governed by our own customs, culture and traditions. We do not require the Government to make rules and regulations. Village Authority Act (1956) should be opposed tooth and nail. Our customs and traditions of governance should be enforced."[14] While sharing his views on the implementation of the provisions of the Village Authority Act 1956, Pu Haokholian states the "the Village Authority Act 1956 is an imposed act and the question of implementation or non-implementation does not arise."[15] It appears that not only the Kuki chiefs but also many Kuki leaders felt that the Village Authority Act, 1956 is an imposed one upon the Kukis without any acknowledgement of the ground reality. The ground reality is that while Act is still in force in the hill areas, its implementation has not been satisfactory over the past years. Their main objective in following the Act of 1956 has been to avail the benefits of various development schemes.

Acquisition of Chiefs' Right Bill, 1966

The institution of chiefship was abolished in the Chin Hills of Burma (Myanmar) as per the recommendation of the Commission of Enquiry in February 1948. Similarly, the Government of Assam passed "The Assam Lushai Hills District (Acquisition of Chiefs' Rights) Bill 1954," in March 1954. As a result, the rights and interests of 259 Mizo chiefs and 50 Pawi- Lakher chiefs were vested in the government.[16] Encouraged by the steps taken in Chin Hills and Lushai Hills, some people in Manipur started to demand for the abolition of chiefship and refused to pay tax to the chiefs. However, following the appeals of the chiefs, Shri R. G. Menzis, the last British S. D. O. (West Tamenglong) issued an order that all paddy tax were to be paid to the chiefs by the villagers.[17] Ever since then, the demand for abolition of chiefship became a debatable issue in Manipur. It was in this background that the Manipur Hill Areas Chiefs' Rights Acquisition Bill was first introduced in the Manipur Legislative Assembly in 1966 to acquire the rights and privileges of the chiefs and introduce land reforms with a view to distribute land to the tillers. All the members, ruling as well as opposition, who spoke on the Bill, termed it as 'progressive' and 'revolutionary'.[18] However, majority members were against payment of compensation to the chiefs on the ground that the State Government appointed them as their agents and argued that the government was dealing with the people directly and not through the chiefs.[19] The issue is if compensation was given to the chiefs of the Lushai Hills, Chin Hills, and the Maharaja of Manipur, why not to the tribal chiefs of Manipur.[20] The main objective of the majority members were to ensure the abolition of chiefship in order to enable the state government to extend the Manipur Land Revenue and Land Reforms Act 1960 to the Hill Areas to allow people from the plain to possess land and settle in the hill areas.[21]

The major defect of the policy of the government was the refusal to pay compensation to the chiefs when the move for abolition of Chiefship was initiated. The claim that the king of Manipur was the owner of all lands in Manipur is denial of corporate rights of tribal communities on lands. The theory of absolute ownership of right of king over all lands in Manipur and the policy in the matter of land reforms that follows from this theory is found to be unconvincing to the tribals. The issue of land reforms and abolition of chiefship are likely to dominate Manipur political scene in the near future. The Bill that was introduced again in 1967 divided the tribal and non-tribal members of the Manipur Assembly. While the tribal members were in favour of re-drafting the bill, other members of the Assembly wanted the Bill to be passed without any amendment. As a result, the chiefs continue to be the owners of the village land. This becomes clear from the orders of the Deputy Commissioner, Churachandpur District. "Regarding titles and ownership of the lands in the Hills Areas of Manipur, the chiefs of the respective villages are the owners of their respective lands."[22]

Unlike the Mizos and Chins, the Kukis wielded no effective political organization against their chiefs, which in turn gave them a relative advantage in the struggle of their status quo. In the absence of any organized opposition, the Kuki chiefs could carry the people with them in the struggle for the preservation of their customary rights and privileges. The majority opinion at present is retention of the traditional chiefship until such time when the tribal could look after their lands without any interference from the plain people. This can be achieved either by extending the provisions of the VI Schedule to the Hill Areas of Manipur or by introducing new provisions in the Manipur Land Revenue and Land Reforms Act, 1960.

Manipur Land Revenue and Land Reforms Act, 1960

The Manipur Land Revenue and Land Reforms Act, 1960, was an Act to consolidate and amend the law relating to land revenue in the then Union Territory of Manipur and to provide certain measures of land reforms. Though this Act was for the whole of the Union Territory of Manipur, the Hill areas were exempted from the purview of this Act. Section 1(2) of the Manipur Land Revenue and Land Reforms Act, 1960, categorically stated: "it extends to the whole of the Union Territory of Manipur except the hill areas thereof."[23] It allowed the prevailing land ownership system in the hill areas unchanged and provided a major impetus to perpetuate their present land ownership system with all its maladies. It was only in 1975 that an amendment was made in this Act in line with the changing socio-economic scenario of the country. Section 1(3) of the Manipur Land Revenue and Land Reforms (Amendment) Act, 1975, empowered the State

Government to extend, by notification in the official gazette, the whole or any part of this Act to any of the hill areas of Manipur as also might be specified in such notification.[24] In spite of this legal enactment, the Act has not been implemented in the Kuki areas of Manipur. It could not make any major impact on the land holding system in the hills. The only possible breakthrough that could have been initiated in the existing land ownership system of the Kukis was through vigorous land survey in the hills and increasing decentralization of ownership system through land distribution. The marginal distribution of land that has been initiated so far with the recorded rights to individuals over wet land is unsatisfactory. In the meantime, a serious problem arising out of the apprehension of alienation of land from the tribal to the non-tribal came to the forefront. Although the Manipur Land Revenue and Land Reforms Act, 1960, as amended by the Second Amendment in 1976,[25] provides adequate legal safeguard against alienation of tribal land, yet there has been alienation. Before 1960, alienation of land continued. There are two modes of alienation; one from the top and another from the bottom. A memorandum submitted by the members of the Tribal Land Protection and Restoration Committee of Manipur to the Chief Minister of Manipur in 1976 observed: We are aware of the proposed extension of MLR and LR Act, 1975, to the hill areas and we are in full hope of getting agricultural lands for wet field purpose, though the results seem not beneficial to the hill people who have got very negligible proportion out of the ten thousand hectares of land distribution so far.[26] In the same memorandum, the committee had blamed the 'top' for alienation of land from the tribal. Alienation from the bottom was affected through sale of land to the non-tribal. For this type of sale, the tribal sellers might have obviously got higher price, which they would never get from a tribal buyer.

The major constraint in land reforms in the Kuki areas of Manipur came from the chiefs who have under them not only the jhum land but also large areas of wet land. In the present context, it is true that the rationale behind traditional land holding system has lost ground. From the very beginning, the Kuki chiefs stood for the inalienable title of the chiefs to land including forests. Forest as such is a non-jhuming sector and there are cases in point that the latter could cash in on this non-jhuming sector in the hills. However, the Kuki chiefs have been constantly giving protest notes pleading for status quo. Thus, when the Congress Committee of Manipur took a resolution against the chiefs in 1949, one of the Kuki chiefs gave a strong protest note that 'Changseo' and 'Samal' customarily paid to the Kuki chiefs were in consonance with a Kuki custom and could never be regarded as taxes.[27] The Manipur Land Revenue and Land Reform Act despite all its pious wishes to bring about an egalitarian society could hardly make any impact in the hill areas. The Kuki chiefs have interpreted the government policy on tribal land protection as a threat to the inalienable rights of the chiefs over land. The customary rules on land ownership system has become so strong a force, though not properly defined and codified by the government, that it is very difficult to initiate any major change through the application of land reform rules. In such a situation a comprehensive land reforms as a part of an 'all round development' requires a change in the basic change of attitude.

Continuty and Change

The Kuki chiefship and its ownership over land have undergone changes at different periods, although critics do not see any justification in their socio-economic dominance in a democratic polity. The Kuki land system in the hills is still governed by unwritten customs and traditions with built in disincentives against individual land ownership. No individual household can lay claim to any land. The Kuki inheritance still goes by the male line through the law of primogeniture. Thus, the traditional values[28] still persists in the Kuki society. Thus, while some see the Kuki land system as backward instruments of social oppression and lack of progress in such areas as political organization, women's rights, social mobility, and economic rights, others see them as instruments of exclusion and domination by one social or clan group over others. The most significant change is that the Kuki chiefs no longer claim certain privileges as they enjoyed in the past. In some villages, even the terrace lands are allowed to own individually and the same could be sold to anyone within the village. Generally, transactions with people outside the village are allowed in rare situations. Another significant change at the institutional level in Kuki society is the emergence of another category of chiefs unofficially known as 'absentee chiefs' or the 'non-resident chiefs' (NRS) and the establishment of new villages by some elites. The 'absentee chiefs' or the 'non-resident chiefs' (NRS) have settled in urban areas far away from their villages, which has created a big communication gap between the chief and the villagers. Surprisingly, such category of chiefs managed to avail all the development schemes from either the government or other agencies by virtue of being chiefs. Similarly, the main objective of the elites in establishing new villages is just to avail development schemes from government and other agencies. Further, since the various development schemes are generally channelized through the village chiefs, many a time the share of the villagers are not given. Again, some Kuki chiefs have shown partiality in distributing goods to his villagers, which resulted in conflicts between the village chief and the villagers. Increasing landlessness and differentiation among the Kukis have sometimes led to tussles between chiefs and other villagers for control over land resources and implementations of government schemes. Thus, unlike in the past, villagers began in some cases began to question the legitimacy and authority of the chiefs. In contrast, the villagers from where there are enough fertile lands for shifting cultivation have not protested against the land ownership of the Kuki chiefs. However, scarcity of land for shifting cultivation and keenness on the part of villagers to grow commercial crops and the difficulty in using land as collateral for loan have led many people to question the validity of Kuki land system in the contemporary Kuki society. The common villagers in order to cope with development programmes, need money and to supplement their credit need, they will have to avail loan from the banks. The banks however could not advance the needed loan on the ground that there is no properly registered landed property to stand as surety. The most valuable, and sometimes, the only asset owned by individuals is their customary share of land for cultivation. Since the chief owns the land, this situation precludes using land as collateral for credit as lenders cannot take possession of the asset in the event of a loan default. Consequently, the villagers' loyalty towards the chiefs has eroded, according to Pu N. Lhungdim, because the chief has lost interest in the welfare of the people. They became selfish, wanted to take all the benefits of the village at the expanse of the people. The present system and practice of Chiefship has become more or less a hindrance to village development. No meaningful social and educational development can be taken up as most of the chief's stand on the way of such development.[29] In the opinion of Pu P. T. Yamthang, the main reason for erosion of loyalty on the part of the people towards Kuki chiefship is mainly due to social, agricultural and political revolution in the society and the chief's failure to meet the demands and requirements of the people in the complex society of the 20th century.[30] Again, Pu C. Haojakam states: The individual freedom is not properly protected. Rights of individuals are not safeguarded. The chief does not do justice to each individual. This has resulted in conflict between the chiefs and the villagers and hence the erosion.[31] Many educated people in the Kuki society share almost similar views today. In fact, some of the Kuki chiefs are not interested in the welfare of the villagers and take advantage of their status for achieving their own benefits. A few educated Kukis view the institution of Chiefship as a hindrance to development. Since the village chief is the owner of the village land, no government project could be taken up in the land without the chief's consent. However, the village chiefs often demand compensation without taking into consideration the benefits of such project. Thus in some areas the chiefs act as a hindrance to village development. In this respect, the views of Pu D. Singson may be stated who says, "Many chiefs think only for themselves. They always try to have a lion's share of all benefits from the Government. They are not chiefs in the real sense. They are like landlords and exploiters."[32] Though the total outlay in various sectors of the economy has registered a sharp rise in Manipur under successive five-year plans, the share of the Village Council in the development activities has not shown any corresponding increase. The State Government controls all the important areas of development administration and hence real decentralization has remained very different in the case of Kuki Village Council. The Kuki chiefs in their various memoranda to the State Government have pleaded either for decentralization of power on the pattern of Panchayati Raj bodies or on the extension of Sixth Schedule framework to the tribal areas.

Nevertheless, the institution of Kuki chiefship and its control over land could not be given a go-by as it is considered Kuki identity. According to Rev. T. Lunkim 'Kuki chiefship is culture and hence nothing can replace it'.[33] The institution of chiefship remains firmly entrenched among the Kukis as it has been considered the fountainhead of all customs and retainer of tradition. Mr. Shonkhothong Haokip[34] theologizes it as God's blessing to the Kukis as the Israelite Kings were to their people. Notwithstanding some inherent defects in the chiefship system, the Kukis are not yet ready to do away with it. The Kuki chiefship system has come to stay as a perennial source of custom and tradition, in that, in spite of the onslaught of modernism and advancement in all works of life, they are able to inherit a rich cultural and traditional heritage. The chiefship system be it on matters relating to economic, political, religious, judiciary has its bases on the proper interpretation of the customary law and tradition. This is the main reason why the system of chiefship and its control and ownership over land could not be given a go-by, despite varied changes all around. The general opinion seems to be in favour of retaining the institution of chiefship by limiting the powers and functions over land primarily for safeguarding and preserving the cultural values of the society, for the origin of chiefship lay in the general recognition of the socially useful role of the chief in the community.

Options and Challenges

Is Sixth Schedule an option? While there have been intense debates over the validity of Sixth Schedule within states where it is applicable, there is a strong demand for its introduction from the Kukis and Nagas of Manipur. The Hill Areas Committee of the Manipur State Assembly, keeping in mind the limitations of Fifth schedule,[35] passed a resolution in 1974 recommending the replacement of district councils by the Sixth Schedule. However, the issue of Sixth Schedule has always been a contentious issue in Manipur as the majority Meiteis opposes the Sixth Schedule on the ground that this will be precursor to the attainment of Kuki state and Nagalim(Greater Nagaland). In addition, while the Kukis demanded for six district councils from the existing five, the Nagas proposed for two councils for the existing five hill districts, one consisting of the four Naga- dominated hill districts and the other constituted by the Kuki-dominated Churachandpur district. Thus, the issue of Sixth Schedule has been politicized in Manipur. Of late, the Naga and Kuki insurgents see the Sixth Schedule as a means of suppressing their demands for greater Nagaland and Kuki state respectively. The consultation paper on National Committee for the Review of the Indian Constitution recommended the Sixth Schedule for Manipur's councils, with certain changes based on experience in other northeastern states. A critical assessment of the Sixth Schedule demonstrates that it is subject to interference, supersession and dissolution by the Central government through the Governor. The Sixth Schedule, which has a long history of tribal struggle for identity assertion, will have to be carefully examined and a substantially altered Sixth Schedule on the line of Panchajati Raj needs to be evolved. The main challenges for restructuring the land systems in Manipur will come from the three major communities namely the Meiteis, Nagas, and Kukis who have not only different viewpoints but also contesting aspirations on land issue.

Concluding Remarks

The general perception is that traditional institutions predates colonialism and represented early forms of societal organizations. However, there are different perceptions. The conservative Burkean perception of society views tradition as the accumulated wisdom of the past and Andrew Heywood, maintains that tradition stands for absence of change. Sociologists went further and viewed tradition in terms of different aspects of social structure and the organisation of individual behaviour and beliefs or of cultural symbols. Sociological theories raised the issues that tradition can be both dynamic as well as static but have not located the historical origin of traditions. On the other hand, historians and other social scientists such as Eric Hobsbawn, Ramila Thapar, and Terence Ranger have argued that it is not only important and necessary but also possible to locate the historical origin of traditions. For instance, Hobsbawn argued that traditions could be constructed and that what sometimes has been considered as very ancient tradition is in fact of quite recent origin if one traces the history of tradition. Thus, traditions or traditional institutions need not be very old and exist from time immemorial. Indeed, people created or invented traditions or traditional institutions at a particular time to suit their interests, although the importance of traditions is not uniform in all societies. In the post-colonial period, efforts have also been made in some countries to accord constitutional recognition to these institutions.[36] Moreover, in some countries the traditional leaders on their part have tended to adjust themselves with winds of change. Nevertheless, most of the tribal societies of the Northeast India, are today at serious socio-political crossroads. The two sets of authority- traditional and modern have interacted with each other in different ways at different junctures.[37] This has resulted in further confusion on the part of traditional leaders and the policy makers. In the process, there seems to be a tussle between the traditional institutions and the democratic institutions for power and control over resources leading to crisis in governance.

The indigenously conceived Kuki land system had a force of the wisdom of the people. It is therefore not surprising that the customary rules on land ownership system have become so strong a force, though not properly defined and codified by the government, that it is very difficult to initiate a major change through the application of land reform. The old theory of change and modernization commonly assume tradition as something static, frozen in time, and cannot be modified. In contrast, the new theory holds the view that the traditional values need not necessarily be inconsistent with the modern values. Land systems, whether customary or western, are social constructs modified over time to accommodate society's particular needs. Similarly, when they are not serving the interests of the community, they are modified or replaced. In the present context, it is true that the rationale behind traditional Kuki land systems is no longer ideal for commercial farming in a modern economy. Thus, the communities in question need to take the initiative in reforming the land system before the state intervenes. However, at the same time, one must realize that the process of changing land systems has always been a complicated, technical and political subject. The efforts to change land ownership throughout the world have failed more often than they have succeeded. In the context of Manipur, the roles of the state government, the communities in question and the chiefs will be central in the success of restructuring land systems in the hill areas. Until and unless, the tribals are convinced and instill in them new values of democratisation process, legalistic approach is likely to remain futile for any time to come. Therefore, what is more important than acts and legislations in the context of Manipur is the gradual refinement of the fundamental ways of thinking of the people. The blanket application of the Manipur Land Revenue and Land Reforms Acts and the Manipur Village Authority Act, 1956 to hill areas will create political turmoil without achieving the stated aims. The MLR&LR Act sixth Amendment Bill (1989) which intends to delete the word "except hill areas" if implemented in its present form is likely to threaten tribal land rights, exposing them to the risk of losing their land without creating an alternative livelihood system. The Manipur government and people of Manipur have to acknowledge the sensitivity and complexity of land issue that can divide communities along ethnic lines especially in a multi-lingual society like Manipur. The most important issue is how to design a land system that unlocks the value of land while preserving its associated traditional values. The present land system of the Kukis precludes using land as collateral for credit as lenders cannot take possession of the asset in the event of a loan default. The new land system must incorporate the customary system of land rights, yet permit more land to serve as collateral.

NOTES

1. For details, See, Das, J.N, *A Study of the Land Systems of Manipur*, Gauhati, 1989. Chapter 2, pp.14-22.
2. The Nagas and Kuki demand for Nagalim (Greater Nagaland) and Kuki state respectively over the same territory have created misunderstanding and conflicts between the two ethnic groups. In contrast, the Meiteis endeavor for the territorial integrity of Manipur.
3. For details, See, Haokip, T.T., *The Kuki Chiefship and Its Changing Dimensions*, Ph.D. Thesis, submitted to NEHU, Shillong, 1995
4. For details, See, Gangte, T.S., *The Kukis of Manipur*, 2002
5. The minority clans here would mean a non-Haokip living in a village where the Haokips are in majority or verce-versa.
6. The author has examined the privileges of the Kuki chiefs in traditional setting. For further details, See, Haokip, T.T., .Kuki Polity with special reference to village administration, Phil Dissertation, submitted to NEHU, Shillong, 1991.
7. Private Members Resolution by Ngulkhohao, MLA, Saikot, Churachandpur, 1986.
8. *A Handbook of Manipur Hill Village Authority*, Government of Manipur, Law Department, p. 1
9. Section 49 (1) (2), Ibid, p. 121.
10. A petition from the Secretary of Motbung village to the SDO Sadar Hills Administrative Unit, Saikul, Manipur, dated 21. 7. 71.
11. Memorandum submitted to the Hon'ble Chief Minister of Manipur, Shri Rishang Keishing by the Sadar Hills Chiefs' Organization, Dt. Motbung, the 14th April, 1985 (Manipur
12. Letter to the Hon'ble Chairman of the Hill Areas Committee, Manipur Legislative Assembly by the Chairman of the Executive Committee, Chiefs' Union, Manipur, Churachandpur, Manipur, 14th July 1986.
13. Interview with Pu Rev. D. Singson, Imphal, 13. 5. 1994
14. Interview with Pu C. Haujakam, Kangpokpi, 16. 5. 1994
15. Questionnaire Respondent Pu Haokholian, Churachandpur 16. 5.1994

16. Thanga, L.B., *The Mizo—A Study in Racial Personality*, (United Publishers, Gauhati, 1978), p. 171.
17. Details. See Sub-Divisional Magistrates' (West Tamenglong) Order Misc. Case No. 66 of 1024-43 dated 23 April 1946.
18. *Manipur Legislative Assembly Proceedings, Vol.* XXXIX (Fifth Session 1966-1967), Manipur Legislative Assembly, p. 58.
19. *Manipur Legislative Assembly Proceedings* (Fifth Session) 1966-67, p. 64.
20. The Maharaja of Manipur was entitled to receive compensation of Rs. 3, 00,000/- annually after the State of Manipur was merged into the Union of India. According to many tribal leaders, the Maharaja's authority extended to the plain areas and the chiefs and their lands remained untouched by the merger agreement.
21. At present the plain people are not allowed to possess land in the Hill areas except by the special permission of the Deputy Commissioner concerned who shall not give such permission unless he has first secured the consent of the District Council (under Fifth Schedule) within whose jurisdiction the land lies.
22. Order No. 5/20/DC(S)/85 dated 16 March 1985, Government of Manipur.
23. *The Manipur Land Revenue and Land Reforms Act, 1960*, (33 of 60)
24. *The Manipur Land Revenue and Land Reforms Act*, 1975.
25. Section 158 of the Manipur Land Revenue and Land Reforms (Second Amendment). 1976.
26. Memorandum of the Tribal Land Protection and Restoration Committee, 1976.
27. "The Congress – The Political Party in Manipur State has no voice in the affairs of the hill People" – A Statement by S. L. Lunneh, Chief of Motbung, dated 28. 7. 49.
28. Values are informal rule that circumscribe appropriate behavior in a particular context. Values have been considered by many to be crucial for understanding cultures and political behavior.
29. Questionnaire Respondent N. Lhungdim, West Molnom on 25/9/94.
30. Questionnaire Respondent Pu P. T. Yamthang, Imphal on 20/5/94.

31. Questionnaire Respondent Pu C. Haojakam, Kangpokpi on 16/5/94.
32. Questionnaire Respondent Pu D. Singson, Imphal, on 13/5/94.
33. Questionnaire Respondent Rev. T. Lunkim on 13/3/94.
34. Shonkhothong Haokip, *Thugilbu,* (1996), p. 18.
35. The District Councils of Manipur under the Fifth schedule were completely dependent on state government financially. The state government is at liberty to accept, modify, or reject the annual budget of these councils. The District Commissioner is empowered to suspend or modify any decision and function of these councils.

REFERENCES

Das, J.N, (1989), *A Study of the Land Systems of Manipur,* Gauhati, pp.14-22.

Gangte, T.S (2002), *The Kukis of Manipur,* (n.p).

Government of Manipur (n.d), *A Handbook of Manipur Hill Village Authority,* , Law Department, p. 1.

Government of Manipur, *The Manipur Land Revenue and Land Reforms Act, 1960,* (33 of 60)

Government of Manipur, *The Manipur Land Revenue and Land Reforms Act,* 1975.

Haokip, T.T. (1995), 'The Kuki Chiefship and Its Changing Dimensions', Ph.D Thesis, NEHU, Shillong.

Manipur Legislative Assembly Proceedings, Vol. XXXIX, Fifth Session, (1966-1967), Manipur Legislative Assembly, p. 58.

N. Lhungdim *Questionnaire Respondent,* West Molnom on 25/9/94.

Pu C. Haojakam *Questionnaire Respondent,* Kangpokpi on 16/5/94.

Pu C. Haujakam *Personal Interview,* Kangpokpi, 16. 5. 1994.

Pu D. Singson *Questionnaire Respondent,* Imphal, on 13/5/94.

Pu Haokholian, *Questionnaire Respondent,* Churachandpur 16. 5.1994.

Pu P. T. Yamthang *Questionnaire Respondent,* Imphal on 20/5/94.

Pu Rev. D. Singson, *Personal Interview*, Imphal, 13. 5. 1994.

Rev. T. Lunkim *Questionnaire Respondent* on 13/3/94.

Shonkhothong Haokip, (1996) *Thugilbu*, (n.p), p. 18.

Thanga, L.B, (1978), *The Mizo- A Study in Racial Personality*, United Publishers, Gauhati, p. 171.

18

LAND, IDENTITY AND DEVELOPMENT: Perceptions Focusing on the Tribals of Manipur

—S. Kipgen

Introduction

Manipur is a small state. The total area comprises of 22,327 sq. km. out of which the hill area covers 20,089 sq. km. The centrally located tiny valley of the state covers an area of about 2,000 sq. km. The hill area covers $9/10^{th}$ of the total area of the state which indicates that the tribal areas are scarcely populated with a density of 44 people per sq. km. The density in the valley is 631 people per sq. km. It is a land of multi-ethnic mosaic being inhabited by Hindu and Muslim Meiteis in the valley. The tribals can broadly be grouped into the Nagas and the Kukis or 'Kuki-Chin'.

The State Legislative Assembly has 60 member seats out of which 40 seats are allotted to the valley and 19 seats for the tribals and 1 for Schedule Caste. The state of Manipur has nine districts. The valley has four districts viz Imphal

(East), Imphal (West), Thoubal and Bishenpur. The five hill districts are Ukhrul, Senapati, Tamenlong, Churanchandpur and Chandel.

Historical Background

The hills of Manipur surrounding the valley are obviously the abode of the different tribal ethnic groups. The process that activated the nature of the movement of different tribes with the resultant outcome of displacing each other could be seen in the light of the inter-tribal warfare, feuds, natural calamities and shifting cultivation. There were many instances of local migration within the state as the hills of Manipur were an uninhabited region that could easily provide sustenance to their economy. The nature of the tribal dispersal and the area of settlement show that the Kukis are placed in between the Meiteis in the valley and the Nagas in the hills of the northeast and northwest of Manipur. Though some of them are also found along the fringes of the valley, it is obviously never their forte. The fact remains that the smaller tribes of the Manipur, irrespective of Nagas and Kukis, who were pressurised by the powerful ones, were almost instantaneously drawn towards the Meitei community in the valley and also sought the protective cover of the king.

Prior to the coming of the British on the soil of Manipur, the tribal chiefs ruled their respective chiefdoms independently without any fear of outside interference. They had the land to rule over and to fight for the protection of their land. Conquering virgin land for their settlement was also not uncommon. They occupied the land which they could claim for themselves. There had been acts of treachery, raids, outrages etc. but in spite of that they generally continued to live together for centuries. Inter-tribal feuds in those days were not simply a manifestation of senseless killings but had valid political and economic reasons. The history of relationship between the Nagas and the Kukis is marked by a mixture of amity and enmity which nevertheless continued to play an important role in the politics of the state.

The multifarious problems of the internal administration of the village were solely in the hands of their chiefs who had strong bonds of unity with the Meitei kings. They had mutual respect for each other. The Meitei kings developed friendly relation with the hill chiefs instead of provoking them. It needs particular mention here that the Kuki warriors used to assist the Maharaja of Manipur as loyal sentinels. Undoubtedly they were the sole protectors of the Manipur frontiers. In many instances the king sought military assistance from them to thwart external aggression or for certain missions abroad. In spite of various successful military expeditions the erstwhile Meitei kings failed to institutionalize political domination in the hills. The Meitei kings fought against the hill chiefs for several centuries and exacted tributes from the subjugated tribes. It is also a fact that the Naga and Kuki chieftains were not always defeated. There were also a series of reprisals from them.

The politico-administrative machineries of the Meitei kings had also failed to penetrate into the interior part of the hills. The activities of the kings were limited to collecting tributes from the subjugated tribes. Besides, the political administration was confined wholly in the valley. No hill people were represented in the royal *durbar*. The non-participation of tribals in the political mainstream led to the incomprehensive process of state and nation building. The hill people continued to enjoy an exclusive and independent political existence. All these historical realities were the causative factors in developing the isolationist tendencies or ethnic insularity among the tribals. When the British consolidated their foothold in the valley, the defiant tribal chieftains were reduced to submission. Consequently, they brought the administration of the hill areas under their direct control leaving the administration of the valley in the hand of the Raja.

In living together for centuries, absorption of the tribal into Meitei society was always a possibility. Cultural elements were borrowed out of social interaction. To maintain friendly relations with the hill chiefs and to collect tribute from the subjugated tribes the Meitei kings used to organize *Haochongba* (tribal dance festival) in the palace. On this occasion, the Meitei kings received tributes, offerings, and the king in return offered them drinks and food. In fact the subjugated tribals in general shared the common joys and sufferings of the state with the Meitei kings through ages. Thus in the early centuries they were interacting with each other. It is only a later development where segregation and individual identity was stressed and common factors were suppressed between the hill and the valley people.

ADMINISTRATIVE CHANGES

The British Period

When Manipur came under the control of the British after the Anglo-Manipur War of 1891, the hill areas were also brought under the British rule by keeping the hill administration under the personal responsibility of the Political Agent. The British subjugation of the hill tribes brought changes in the administrative pattern of the tribals. The *sanad* issued by the British authority to Raja Churachand Singh clearly stated the final authoritative control rested with the British. With the formation of the *durbar* headed by the Raja, an officer especially selected by the government of East Bengal and Assam was made the vice-president who was allotted the portfolios of finance and revenue. Besides, the administration and control of the hill tribes were also left in the hands of the vice-president. The real administrator of the hill tribes of Manipur was the durbar's vice-president. The *durbar* was also the highest criminal court in the state and tried all criminal cases not covered by the jurisdiction of the *Cheirap* court. In this connection cases relating to hill tribes were tried independently by the political agent. In other words, cases related to the hill-men were excluded from the civil and criminal jurisdiction of the *Durbar*. The Maharaja of Manipur was divested of all his powers over the administration of the hill areas despite being the president of the *durbar*. Later amendments removed the Maharaja from the post of the president and the British officer who was appointed president of the *durbar* administered the hill areas on behalf of the Maharaja.

Thus, there were separate rules to govern and administer the tribals according to their traditions and religious beliefs, under the vigilant supervision of the British. The tribal chiefs were not deprived of the rights of ownership from the land. Instead of tampering and hampering the tribal customary land ownership and social institutions set up by the tribal chiefs, the British administrators preserved and refrained from direct interference from the legislation power of British India in Manipur. The British political agents or authorities recognized and utilized the institution of chieftainship as part of their administrative machinery to serve the interest of the state in general and the tribe in particular. So their office was retained as part of an administrative empowerment. This indicates that the institutions of administrative machinery under the chiefs of the tribals were preserved.

Impact of Anti-British Movement

The Anglo-Kuki war, 'Kuki Rebellion,' of 1917-19 was a watershed in the administration of Manipur. The administration of the hill areas was transformed. The British authority started taking more vigorous administrative steps in the hills. The anti-British movement of Rani Gaidinliu brought further changes. The President of the Manipur State *durbar* became the sole authority of hill administration. A policy of administrative decentralization was adopted. The

Maharaja and the State *durbar* were completely eliminated in the administration of the hill areas. It is clear that the *durbar* exercised no direct control but from time to time it tried to claim their indirect control through its power over the budget. It shows that only in theory the tribal people were under the Government of the Maharaja. The exclusion of the Maharaja's authority was so complete and thorough that the tribal people tended to forget that they were the subjects of the state of Manipur. In short, the hill people were given separate treatment though they were theoretically within the political state boundaries of Manipur. The policy of 'Divide and Rule' had been enforced. In such situation there was no question of extending or establishing modern system of administration in the hill areas either by the Maharaja or the British. The Maharaja of Manipur was rightly blamed for neglecting development in the hill areas. Even after 1891 there was no proper administration of the hill tribes and no provision for them in the budget. After assuming the administration of the hill tribes, the British authorities justified the action on the ground that only by maintaining a decent standard of administration can peace be preserved. The motive behind the British to keep the tribes divided and to create a 'barrier of wall' between the hill men and the plainsmen was achieved. The integrated social fabric of Manipur thus got fractured and fractionalized. A frustrated and outmaneuvered society remained no match for the cunning and cleverly executed policies of the British. It was indeed a sad state of affairs for Manipur. The politics in Manipur got manipulated ever since the Anglo-Kuki war. A section of the common masses always remained suppressed and deprived of welfare measures.

Post-Independent and Contemporary Changes

With the passing of the Indian Independence Act in 1947, Manipur became independent along with other princely states of India. With the lapse of British supremacy the administration of the hill areas was in the hands of the Maharaja of Manipur. After this a series of Acts were passed regarding the improvement of the administration in the hill areas. These were-

i. "The Manipur State Hill Peoples (Administration) Regulation Act, 1947" which introduced a well formulated local government system in the hill areas by constituting a village authority to replace the traditional village council;

ii. "The Manipur (Village Authority in Hill Areas) Act, 1956," passed by the Parliament to initiate peoples' representation at the grass root level for better administration. According to this Act, the village chief became the ex—officio chairman of the village authorities and its members were elected on the basis of adult franchise by repealing the hill people's regulation of 1947;

iii. "The Manipur Hill Areas (Acquisition of Chiefs Rights) Act, 1967," passed by the state legislature on 10th, 1967.[5] It was an attempt to abolish chieftainship in the hill areas of Manipur by paying land compensation. However, the Act could not be implemented due to the objection of the chief's union. What is more proper here is that the acquisition of the chief's rights over the land is to be done by the people themselves who are the rightful custodians of village lands as per the age-old customary practice of the tribal people in pre-colonial days;

iv. "The Manipur (Hill Areas) District Council Act, 1971", which the Parliament passed in 1971 on the eve of Manipur's attainment of statehood to establish Autonomous District Councils in the hill areas of Manipur with a view to decentralization of power. There are six Autonomous District Councils for five districts- two in Senapati and one each in Ukhrul, Churachandpur, Chandel, and Tamenglong. However all the six Autonomous District Councils had been kept under suspension even after the lapse of more than fifteen years. Our findings have revealed that the autonomy granted to the district council under the Act is only in name. The survival and working of the district council greatly depends on the government of Manipur through the district administration. The Councils does not have any power of legislation. In other words, the Sixth Schedule provision of the Indian Constitution is not extended to the District Autonomous Council; and lastly

v. "The Manipur (Village Authorities) in Hill Areas (Amendment) Act, 1983". The most important feature among others of the amended Act is that no transfer or allotment of land be made to the non-tribal without the previous permission in writing of the deputy commissioner of the concerned district. In other words, the deputy commissioner has to secure the consent of the council as per the existing rules of the district council.

As of now neither the Manipur (Hill Areas) District Council Act, 1971, is in operation nor is the demand for the extension of the provisions of the Sixth Schedule under Article 244(2) of the Constitution in the tribal areas of Manipur conceded. Economic backwardness, lack of development infrastructure, poverty and shortage of educational facilities in the hill areas of Manipur has greatly enhanced the sense of alienation among the tribals from the political mainstream of the state. The tribals feel that they were deprived of their right to economic development. The non-constitution of the District Council for many years is a glaring example of wanton violation of the statutory Act and "rape of district autonomy and democracy" leading to a sort of political vacuum, which trampled the interest and legitimate aspiration of the tribal people. Presently it appears that the extension of the provisions of the Sixth Schedule will satisfy the interest and aspiration of the tribal people of Manipur. Hence, in conformity with the principle of genuine democracy and federation, the Sixth Schedule, if extended, would serve as a basis for working out the principle of internal self-determination of the tribals, which in turn will serve further as the cementing force for the integrity of Manipur. Probably, it will also help to arrest the fissiparous tendencies and mushrooming of different tribal movement for separate homeland in Manipur.

There has been a demand for upgrading the present Autonomous District Councils in accordance with the provisions of the Sixth Schedule of the Constitution of India. In the absence of elected Members of District Councils, the hills of Manipur today remain utterly neglected, deprived and devoid of any concrete development. In contrast, the Panchayati Raj system functions properly without any hitch in the valley of Manipur including in the Nepali inhabited regions of Senapati district.

All the above Acts establish the fact that the tribals of Manipur have been given separate treatment. They are out of the purview of general administration. In the preamble of the Constitution of Manipur, 1947 it is stated that it extends to the State of Manipur as a whole including the Hill Areas thereof, whereas the Manipur Land Revenue and Land Reform Act, 1960 states that, this Act extends to the whole State of Manipur 'except the Hill Areas thereof'. It may be noted here that when the country gained Independence in August 1947 the founding fathers of the constitution recognized the uniqueness of certain traditional and customary institutions of the tribal areas in this region such as the self-governing village administration. They felt the needs for political and administrative framework, which would work to safeguard and promote the rights and interest of tribals in these areas.

Land-Ownership and Land-Use System

The subject matter calls for a brief highlight of the traditional institution of chieftainship and the manner in which land is used. Every Kuki village has inevitably got a chief called *Haosa*. The Mizos called it *Lal*. It is usually hereditary. Kuki traditional form of governance is based on chieftainship. The Kuki chiefs are owners of the ancestral lands and traditionally they are the repositories of all powers of administration dealing with the village. Land ownership is the exclusive right and prerogative of the chief. Individual villagers have no rights over the land whatsoever. The villagers are at the mercy of the chief. The land allotted to the village people cannot be sold. If a family in the village wishes to migrate to another village, the land will automatically return to the chief.

The chief of the village and his council of ministers wield great authority and prerogatives over the villagers within the limit of their territorial jurisdiction. The chief performs judiciary, executive and legislative functions in consultation with his council of ministers. The Kuki chiefs are vested with absolute power. Chieftainship as an institution is the perennial source of customary laws and retainer of tradition. It has come to stay as the mechanism by which such customary laws are interpreted in the social system. This makes chiefship a living force enabling the maintenance of the separate identity of the Kukis.

Unlike the Kukis the system prevalent among the Nagas is essentially democratic. A village has an elected head or chief called *Khullakpa* and a council of elders who had wisdom and experience representing the clans. The office is held by election for a specific term. Among the Nagas land ownerships are allowed to individuals, clans and to groups or villagers collectively with equal rights.

From the earliest times, the hill tribes practiced different land use system in their domain. Though the entire land of the village theoretically belonged to the chief in the case of Kukis, the village community who shared the land among themselves did the actual cultivation. The general condition that prevailed among the Kukis from the earliest times is that the land within the chiefdom is distributed to the villager for cultivation and homestead. The member of the chief's council, with the approval of the chief, superintend and transact all business matters in connection with the land cultivation, measurement, collection of tax, etc. When a particular land is to be cultivated for Jhumming purposes by a villager it has to be brought into the knowledge of the chief for approval. This shifting cultivation is necessitated by the absence of permanent allotment to the villagers. This old devilish system will continue until a new approach to do away with the said system of cultivation is taken up with earnestness by the authorities directly concerned with the problem thus posed.

The most important factor of tribal life-style in respect of 'land use system' is to maintain subsistence of their life based on Jhumming or shifting system of cultivation. It is a rain fed agricultural practice for economic sustenance to which they are adapted. They produced almost everything they needed from the Jhum land. Normally it is an important factor of tribal lifestyle in respect of their 'land use' system. It served as the economic mainstay. Traditionally the tribal were totally dependent on it for their survival. However, the end result of the system is considered as obsolete, destructive and devastating. It is more heavily practiced in the areas where the Kukis inhabit preponderantly than in the areas inhabited by the Nagas. As of now terraced cultivation is found successful and it has been increasingly practiced as a viable method of cultivation among the Nagas. Of course, the Kukis too are not an exception to this terrace farming method of cultivation.

Brief analysis

The institution of the chieftainship among the Kukis is autocratic in nature. It has a direct bearing on the socio-economic life of the people. Unlike the Naga system of village administration, the people cannot enjoy liberty and freedom. As he is the sole owner of the land, the villager has to please him. He has the right to sell off the land without the consent of the villagers or the public. In many cases the chiefs have done so. The nuisance created by the chief in all matters has diminished the incentives of the individuals. As free hand is not given to the individuals there is no room to exhibit their talent to strive for development. Though most of the Kuki chiefs no longer enjoy the traditional privileges and customary entitlement, however in matters of land ownership he continues to be the sole authority. The weak economic base and their fragile nature of their subsistence is due to the existing systems of land use and ownership pattern which needs serious introspection and experimentation with the system of individual holding and ownership of land. Owing to the absence of individual rights over the land, credit facilities and financial assistance either from the government or from other financial institution is hard to come. It is imperative on the part of the Kuki community to switch over and explore ways and means for attaining sustained economic viability in the hill areas. Chieftainship is instrumental in the preservation of customary laws and identity no doubt, but its continuation as it was without any changes in its structure may no longer be favoured. The past trends suggest that chieftainship needs reformation from within to pave the way conducive to economic growth and development to suit the changed situation. At the same time certain measures should also be adopted to retain traditional value system in order to preserve the culture and identity.

MLR & LR ACT, 1960 vis-a-vis Tribals

The MLR & LR Act-1960 is another significant legislative measure that has an important bearing on the land ownership or holding system of the tribals. The tribal people by and large were opposing the extension of Manipur Land Reform and Land Revenue Act of 1960 in the hill areas. According to this provision all land including forests, mines and minerals therein are not the property of any person but are the property of the state. This is in conformity with the Manipuri tradition that the king was the absolute proprietor of all land within his territory in the valley. But for the protection of the tribals, the Act incorporated 'special provision' under Sec. 158 according to which it prohibited the sale or transfer of tribal's land to a non-tribal without the prior permission of the Deputy Commissioner and the previous consent of the District Council.

The act does not apply to the hill areas of the State but the State government may extend the whole or any part or any section of the Act to any part of the hill areas of Manipur by calling upon section (2) 1 of the Act. According to this section the term hill areas means such areas in the hill-tracts of the state of Manipur as the state government may by notification in the official gazette declare to be 'hill areas'. The hill district do not automatically become 'hill areas' by virtue of its location in the hill districts as it requires declaration by notification in the form of official gazette. This section empowers the government to extent the Act in the hill areas in a planned and calculated manner.

In this connection many attempts have been made to remove the restriction of transfers of land to non-tribals by inserting the relevant provisions in the sections and clauses. The next attempt to remove this restriction on the transfer is the MLR & LR Act 6th Amendment bill 1989, by inserting new sections i.e. 158-A,158-B,158-C, and 159-D.

The new 6th Amendment Bill intends to remove the word 'except hill areas thereof' mentioned earlier and the provision thereto in sub-section (2) of section 1, above which means that the extension of the Act is to be made absolute or statutory, including the hill areas of Manipur. The tribals vehemently opposed the proposed amendment bill and demanded the withdrawal of the bill. Due to such opposition from the hill people, the bill awaits the assent of the Governor.

The 7th Amendment Bill 1992 introduced new sections for removing the restriction of land transfer in the hills and making the revenue tribunal the highest authority under the MLR & LR Act retrospectively from the 1975 Amendment and no further appeal shall lie from this court. This means that concerning revenue matters one cannot go to appeal in the high court or Supreme Court, as the tribunal is the highest court as per the proposed amendment.

As of now the Act has been extended in many parts of the hill districts. In spite of the restriction, some landholders in Sadar Hills of Senapati district and Churachandpur are found selling their lands to the non-tribal without prior permission from the concerned Deputy Commissioner. This has made the system more complex and complicated. In this way the tribal settlers are gradually becoming landless. It may be noted that under the 6th Schedule of the Indian Constitution and the Manipur Hill Areas District Council Act, 1971, power to allot land is vested in the District Council.

Article 371 (C) of the Indian Constitution has special provision 'to look after the interest of the hill areas' with respect to the state of Manipur. However, this provision has been reduced to the status of other committees of the state assembly. All relevant bills and projects excepting those related to finance should always be referred to the chairman of the Hill Areas Committee who represents all the twenty MLAs of the hills of Manipur.

Further, the Hill Village Authority Act, 1956, which does not synchronize with the present day realities should also be amended, based on their customs, culture and traditions. This is essential to remedy the deprivations that have so far affected the hill people. Long overdue compensation by way of appropriate development needs to be brought in order to keep the tribal economically at par with other people of the hills in the country who have enjoyed the benefits of Autonomous District Councils. The Meiteis who are economically and socially advanced should take more interest in the development of their tribal brethren.

Cultural Value of Land

Land to us means identity, culture, uniqueness, heritage, etc. To human beings air, birds, flowers, trees, fish etc. represent the cosmos and the universe. We refer to "Mother Earth" as the provider. We are but temporary tenants who live off with what she provides to sustain ourselves. What remains is for future generations. The tribal generally thought that outsiders might not share the same sentiments as they have toward their land. The lands and forests are the people and they are them. This rather unique attachment to the land is almost religious and emotional to the extent that when trees are cut, dams are built etc. the environment is polluted; they share the same pain that the land feels. Each group is given the land to cultivate and to take care of in the same way they take care of their very life and survival. They co-exist harmoniously with the land, forest, and mountains that provided their life's sustainability and nourishment. This may sound weird to other's ear but that is their unique heritage and relationship with Mother Nature - the provider. They belong to the land and not the land belongs to them. In fact, the bottom line of conflict between the Nagas and the Kukis in the recent past is also mainly due to the issue of land ownership which they occupied. Therefore, it is very natural that the tribals are conscious of their ancestral land.

Further suggestions have been made below:

i. Election to the District Councils should be held as early as possible and the powers and functions given under the 6th Schedule such as - the power of allotment of land and others should be transferred to the Council in totality.

ii. All relevant land records of the respective hill districts, which had been maintained by the State revenue departments and settlement, should be handed over to the District Councils.

iii. Protective measures like framing of separate land laws for the hill districts should be enacted to avoid any kind of encroachment except in exceptional cases like acquisition by the Government.

The problems of lack of development and mal-administration in the hills especially in the Kuki villages have its roots with the application of unsuitable acts and laws by the government who has no idea other than their own traditional administrative system. Besides, the apathetic and lackadaisical attitude of the State/Central governments towards the aspiration of the tribal for their internal self-determination at the village level is to be blamed. It is to note that the tribals are the best judges of their own development. Thus, in order to bestow equal justice to the tribal, the government should delegate powers to the district council to promote national integration. The politics of deprivation should be stopped.

Indian Forest Laws vis-a-vis the Tribal

Only when Manipur became part of India the Indian Forest Act was then adopted for the first time in 1950 and no Act of its own has been framed. Manipur then adopted the Assam Forest Regulation vide Notification dated 01-10-1958. The State framed its own transit rules in its present form in the year 1971. Forest areas as per 2003 are classified as –

Reserved Forest – 1, 567 sq. km.
Protected Forest – 4, 171 sq. km.
Unclassed Forest – 11,581 sq. km. = Total- 17, 219 sq. km.

The traditional system of community forest and resource management has long existed in the Northeast, defended by decades of struggle against British and Indian forces. This struggle has in turn been reflected in a complex set of legal protection in the form of Acts 371-A, 371-G, in the 6th Schedule, Manipur Hill District Acts and similar laws. These structures are now under serious threat. Supreme Court rulings, changes in national forest laws and moves by the Forest Department are threatening community forest control. The Center can control all such land which was previously held by the state Government. In the event of centralization of control, traditional community activities like jhumming, cutting of trees, etc. will be deemed illegal. The Central government will not only restrict these activities but will also seize control of lands that it wishes to use for mines, dams or similar projects, depriving communities of their homelands and their resources. When any land is classified, Indian Forest Act and Forest Conservation Act will apply. The rights of these lands are with the community and it will be against constitutional provision if the Centre declares these areas as forest since the land in the North East fall within Schedule VI of the Constitution. As of now the tribal communities in the Northeast have not suffered the whole seizure of their resources that were inflicted on mainland where lakhs of forest dwelling communities became the victims of brutal eviction drives. However, it may be noted that the same process of seizing forests and land is now beginning in the Northeast as well and two threats can be identified.

Unclassed State Forest: The first threat to the Northeast has come through Forest Department records in which every state forest departments maintain forests maps of their respective states. These maps largely record the areas controlled by communities and ADCs as "unclassed state forest" a classification that does not exist in any forest law or regulation. Since these lands are recorded as 'forests' Forest Conservation Act applies and any non-forestry activity like jhuming is barred. In the Supreme Court's mind community use of these 'forest lands' is already illegal notwithstanding the existing constitutional or legal provisions.

Joint Forest Management (JFM) Committee: The second threat comes from the JFM policy introduced in 1980s. The moves for the formation of this committee appear to be more dangerous as it aimed at reducing community management and control over the forest. In areas considered 'degraded' the Forest Department creates local JFM committees that are to assist with forest management, protection, regeneration etc. and the said committee has agreed to be the agent of Forest Dept. These Committees signed a Memorandum of understanding with the Forest Department. The Committee will allow only those forest activities that the Department permits and any violation will be dealt with under the Indian Forest Act- a law that did not in any sense apply to community forests. This process is in the initial stages in Northeast. It is to note that the very extension of the JFM will later be used by the Forest Department as evidence that these lands are "state forests" as per the Supreme Court's definition. This gave the Forest Department a support base for itself who have vested interest in serving the Department and breaking community control.

Few suggestions for local strategies:

1. Communities need to be sensitized and they should be mobilized to stop JFM and to bring forest regeneration and protection under their control.
2. District Councils or State Government and other bodies should pass laws against such classification. Forest Rights Acts (recognizing the rights of STs and Forest

Dwellers) should be supported and the rights in the NE and elsewhere, reaffirmed.

3. MPs and MLAs should demand that their government oppose the Supreme Court's action.

Over the past three decades there has been a gradual process of bringing all forests in India under centralized control in Delhi. In 1975 forests were made a concurrent subject and in 1980 the Forest Conservation Act was passed. Hence, both the Centre and the States can make any legislation. Now all forests and large areas have been brought under the direct control of the Centre and the Supreme Court. The process of seizing control over forests is still in its initial stages in the Northeast and there is a possibility of resisting it. It is a legal problem and political solution may also be needed.

REFERENCES

Gangte T.S (n.d), 'Retrospective of land use system under chieftainship among the tribals of Manipur', *A paper presented in a seminar* held at Manipur University.

Government of India,(n.d.) *The Supreme Court of India Civil Original Jurisdiction in T.N. Godavarman Thirumalpad vs Union of India & others writ petition (civil) 202/1995 & Jammu & Kashmir Environment Forum writ petition (civil) no.171/1996.*

Government of Manipur (2000), *Notification no. 55/4/95 Forests (Pt):* - Secretariat: Forest & Environment Department – Imphal, the 8th June.

——— (1967), Bill No.2 of 1967- The Manipur Hill Areas (Acquisition of Chiefs' Rights) Bill.

——— (1963) Manipur Land Revenue and Land Reforms Act, 1960. Directorate of Printing and Stationery Manipur-Sept 13,.

——— (1975), Report of the Manipur Legislative Assembly Hill Areas Committee on the MLR & LR (Amendment) Bill.

——— (n.d.) A Hand Book of Manipur Hill Village Authority Act, 1956- Law Dept.

——— (n.d) The Manipur State Hill Peoples (Administration) Regulation Act, 1947.

Horam, M. (2000) (ed.), *The Rising Manipur- Including other North Eastern States*, Manas Publication, Delhi.

Reid, Robert (1983), *History of the Frontier Areas Bordering on Assam from 1883-1941.*Delhi.

Sanatomba Kangujam (2003), 'An analytical perspective of Manipur Territorial Question' *Sangai Express*, March 06.

19

LAND, IDENTITY AND DEVELOPMENT: Kuki Experience

—*T. Misao*

Introduction

A brief narration on the administrative system of the Kuki community is essential to appreciate matters connected with land, land holdings and its utilization. The State Government's participation or jurisdiction is negligible in Kuki areas.

Every village has a council where the Chief (Haosa) is the head of the council and is assisted by the Semang, Pachong, Lhangsam and Record Keeper (recently introduced) and Thempu exists. The Chief for all purposes is the head of the Village administration in all aspects. The Semang functions something like the Chief Minister (Prime Minister). The Pachong- assists the Semang in all matters. Lhangsam functions like an information and broadcasting department (Ministry) and record keeping responsibility of all events, decisions and so on concerning the village affairs, lies with him. This is a recent introduction. In the light of the changes of the present age, this newly created portfolio is welcome. In the past all events were kept in memory and not documented.

The Thempu is a very important functionary where he is in charge of religious affairs. Before Christianity came, the Thempu dealt with all matters connected with whatever belief system that was in vogue. Matters relating to sickness, death, marriage etc are performed and dealt by this functionary. This brief narration may give an idea of the administrative system that has been followed since centuries in the Kuki village that has a well demarcated land boundary.

A slight variation has been introduced where some Khas (unoccupied) land has been demarcated for settlement after the 2nd World War where the function of the chief has been substituted by a re-designated Chairman, Secretary etc. a body formed on election and consensus of the villagers. The composition of the village council differs, nonetheless the principle remains the same. Such areas are few.

The Chiefship is heriditary and his eldest son succeeds him when he dies. Sometimes by consensus the Chief is succeeded by other relatives of the Chief. All other Council bodies are selected by the chief. The council members hold the assignment for a calendar year but may continue for more. However they are also removed due to various reasons. The prime consideration lies in the opinions and feelings of the villagers. The main reason for removal can be violation of the agreed principles aided by moral turpitude etc.

The village land area is identified by rivers, important land marks and ridges and the next village recognizes this boundary and seldom the land boundaries are encroached or extended. In case, land not belonging to the village is required for cultivation, well set procedures are followed. Only after the approval by the village council, duly approved by the Chief, the area, after verification, is allowed cultivation, for a specific period, normally for a year, by the neighboring village.

What portions of the land should be cultivated is decided beforehand by the village Council and duly consented by the Chief, preferably during November/December, where clearing begins from December/January. There are at times disputes where preferences of area to be cultivated are given. On such occasions, a lottery is adopted and non can complain on this issue.

The Kukis prefer to have a high altitude area identified as Zou, which serve for **(a)** Timberable trees (in the past strictly for building house) **(b)** hunting wild animals **(c)** grazing for Mithuns **(d)** Collecting vegetables (Wild) season wise.

This area, in the past, has been strictly adhered to, where individual interest especially in removing trees has been forbidden other than actually needed for individual household building requirement. In the past this high altitude area was used for vegetable growing, following the pattern of Jhuming.

The Kukis' main staple food is rice. When hard hit they mixed it with maize. There used to be one species locally known as Mim (Available in N.C. Hills) for similar use. This specie is no longer seen and is perhaps extinct in the region. This is comparable to Millet.

With the increase of population and land holdings being limited, the concept of cultivating wet paddy, which hitherto was rarely in practice before the second World War, had reaches the maximum in the late 1950, and today every flat land close to the major rivers has been fully exploited.

Unlike land where Jhum cultivation is practiced, which individuals do not own, wet cultivation area of land belongs to the individuals who cultivate it. The individual may allow other person to cultivate the land on an agreed rent or fee on yearly basis. Rarely this land is disposed off. However in recent past, these land holdings are sold to others or kept in hold by others on an agreed price much to the disadvantage of the holder. Unfortunate circumstances compel them to do so.

In fact if one has to go by events of the past, the land holdings in the Chiefs name or village is for the fear that a portion of the land may be disposed off by the villagers to third parties which will be of immense detriment to the village administration and polity.

Collective ownership under the chief has distinct advantages in the case of Jhum cultivation. Jhum Land cultivated by an individual cannot be utilized continuously. At the most after two consecutive years of cultivation, diminishing returns sets in and that area has to wait for 5 years for trees to grow and mature and the soils to replenish for the next Jhum cultivation, preferably after 9/10 years. The individual farmer cannot wait for so long. Hence collective ownership is to the individual's advantage where an individual can be allotted a land for the next year's cultivation at another site.

Some writers lamented that Manipur Land Revenue and Land reforms Act 1960 could not be extended to the hills, *"depriving the hill people from enjoying the benefit of the popular act"*. This is not correct. This Act is neither popular nor unpopular. Once this Act is extended in a matter of a few years, all the land will be sold out. Individuals who purchase the land can be outsiders whereby they will not fall within the administrative council and will seriously affect not only land management but other administrative affairs of the village. The case of the Lungphou land is an example. In the year 1958 a portion of this land was given on lease to Nepalese for a period of 30 years. A written undertaking was made by the lesees to follow Tribal customary laws viz. a) to contribute a days labour by each household b) to pay Hill house Tax annually c) not to dispose off the portion of the lease land.

Manipur, being known for invention of ingenious means of corruption, these Nepalese quite obviously in connivance with concerned State officials, had the land surveyed and obtained "Dag Chitha" (ownership document) and survey maps with individual land marks.

They refused to comply with their written commitments and any further discussion on the future of the lease portion and with indignant posture, discarded all the commitments. Further, grazing of their cattle at any place they choose, had detrimental effects on the various adjacent tribal lands.

In spite of repeated appeals to the appropriate authorities, no action has been taken. This is one glaring example of the consequences when land of the hill Tribal people changes hands. Would such consequences conform to development goals?

The Development Path

Multiple cropping

1) More villagers have now resorted to wet paddy field cultivations in flat land close to the rivers and every possible space is now utilized. The ownership lies with the cultivator who develops the land for the purpose and the chiefs do not interfere in the ownership. This space however is not sufficient in most cases (sufficient to support the family of the cultivator). In some cases the land is cultivated on sharing basis between the cultivators owning large holdings and those with less.

The issue of development on this limited land, lies in applying different methods or by introducing a second crop.

2) The concept of cultivating a second crop is very much possible. These fields are cultivated for rice only. From May/June preparation for planting, clearing of the

unwanted weeds, begin. Harvesting takes place after seven months and for the remaining five months, the land lies idle. Yet the concept is very much alien to the villagers. An example- a seminar, surprisingly well attended, was held some years ago on how to improve our economy and usher in a better living standard among the Tribals in Manipur.

I was invited to speak and on great length I narrated the various places I have visited in several States of India, quoting instance of successes like Punjab farmers and so on. To my surprise the speakers with who I interacted, sounded very knowledgeable as to why another crop should not be introduced after rice harvesting. Eight of my villagers had such wet paddy fields and they refused to introduce another crop more or less on the same logic of the Chiefs Seminar on the subject.

3) Wet paddy fields in the flat land area have a great scope for successful undertaking of second crop within December to April, where varieties of cash crops can be cultivated. The weather is good, and ideal for cash crops. Since these crops will not be cultivated in larger scales, it can be marketed locally where there is sufficient demand at a cheaper rate. Instead of depending for these products on imports from Assam/ West Bengal, these could be gainfully produced locally. In the plains of Manipur it has picked up now.

The problems of multiple cropping however will be uncontrolled grazing, insufficient water and guarding of this field. These problems can be overcome. The biggest hurdle is how to educate and make the common farmers understand the possible bonanzas from multiple cropping. One suggestion is to make a documentary or feature film. This however will require innovative ideas, experts on the field and a lot of funds.

The strategy of development should be to target self sufficiency in the initial years and strive for commercial purposes latter on.

For the common farmer's category, the vision is only for rice cultivation and alternatives like wheat still has not attracted them. Other cash crops like Potatoes, mustard, cabbages, Tomatoes, Chilies, maize etc. have not been considered for the flat lands. However, a number of villagers now grow varieties of the above and different vegetables in the upper region of the hills and in fact some are depending for their livelihood on cultivating these cash crops. In the high altitudes, though it can be commercially cultivated, it has its limitations, the main reason being limited space and transport problems.

Collective Farming/Marketing

The Concept of collective farming/cultivation is absents amongst the Kuki Community, specially work relating to farming, be it rice or vegetable, whether in the plain or in the hill areas. Individual effort apparently is an ideal situation for them. For example, quite a big area had been earmarked for plantations of passion fruit, and it was made very clear to them that all villagers should be involved in cleaning, harvesting and marketing and everyone was to share the profits equally after deducting the cost of labour contributed. It did not work, the area after plantation was left unattended and nothing could be harvested. So the same applies to "Yongchak" (Parkia), which has a high commercial yield. This is a popular vegetable bearing tree, not cultivated in low lying areas like Imphal Valley.

Such is the attitude. Pea plantation is very popular among the tribes, fetching very handsome profits during the Meitie festival of Ningol Chakkouba in November where married daughters/sisters, are invited for lunch. Instead of collective cultivation and harvesting where more yield and marketing benefits could have been reaped, everyone prefers individual efforts. For example Ginger cannot be grown in water logging areas and are doing well in the hills. In Manipur also two local species have been cultivated and in the last two years another one has been introduced. Here, traders from outside play havoc. During difficult periods (July-September), money is advanced to the villagers and after harvesting they are under paid, anything from Rs. 4 to Rs 5 a kilo (data of the last 4 years). Earlier in the 1990's payment was as low as Rs.2 a Kg.

A few young persons wanted to break the monopoly and collected 4/5 truck loads of ginger. The ginger lobby was so powerful that these truck loads were made to perish outside the limits of the local market, about a decade ago, and the idea has been abandoned.

In other states (Sikkim), I have seen how the lion's share of the middle man is whittled down for the advantage of the farmers. At selected locations of ginger growing areas, Rural Marketing Centers have been established with full fledged functionaries under D.R.D.A. in recent times. This centre also will cater to Oranges, Cardamoms etc. In Manipur such an idea however seems to be a far cry. Terrace cultivation was introduced 50 years ago and it has not picked up amongst the Kuki community. Only a very few persons have adopted it and on limited space only. This could be an alternative means of space besides the riverside flat lands and a means of avoiding Jhum cultivation.

After the late 1950's when the Nepalese settled in the hill areas, most of the areas occupied by them have been turned into terrace cultivation. Someday the Kuki community will pick up and the maxim, necessity knows no laws, and will perhaps resort to larger terrace cultivation. In what shape the situation will turn cannot be predicted but it will be rewarding.

Land and Ethnic Relation

Hitherto, respect for one community by another and living in harmonious existence amongst neighbours or even distant far flung areas, has become a nessesity in Manipur.

Amongst the Nagas and Kukis, this harmonious existance has been turned upside down (whatever may be the political ambition). The wounds of the last century of conflicts were opened and the nature of their migrant character rekindled when the small village households were resettled in different places in the state amongst relatives, in the aftermath of the Kuki- Naga conflict. And very few understood the larger implication which followed in subsequent years.

The uprooting of small villages and land holdings in confined limited areas had dire consequences in the lives of many Kuki villages. The fallout of Inter-Ethnic violence in the 1990's has left a number of villagers, fatherless, homeless and landless.

Thousands of Nepalese have been allowed to enter and settle in Manipur without any R.A.P (restricted area permit) in Sadar Hill areas. Koubru Hill had been known for its rich forests and wild life. Today one can see the rich lands mercilessly destroyed even from a distance.

The displaced Kuki persons are now living in and around Kangpokpi a Napali settlement area. The future is uncertain. The Naga-Kuki-Napali conflict over land has dangerous portents for the future as the produce of the soil and the agrarian base is the fundamental basis for the existence of the people.

The wealth in the hills

1. The rivers in the hill areas of Manipur were not utilized other than for drinking and irrigational purposes. Now stone boulders and sands from these

rivers have been extensively exploited for domestic and commercial purposes. Some control measures are necessary. The importance of preserving the varieties of Fish in these rivers have not been understood, on the contrary, short term measures of fishing by poisonous weeds/chemicals, use of explosives etc. has destroyed fish and other marine lives. Trout and Mahsher studies are very important sports today and are attracting visitors from all over.

2. Forest Land: This forest land is situated in the high altitude regions where varieties of trees, canes, bananas, bamboos to name a few, were abundantly found, including edible plants. The Kukis prefer to settle below the fringe of these places. The forest lands are disappearing fast. To name a few villages, Chahsad (Ukhrul), Laiyang (Tamenglong), Chalwa/ Tujang Waichong, Old Haipi (shifted to Saa Hills) Thanlon (Churachandpur district) Lungphou/ Maohing/Changoubung/Hengbung(Senapati district-Sadar Hills) are villages where the forests have disappeared forever.. Till the 1950's these forest were so thick that for a visit even in daytime the sun is hardly visible.

3. These regions were utilized for hunting, collecting vegetables and fruits. Wild life was abundant. Till the 1950's, elephant, tigers and all known animals roamed the forests including a wide varieties of birds. Most of these wild life no longer exist.

4. With the increase in population, including the influx of Nepalese these forests (particularly Sadar Hills) in the main area of the Koubru Forest, are diminishing at a very fast rate due to commercial exploitation, specially of trees for timber and canes for furniture.

5. Some villagers whose daily lives depend on collecting a wide variety of vegetables are facing livelihood dillemas. Most of the fruit bearing trees have been done away with. Thanks to shortsightedness of the villagers.

6. Manipur forest once boasted of as many as 250 species of orchids and today these exotic flowers are reduced to around fifty varieties only as of my own studies in the 1980's. The pity is the ignorance of the locals both Naga/Kuki Community living in these regions. Till recently highly valuable species are collected and sold for a song in the Imphal market.

2 (a) There are still a lot of spaces not utilized in the hill regions of Manipur

I recollect an incident which will perhaps enlighten those not familiar. Sometime in the 1980's, a group of Japanese relatives of soldiers who fought during the last war, visited Manipur, to collect bones of these dead soldiers. On the eve of their departure, The Japanese profusely thanked the officer (since deceased) who assisted the visitors. Curious, the officer enquired why so much praise and the Japanese visitors replied that keeping the hills and the forests in good shape was commendable. The officer had a good laugh having shown the visitors the virgin areas and not theover exploited ones where the Government had done nothing.

(b) These region is a gold mine as the lying vacant is suitable for many crops like tea, coffee, horticulture, vegetable of all varieties, the list is endless. Even jungle vegetables can be domesticated, one species is now successfully grown in the kitchen gardens (Changkhot).

Problems associated with development: - Flat lands in the riverside

(c) On the available land cultivated for paddy, mainly

for domestic/local consumption, the yield is decreasing. Wet paddy cultivation is however not very old, perhaps seventy years old. Farmers have started using chemical fertilizer, much to the detriments of the lands cultivated. The answer for this problem lies in the application of composted manures which can be produced/manufacture locally by individuals. Sikkims State bans the use of industrially produced fertilizer. For Manipur such measures may not come at all.

(d) To enhance further development cultivation of suitable cash crops including wheat is very much essential. This has been discussed earlier. Within the hill range, varieties of flowers can be cultivated like gladolies. Gladolies have a huge demand in Kolkata, Delhi and other big Cities. Kalimpong (Darjeeling) and Sikkim where such flowers are successfully cultivated, have the terrain, the soil and the weather similar to the hill regions of Manipur. It has been successfully grown in small scales as a pilot project. The problem faced is that of marketing outside the State. It may be mentioned that the seeds of gladolies planted in this altitude multiplies, which is not the case in valley areas. Seeds export has handsome profit potential. Foothills in the region are doing well and the commercial prospects are large as they fetch handsome prices. Dahlias and other varieties can also be cultivated.

(e) Antharium has been successfully cultivated and marketed in Mizoram. As of 2006, the Mizoram Government imported as many as 40 (Forty) species of this flower from Holland trained willing persons and provided infrastructure to them. They have no problem of marketing and are doing well. There is a vast venue to develop on this front. However under the present situations in this State it is doubtful such ventures can be undertaken. A pilot project was undertaken on cardamon, the price fetched was only Rs. 12 to Rs 15 a kg as compared to Sikkim where minimum price is Rs.90 a kg (as of 2005).

I am quite familiar with Tea and the projects, having spent a considerable time during service both in Darjeeling and Jalpaipuri districts of West Bengal. As far back as the 1980's, a small pilot project was initiated. One specie from Springfield (Kurseong-Darjeeling) of 50 plants and another from the plain regions of Kalchini (Jalpaiguri West Bengal) and Dibrugarh (Assam) of 120 plants were brought and planted. Since the plants were doing well, I was encouraged to seriously start a Tea garden after retirement. A Tea garden consisting of about 400 acres can employ 300 permanent workers apart from several other hundreds as casual workers.

I had several meetings with Tea Board officials in Kolkata and to involve the Board a few requirements are to be met i.e. mapping, soil testing, weather data throughout the 12 month period etc. The first step is mapping of the proposed area, the land holding boundary and the proposed area for plantation are to be specified. Since the Manipur Land Revenue Act does not extend in my land (Lungphou Sadar Hills), there is no mapping though there is a document defining the land boundary, I met several times the concerned officials to undertake the survey. However, during the President's rule one of the Advisors was familiar with the requirement of the Tea Board and consented, and a survey was conducted and all expenses of the team was at my cost. Several requests were made to provide me the results of the survey, and finally I had the answer –all documents had been destroy by arson. There have been several outrageous events targeting me over this issue. This is very frustrating.

Nonetheless a very young energetic entrepreneur amongst this Community has started a tea plantation and doing well on his own cost. To have successful undertaking machinery is required, quite expensive though. In the midst of fruitation of his venture, he was unable to meet the extraordinary demands of a particular militant group and was imprisoned by this outfit for several days. What next now should be any persons guess.

During my service tenure I had a wide range of contacts and one such person was an expert on Fish. Besides my rudimentary knowledge about breeding of fish, this expert confirmed and refined on my rudimentary understanding of the subject. Since I had the land with sufficient water, fish breeding suitable for the region was a distinct possibility. I proposed to start a pilot project in the public interest. The project required the recommendation of the State government and was to be financed by the Govt. of India. After completing all the technical and other formalities, an outrageous monetary demand in advance was made for recommendation of the project, hence the project was abandoned.

It has been my personal interest to preserve the trees and develop areas which will be beneficial to my Village in particular, the public in general. All my saving and efforts put in to start a horticulture venture has faded due to indiscriminate, grazing in spite of a ban order to confine grazing within the house premises. My several requests even to the highest official remain unattended. Events prevailing in this part of the country are indeed unfortunate.

20

CUSTOMARY LAWS ON LAND OWNERSHIP AND RESOURCES MANAGEMENT IN THE THOUBAL DAM AREA:

The Kuki Experience

—D. Letkhojam Haokip

Introduction

Manipur was once so fondly described as the 'land of Jewel'. Broadly three ethnic groups viz. the Kukis, the Meiteis and the Nagas inhabited from the early times. The ethnic composition of the Thoubal Dam area followed this pattern. Based on the ethnic composition and distribution of population, the area can rightly be called 'Mini Manipur'. They have lived peacefully for centuries. The Kuki and the Nagas were inhabited in the foot hills and mountains.[1] The Meiteis spread along the Thoubal River bank.[2] The Kuki and the Naga villages were located either on the slope of the foothills or on the top of the hills. The Meitei villages were mainly concentrated on the plains. On the south eastern side of the river lies the most popular eastern Hills of the Manipur called *Mapithel.*[3] On the western side of the area lies the *Chandrakhong* noted for its salt well and *Langmaiching* Hills. The Maphou Dam is only 30 km from Imphal. This area shows different types of landholding system which are found in the entire Manipur. The indegenious landholding system and tenancy system of these three sections of communities (The Kuki, the Naga and the Meiteis) could be found here. Both shifting and terrace cultivation were practiced since time immemorial. Educationally, the area seems to be one of the most backward regions of the state.

Oral history reveals that the area was first inhabited by the *Hundung, Itham, Monglham and Saichang*. Due to lack of written record it is not possible to establish the date of establishment of these villages. *Monglham* was founded by Tolseng in 1707 AD.[4] By 1886, it was inhibited by 50 houses. It is not possible to say accurately which villages of the Kuki have been living in the area from the remote past. However, the oral traditions of the Kuki of the areas reveal how the chiefs of the *Monglham* influence other villages of the areas for centuries. In the olden days where there were no definite and proper boundaries between villages, many powerful chiefs claim as their territory where their mithun or cattle freely move and graze. This papér attempts to reflect the traditional land ownership or holding system and resource managements found among the Kukis of the area in historical perspective and also the problems and prospects of reforming the traditional system of the area in particular and the other Kuki territory of the state of Manipur.

Controversy Over Bulpi and the Traditional Land Owership of the Kuki

Traditionally there are no substitutes for *Upa* or head clan as far as land ownership is concerned. Every families and clans have their own *upas*. Question arises over who is or who are the *Upa(s)*? The answer is very simple. The eldest of a family is the upa of a family. A number of families again have their own *Upa*, called *Inkon Upa*. Still a number of *Inkon upa* have their own upa called *Phungkhai Upa*. *Phungbul* or phungpi *Upas* are again the *upas* of the *Phungkhai Upas*. *Bulpi* is supposed to be the most superior over all the *Phungbul Upas*. *Phungkhai Upas* are commonly known as Head or pricipal clans.[5] The position of the *Upas* therefore has several layers. The number of *upas* are nots same in each and every clan.[6] All the Kuki clans have their own *Phungbul upas* and Bulpi is the most powerful as far as the Kuki society is concerned. There are writers and authors who projected the position of Bulpi equivalent to that of the Emperor. The oral history of the Kukis of Manipur reflected controversy over Bulpi between the *Lunkim* (MiluiKhongsai) Phungbul and the head clans of the Doungel (Aishan) and also the Phungpi Upa of the Haokip (Chassad) and the Sitlhou Bulpi (Jampi). The claim for Bulpi between the Doungel and Lunkim is reflected by the folk story of their own version and that of Chassad and Jampi is reflected by a folk song handed by both the clans. In this way there were a number of claims and counter claims among Kukis for the position of *Upas* whose position and privileges is unravel with any other section of the Kuki society. The Kukis have clan based organization which is the most primitive form of government but is forceful even in the present century.

Traditionally Landholding or ownership is associated with *Upas*. No alternative or substitution was possible under any circumstances. The different layers of *upas* mention above are the chief of their village. There are a good number of *upas* who don't have village. Still these *upas* are the protector and destination of his clansmen. When the chief of a village died without any heir, his nearest next kin inherited his chiefship.[7] Traditionally there is no room for the common men to become chief. One who is not upa has to handover chiefship to his *upa* if he founded a village[8]. When the chiefdom of a phunkhai upa or phungbul upa is deserted due to tribal blood feud or any other factor thereby causing uninhabitable, his nearest junior chief have to offer the chief ship by abandoning his chief ship. When a chief died leaving minor son, his brother has to look after the minor and when he grows up the chiefship has to be handed over to the legal heir.[9] The tradition on land holding and ownership discussed above reveal us a certain customary laws that regulated the land ownership system of the Kuki from the remote past. The Kukis strongly believed that he who collects tribute from his upa shall face the dire consequences. In the event of his upa living in other village, he should go and summoned him for chief ship. If his upa did not want to take up his responsibility, one can become chief. Therefore, there is no room for an individual who has upa in his village to become chief. The different layers of the chief ship reveal us how the land belong to the chief but passed on to the next of kin when the later expired. This shows that land belong to the chief during his life time and passed on to his eldest son or next of kin after his death. The tradition of land holding system also reveal how he cannot simply passed on or out to the person of his choice. Even if two three layers of upas died without any successor, customarily the next layer of upa has the right to inherit. It is therefore very clear that a chief has no right to disposed off his land out of vested interest. He has a number of successors. This tradition is clearly indicated by the genealogical tree of the Kuki clans. None could become a chief by his skill, intelligence or by any other means but by birth. Chiefship therefore, can rightly bc called the birth right of Upas. None can dispose off or distorted under any circumstances. In the event of the chief becoming lunatic, derange or leprosy, his next kin or able man acts as regency. Thus, chiefship cannot be transferred or disposed off as and when required.

So far there is no plan and thoughts that can easily replace the chief ship or land ownership of the Kuki[10]. It maintained and sustained the identity of the Kuki which depend very much upon the land ownership and its management. It also strengthens the harmony of the village that exists since time immemorial. The traditional land holding system too is good for controlling the forest. It was the traditional land custom that regulated and preserved the landholding system through the ages for the posterity of the people. Proper regulation and utilization of the land make them survived them from natural and man made calamities. Such a unique land ownership system protects them from the outside threats and also lessens disputes over land ownership and property(s). The chief lineage could be compared to the royal lineage of the United Kingdom and many of the Kingdoms that work.[11] The place and importance of the Kuki Head clans or *Upas* are very important. To avoid confusion, controversy and the possible conflicts over the chief ship, each clan maintains their own genealogical tree from their ancestors.[12] Even women folk and children knew who is to be the next chief even if the chief did not have his own son. The chief is also the leader of a village both in times of war and peace.

Traditional Resource Management

By resources management we will confine to the primary and secondary products and the mode of controlling land, forest and agricultural productions that is considered to be the most efficient procedures practiced in the Thoubal Dam area.[13]

Different Types of Village Reserved

The land belongs to the chief. However, in practice, it is set apart for different purposes. All the cultivable land is reserved to meet the foodstuff of the people. *Gamkhat* is one of the reserved which is not so much good for Jhum cultivation but provides housing materials, like bamboo, fibre, thatch and other wild creeper commonly used for construction of houses. *Ujoh* or village reserved surrounding the village is made to protect themselves from the forest fire. Another forest reserved found in the area is *Luikhuh kim*. It is necessary to get water from the natural tank or spring through out the year. Felling tree that surround the source of water could cause drought. Villages that rear huge number of cattle or mithun shifted pasture land from year to year to a void exploitation of forest. Exploitation of forest threats the village economy.[14]

Land Distribution for Jhum Cultivation

The land is set apart for paddy and maize cultivation based on the climatic conditions and soil formations. The area is suitable for cotton cultivation as well. Every household is given two units viz. *Bulei* (Paddy field) and *Joulei* (Maize field). Distribution of jhum field during the pre-Christian society was the toughest subjects of the village authority. Many householders were sure to fight over Jhum land annually. We come across how such quarrel turn into violent form. Regarding land distribution among the Tibeto Burman group, JB Lyall's comment may be reproduced here.

Every family or householder had its holding or share of one but such holding is not in the shape of an ancestral or customary share of the fields round the hamlet but rather in the shape of arbitrary allotment from arable and of the whole country. All the arable lands seem to have been divided into lots; each lot being presumably equal value and calculated to be sufficient to provide subsistence for one household.

For Jhum field purpose, only the entire arable land is set apart into nine to ten units. The number of unit depends upon the availability of the land and population density of the village single unit is distributed for each year.[15] In the area we come across how certain families had reclaimed the unit that they tilled in the former recycle. Some of the village authority members choose the area they preferred in a very rare case. Village chief is free to choose the Jhum field he prefers. New immigrants from other villages equally share Jhum field as stated above. In the modern period that is after the coming of Christianity, lottery system is introduced to avoid hatred and conflicts over Jhum field distributions. There is no hard and fast rule regarding distribution of cultivating for cotton and some other vegetable crops. He who is willing to cultivate selects a portion of land suitable for it, provided it is not within the portion of land set apart for paddy and maize cultivation. All the villagers except the close kin of the chief had to pay *Changseo*[16] or land tax to the village chief. In the remote past *Changseo* constitutes the corpus fund of the village authority. With the passage of time it becomes the property of the chief. We also come across lots of middle men who came in the region for trade. Maize is sold out for purchasing basic needs while paddy is consumed in the village.

Unit used for Mesuring Land

Lam is the smallest and the most suitable unit used for measuring Jhum land. It is roughly equal to five half feet to six feet. The tallest man or the village chief stretches his arm. Ten *Lam* or such stretches is equal to *Khaokhat*.[17] Three to five *Khao* is calculated to meet the food requirement of a medium and big family. Whereas seven to ten Khao square are is usually assumed for maize and other cash crops. The Meitei called it *Sanalamjei*[18]. The King stretches his arm long with his four finger tips.

Forest Resources and Mode of Hunting

The area is the home for different birds and wild animals. Interviews with village elders reflected the existence of elephant, tiger and various types of wild animals, like porcupine, fox, varieties of deer, stag, tortoise bear, wild boar squirrel etc are the common animal found in this region[19]. Among the birds, wild fowl, peacock, vulture, kite, Owls and many varieties are found. Bee hives and several medicinal herbs or bark of tree and fishes and other animals that lived in the water and also streams or rivers are considered as forest resources. Salt well at Chandrakhong is not less significant. Presently stone and sand of the area constituted an important sources of forest products. Each chief is given one of the hind legs of animal killed in the forest.

Hunting is regulated by local or inter village agreement or any other synthesis brought out for the purpose. On every caught of wild beast or big animals the chief is given one of the hind leg. Each village authority has a set of rules that regulated hunting. In group hunting he, whose bullet hits the animal first get the head and all the customary defined portion of the animal.[20] In group trapping, the senior most men or one who has *salung* becomes the leader. Widows, destitute or aged people joined the *salam dawt* ceremony that usually took place at the residence of the chiefs or at khomol by bringing their own wine to refresh their hunting team or the hunter. They get their own share on the occasion of hunting wild beast. The priest, who did rites in favour of the hunters, gets a portion of the chest called *Sachegu.* Group hunting is like a corporate body. Lost of life due to accident in the course of hunting is paid ex-gratia (Longman). Hunters from outside the village are checked and deal severely. One who secretly harvests bee hives marked by some others is treated as thieves or robber. He who sees and marked first becomes the sole owner of it. Hunting in the pre Christian society is purely for food. The skin of animals hunted is used in making drums, seat and war amour and to strengthen many domestic properties.

Fishing is another dry seasonal and secondary occupation of the people of the area. Fishes are caught either in bamboo traps, cut with a sharp knife at night or when they bask in the sun and through poisoning by a poisoning tree leaves or creepers or by draining off a stream into the other channel, weirs and baling out the deep portion of a river. The rivers flowing between the villages and Thoubal River are favourable for fishing. If two or more parties meet at the same spot for fishing, the party who comes first has the right to hunt at the spot of their choice. Wild animals are the most important source of high quality of food. Most rivers are flowing between two villages. They also mark village boundary. Such rivers become the common property of the villages who share it. Later on, the village chiefs share revenue from stones and sand.[21]

Merits and Demerits of the Chiefship

The laws of inheritance, position of the *upas*, the tribute collection and also the free labour/service called *Khotha*[22] rendered by the villagers in favour of the chiefs sustain the continuity of the Kuki chiefship, their identity culture, custom and traditions of the Kukis through the ages. It also protects their territory. The layers of the Kuki chiefs or upa that control and sustain ownership of land integrate the Kuki society since time immemorial. Such connections which worked like chains unite them during the Anglo- Kuki war during 1917- 1919 AD and during the Second World War.

We also come across how the different layers of the *Upas* who did not become the village chiefs constantly strive for foundation of new villages for them and their clansmen. For instance in 1886, the present Monglham village has 50 fifty houses. Now it becomes about 30 houses[23]. This is mainly due to the growth of population, the tendency of some *upas* and their clansmen towards establishment of new villages and the decrease of soil fertility. Today many of the mother villages of the area in particular and many other Kuki villages become moribund. New villages come up on the foot print of the same and input of modern technology and other development programmes become impossible. The attitudes of the common men are not considered. None could plan for sustainable development. They still thought that the entire land belongs to the chief. The mindset of the common men centres around the traditional methods. The common people thought that the chief has the right of ownership over all the development schemes sanction by the government. They did not undertake long term policy, as they fear that one day the chief could forcibly turn them out. The thinking of the common people is again consolidated by the present scenario of forest and land management the Kuki experience. The chiefs sold forest products and land that caused erosion of the traditional chiefship. The legacy of the British administration, over the village administration among the Kuki after the Anglo-Kuki War and the large scale circulation of modern currency has its own negative aspects. The chiefs thought that they are the sole owner of the land and started selling forest products and the land. Powerful chiefs and candidates for the Manipur Legislative Assembly Member and many MP candidates frequently disturbed the democratic processes of the Manipur state. Many villagers never cast their vote even till today. The common people are yet to exercise their right in the democratic processes that India has. We also come across how some people established villages for securing government development schemes for their vested interest. The traditional chiefship therefore has a good number of merit and its own demerit. It is very clear that unless modification of land ownership and holding or management system within the villages that could suit the changing time is done and regulated, the traditional land ownership that sustains the custom, identity and culture is under threats. The erosion of the traditional chiefship eroded the fertility of the soil that affects the economy of the entire villages. Poverty is now greatly responsible for the outbreak of different forms of conflicts in the region. Besides many internal problems that hamper the economic growth of the area, the conflicts between the Kuki and the Nagas further destroyed the slow pace of development in the area. Many Kuki and Naga villages were burnt down during 1993-96[24].

Suggestion for Reforming Land Holding System

The proposal for bringing land reforms on the line of Manipur Land Revenue Act is opposed by all the tribal. Whenever it is introduced, it hurts the sentiment of the tribal. There is possibility of conflicts between the hill dwellers and the people of valley once it is moved for introduction in the Hill areas. However, reformation or restructuring of the present land management system is the need of the hour. To bring changes that could meet the common people in particular and the entire Kuki population some concrete steps must be taken. The state, the centre and the Kuki intellectual, social organization, NGOs and the village chiefs should involved. There should be series of debate on the merit and demerits of the present scenario of the Kuki land holding system and also topics like towards better future. The synthesis that is brought out should be enforced by the state and the central government. For instance if the synthesis is to restore the traditional chiefship, the state government should removed the village chiefs who are illegal[25] and the villagers should not simply exploit forest and the chief who is the *upa* of his clansmen should not utilized forest products and land for his personal gains. The land is not the chiefs' personal property. It was his ancestor's land, which he is responsible to preserved for the posterity of his heir(s) and the next generation of his clans men. One must keep in mind that the laws frame for bringing changes that best suit the locality should be oriented for input of the fast growing modern technology. In order to sustain the chief ship a chief should always have enough villagers. To have intact number of houses in the villages a chief can do lots. He can even partition the entire territory into a number of units and give permanently or semi permanently to his villagers, who are generally his own clansmen. They can in turn plan for long term policy by cultivating various fruits or plants that can sustain village economy in the long runs.

NOTES

1. Nongdam Kuki, Monglham, Loutei, Kholep, Mamong, Bongjang, Kamu, Saichang, Songphel , Nungmanbi, Bongbal, Sanaching, Saram patong and N. Mollen are the Kuki villages lying on the southern side of the River. Maphou, Chaningpokpi, Molkon, Molnom, Beulahlane, Kamuching, Kamutampak etcs, lies on the northern side of the river. Among the Naga villages, Louphong, Nongdam Tangkhul, Monthou, HundungKhullen, Hundung Khonou Itham and Kaihao lies on the southern side of the Thoubal river whereas, Thangjingpokpi Island and Rishophung lies on the Northern side.

2. Tumukhong,Moirangpurel, Itham, Laikhong and Keithelmanbi are the Meitei villages that lie on the Thoubal river bank.

3. EW Dun, *Gazetteer of Manipur*, 1886,

4. Monglham Baptist Silver Jubilee Souvenir, 1981, Imphal Chassad chief is the head or principal clans of the Haokip; Jampi chief that of the Sitlhou clans, Aishan chief is the Headclan/ principal clans of the Doungel, Lunkim is the head or principal clans of the Khongsai, Leikot chief is the head of the Kipgen, Tuithang Chief is the head of the singson clan, so on and so forth.

6. The Haokip of Manipur has about seven Phungkhai Upas and Mangkholet Haokip is the present Phunbul Upa of the Haokip of Indo Myanmar.

7. On the expiry of the Chassad chief Tonglhu, without any heir his nearest next of kin Lhukhomang from Myanmar inherited the chiefship of the Chassad. Similarly, the present chief of Monglham village in sadar hills is the next of kin of the Monglham chief who expired without any heir.

8. Tolseng founded Monglham village in the year 1707 AD but hand over the chief ship to his upa. Letkhoneh Haokip also founded K. Salbung village in 1960s but handed over the chief ship to his upa Haokhothong.

9. Ngamjapao Lupho looks after the chief ship of the Maphoudam for many years at the time when the present chief Haokhomang was a minor. He hands over the chief ship to Haokhomang in the years 1990 by hosting a big feast inviting the neigbouring tribal chiefs including the Naga and the Kukis.

10. PC Misao; History and custom of the Thadou Kukis, Imphal, 1979,pp.10-15

11. J. Doungel MSS, The responsibility of the Kuki chiefs, A seminar paper

12. Haokip T. Ngamsei, Khanggui thu(Geneaological tree, Homalin Myanmar, 1982

13. Earlier Thoubal Dam is called Maphou Dam after the name of Maphou village. The proper location of the Dam lies within the perimeter of the Maphou village. There is a strong movement for renaming after the name of the Mapithel range by some Nagas.. It can also be called Thoubal Dam after the name of the Thoubal River which is constructed to extract water resources from the Thoubal River.

14. Most of the Kuki and Nagas of the area practice these three types of forest reserves within their own territory.

15. At Mamong village of the area Jhum circles varies for 10 to 15 years. It is about nine to ten years at Monglham and Saichang villages of the area.

16. It is equal to one Sangpai or two half mustard oil tin of modern days.

17. Khao= rope and khat means one.

18. Letkhojam Haokip Historical traditions and customary laws of the Chassad, p.203

19. Till now the presence of wild beast like tiger and many others except elephant that extinct from the region is reported. In 1983-84 a tiger ate the domestic animals of Saichang village. The people of the joint hand in hunting it.

20. The neck of the animal hunted is given to one's maternal uncle the slice backbone flesh is given to one's *upa*. Other customary define portion is retain not applicable in group hunting.

21. Stones and sand constitute a good source of income for the area with the construction of Thoubal Barrage and the Thoubal Multipurpose projects.

22. Kuki Inpi Manipur: *Kuki Customary Laws*, Imphal, July, 2000.

23. For instance the present Monglham village of the area has several offshoot villages in the Churachandpur district. Mong lham village in Henglep subdivision is the direst offshoot of this village. Mongken in Henglep is again the offshoot of the later; Mongken has another two offshoots viz, M. Phaijang and Lajang phai. Pat len, T. Monglham and Chahnou formerly Molnom is also the direct offshoot of the Monglham village in the Sadar hills. In this way the Kuki villages have their own offshoots which centre round the tendency of *upas* to become village chiefs and newer identity on the traditional line where input of modern technology is not successful. It is an established fact that almost all the Kukis originated from the same village. They scattered due to the factors stated here.

24. PS Haokip, A Rejoinder/ counter repose to the NSCN(IM) claim, KNO publication, Imphal, pp. 60-70.

25. Illegal chiefs are those chiefs who established village to suit one's own interest and those chiefs who have *upa* but become chiefs without the consent of his *upa* or one who forcibly dethrone his upa and become village chiefs.

REFERENCES

Doungel, J. MSS (n.d), 'The responsibility of the Kuki chiefs', *A Seminar Paper*.

Dun, E.W. (1886), *Gazetteer of Manipur*.

Haokip T. Ngamsei, Khanggui thu (Geneaological tree, Homalin Myanmar), 1982.

Haokip, PS. (n.d), *Rejoinder/ counter-repose to the NSCN(IM) claim*, KNO publication, Imphal, pp. 60-70

Misao, P.C (1979), *History and Custom of the Thadou Kukis*, Imphal, pp.10-15.

Monglham Baptist Silver Jubilee Souvenir, (1981), Imphal.

INDEX

■■■